POINTMAN

William R. Kimball
&
Roger L. Helle

The accounts depicted in this book are factual and based upon the true life experiences of Roger Helle. Names have been altered to protect the anonymity of certain persons and to safeguard the sensitive nature of isolated events. The dialogue is based on fact.

● **Second Printing 1993**

Cover Art by Ken Norberg

Selected photos courtesy of Charles Gardner, Combat Photographer U.S.M.C.

For additional information contact:

Roger Helle
P.O. Box 185
Colfax, IA 50054
or
William Kimball
%*"Vets With A Mission"*
P.O. Box 9112
So. Lake Tahoe, CA 96158

Printed in the U.S.A.

Dedication

Dedicated to the men and women who answered our nation's call in time of war. Our sincere debt of gratitude is offered for the painful sacrifices you made. We pay special tribute to those who fought and died and have yet to return from a faraway place called Vietnam. We also dedicate this book to those left behind who paid the supreme sacrifice. Know that your loved ones did not die in vain. Their brotherhood, honor, and selfless love will always live in the hearts of us who knew them, and had the honor of serving by their sides.

Greater love has no man than this, than to lay down his life for his friends.

John 15.13

Acknowledgement

I want to thank those who spent endless hours "proofing" this work and offering their constructive criticisms. To Nancy Dickerson, Pat Cluney, and Kathy Olson, my thanks. I also want to thank Todd and Kate Dierdorff for their invaluable editorial assistance. To Tan Phan, a young Vietnamese man who risked his life to flee Vietnam as a teenager, thank you for your help with the Vietnamese language. I want to express my gratitude to my dear friend, Gordon Severance, who has encouraged me to keep writing - and thanks for "Martin Eden"! A thankfulness which cannot be adequately put into words goes to George and Charlotte Stathos for showing the true meaning of "The Good Samaritan" in a time of need. To my precious wife Rose and my daughters Angela and Rachel, know in your hearts that I appreciate you more than ever. And finally, to Roger, a friend and fellow soldier, I thank you for the privilege of writing this book.

William R. Kimball

I want to thank my family for the sacrifices they made to give me time to devote to the development of this book - both in Vietnam and here in America. They gave me the freedom to share "our story" to so many who have been affected by Vietnam. To my lovely wife, Shirley, who, though wounded by my hurt and pain, stayed with me to see the nightmares end and the healing come - you are a gift from God. To Josh and Jamie, the children the doctors said I would never have, what gifts your lives have been to me.

Roger L. Helle

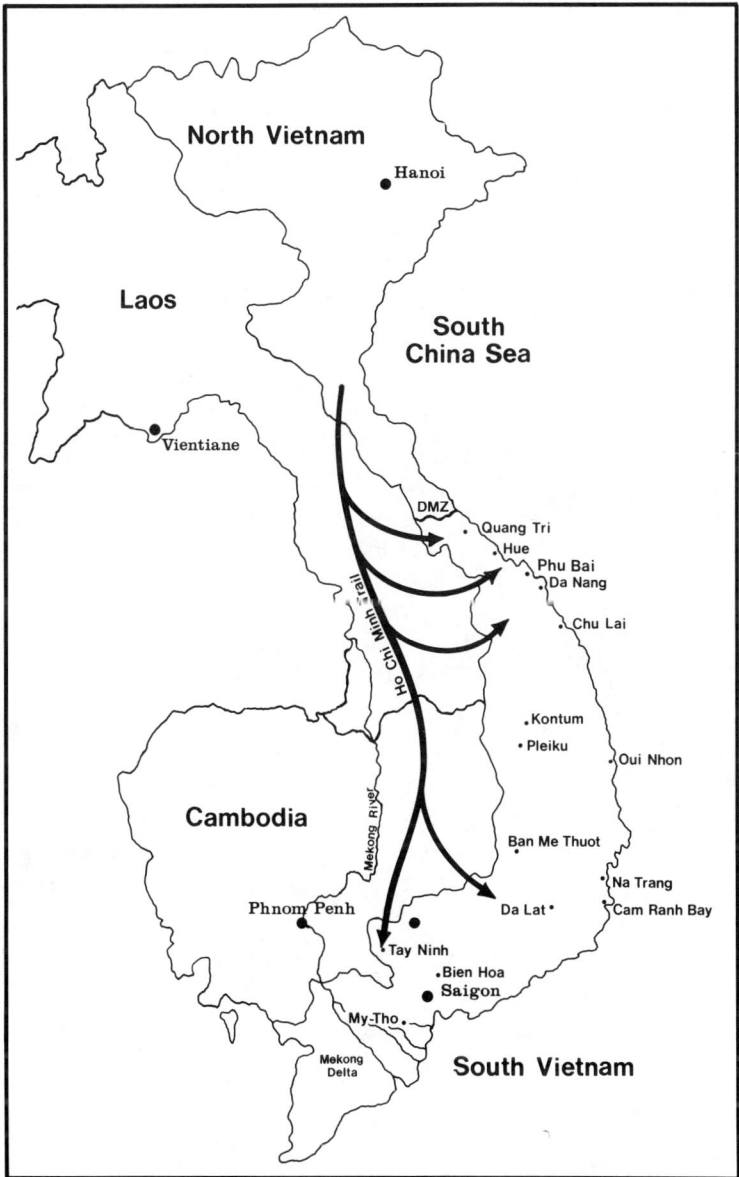

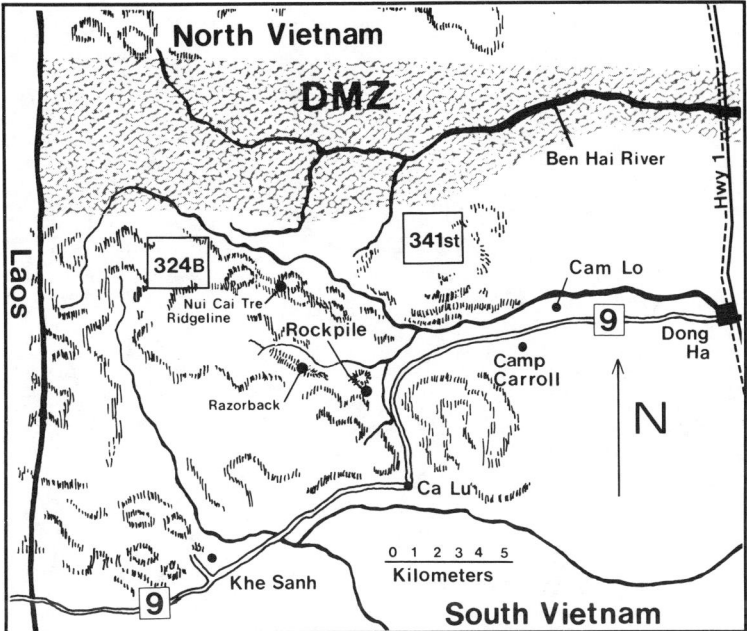

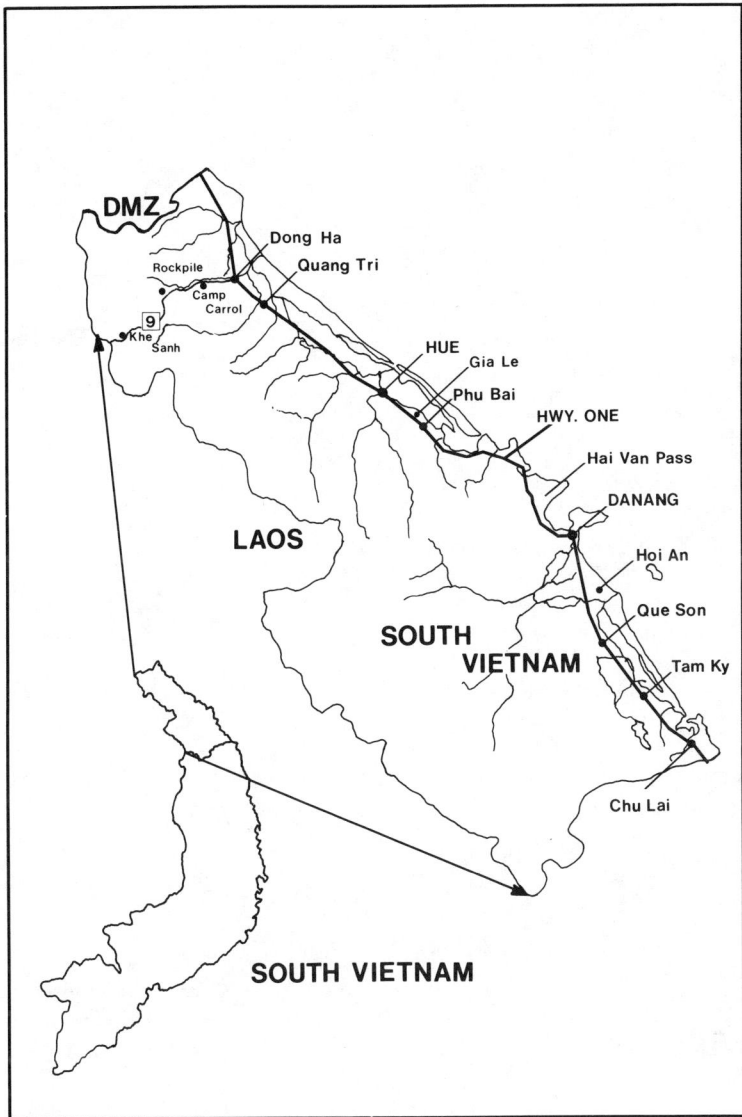

DMZ

Dong Ha
Quang Tri

Rockpile
Camp
Carrol

9
Khe
Sanh

HUE
Gia Le
Phu Bai

HWY. ONE

Hai Van Pass

DANANG

LAOS

Hoi An

Que Son

SOUTH

VIETNAM

Tam Ky

Chu Lai

SOUTH VIETNAM

Vietnam

The sinewy legs of our pedicab drivers pumped up and down like slow motion pistons as they deftly maneuvered through the morning throng of bicycles and scooters in front of the Presidential Palace. They wove us past Notre Dame Cathedral and down *Dong Khoi* Street, the once infamous Tu Do. Like many things in 'Nam, it had been changed since the fall in '75.

It was May, 1990 and my sixth trip back to the place which had played such a pivotal role in each of our lives. Both of us had passed through the long night of 'Nam and returned full circle to the place where it all began - a middle aged soldier and Marine, now, twenty years older.

It was at that moment, under the shade of the Tamarind trees lining the street that Roger planted the seed for this book. He casually leaned over in the seat of his pedicab and said, "Whaddaya think about writing my story?"

"Well," I thought out loud, "I guess this is where it all started."

"Not quite," Roger grinned with typical Marine Corps pride, "The Marines were a little further north."

Preface

Only a split second elapsed between that icy surge of blind, anonymous terror and the realization of what his eyes beheld. A moment before, he was walking point. Under the scorching glare of the early morning heat, glistening beads of sweat had coursed their way down his face, stinging his eyes. He had briefly paused to wipe the briny rivulets from his face when that hot blast of dragon's breath engulfed him.

Only seconds had passed. He regained his footing. His eyes now locked on the figure standing before him. He calculated his odds in that fraction of eternity, but there was no time even to flinch. The Kalashnikov flashed and jerked upwards in quick succession as high velocity rounds slammed into his body, lifting and twisting him backwards. His body was spinning out of control - a dazed blur of confused impressions. The ground was rushing up to meet him.

He was in a world of hurt, of stinging pain and searing flesh. *"Where is he?"* he questioned, as a surge of thoughts shot through his mind. The pain was unforgiving as he struggled to roll to his back. *"Where is he?"* He strained to get up, but unseen hands were holding him down. He was fighting desperately to pull himself free, but a reluctant body would not cooperate. It seemed as if he were pinned and being slowly drawn into the earth. *"But it was one of ours!....Where is he?"* Roger blinked his eyes, barely able to focus as he stared heavenward. A suffocating wave of claustrophobic panic began to build, like the growing swell of an oncoming breaker. *"I've Got to hold it together.....Oh, God He's over me"* The blood blurred specter of a soldier towered over him. Cotton like clouds drifted slowly through a cobalt sea. A brilliant Vietnamese sun was eclipsed by the ominous outline of a pith helmet. He saw the glint of the bayonet and the distinctive silhouette of the AK poised in mid-air like the frozen stop-frame of a camera shot. A slow-motion second passed, before the horrifying plunge of the shadow.

Then the shadow was gone. . .

POINTMAN

William R. Kimball
&
Roger L. Helle

Chapter 1

The first impressions of 'Nam for countless vets came when they emerged from their chartered jet after it had taxied to a stop. For many, those first impressions were offensive. The shock of stepping from the air conditioned comfort of the passenger cabin into the sweltering heat and humidity of Vietnam was like entering an over-heated steam room. The pungent smells of oriental cooking, petroleum products, rusting metal and spent ordnance, intermingled with the stench of burning diesel and human excrement left an impression they would never forget. They were sensations which will be burned in their memories forever.

Roger's introduction differed slightly but was no less offensive. Though he was fortunate to have escaped the tedious two week passage by troop ship across the Pacific endured by earlier Marine units, he wasn't afforded the luxury of a chartered passenger jet either. Instead, his passage to Vietnam was on a noisy, C-130 cargo plane. The flight was long, cramped and mind-numbing. His first vivid memory was of being jolted out of an uneasy sleep when the C-130 suddenly dove in a steep descent during its final approach to the Da Nang air base. He thought the plane was crashing. Roger didn't know that this was standard operating procedure to minimize the hazards of potential ground fire.

The steep descent of the C-130 lasted only a few seconds. It abruptly leveled off and touched down with a rough jar which sent a sudden shock through the entire fuselage, followed by the deafening roar of the air brakes as the plane raced down the runway. A sense of nervous anticipation filled the cargo bay as the transport slowly taxied to a stop, and the pilot shut down the engines.

No sooner had they landed, when a big Gunnery Sergeant entered the cargo bay with a Lance Corporal in tow. The Gunny was barrel chested with muscular arms which bore faded blue tattoos. He quickly surveyed the batch of recruits and started yelling out instructions. "O.K. you men listen up! Pick up your duffle bags and police your loose gear and follow Lance Corporal Cummings here," pointing to the freckled face corporal with thick framed glasses. "I don't want any grab ass'n or jaw-jackin'. We get mortared now and then, so I want you replacements to pick up your gear and move it. Is that clear?"

"Yes, Sergeant!" The Marines responded like a chorus of trained seals.

"O.K. then, c'mon, move it!" the Sergeant barked.

The Marines shuffled down the ramp in a state of numbed curiosity. They were disoriented and worn out from the flight, but keyed up with excitement. They didn't know what to expect. Roger didn't know what was going on or what was going to happen next. All he could think of when he emerged from the dim confines of the cargo bay was, *"Well, I'm finally here!"*

"Looks like this is going to be our home for the next thirteen months," Roger noted to his buddy, Danny.

"Yea," Danny said wryly, "Be it ever so humble, there's no place like home."

Roger and Danny had been together since boot camp and had become close friends. Danny was one of those soft spoken types with curly blond hair and thoughtful blue eyes. He had an inner strength which had been sculpted by the sun and wind and snow on the weathered ranch lands of Wyoming. Countless hours of solitude, riding range, rounding up strays and mending wire had tempered Danny. Maybe the loss of his parents when he was fourteen gave him a sobriety about life of which most nineteen year olds knew nothing. Though mostly quiet, Danny had a dry sense of humor which would come out when you least expected it. Until he received his induction notice from his local draft board, he had never ventured more than a hundred miles from the family cattle ranch he and his elder brother inherited when their parent's pickup was side-swiped on the interstate east of Billings and run into a ditch.

Danny didn't talk much - not because he didn't have anything to say - but because he chose his words carefully. If he was your friend, you knew it. He was loyal and protective. He was the kind of Marine you wanted to cover your rear when the crap hit the fan.

Roger was struck by how gray and gloomy everything seemed. The sky was overcast with dismal gray clouds. A light rain was falling, texturing puddles on the runway with thousands of tiny concentric circles. Westward, he could barely make out some faint green mountains, shrouded in layers of mist. To the east, a driving squall was pelting a distinctive outcropping the Marines called, "Monkey Mountain." It had acquired the name because of a large contingent of Rock Apes which inhabited it.

"Man, this place is depressing."

"I'll bet you, we haven't seen anything yet," Danny stated.

"That's what I'm afraid of, Danny boy!"

"Yeah, me too," he confided. "The whole place looks kinda spooky, if ya know what I mean."

Roger couldn't help noticing how busy the base seemed as he crossed the tarmac. It was crawling with activity. It gave the impression that the war was in overdrive. Every few moments, the roar of afterburners signaled another sortie heading north to one of the Route Packs or in support of friendlies in the south.

All around the runways, a variety of fighters and choppers was resting in reinforced hangers and concrete revetments. Somehow, there was something eerie looking to Roger about a nearby row of olive drab Heuys. They were sitting idle in their revetments - their tilted rotors and bulbous green noses showing a resemblance to some kind of prehistoric insect.

"Those things look like bloated dragon flies to me," Roger nudged Danny.

"Yea," he added. "They are kinda creepy lookin', now that you mention it."

"Wonder if we'll ever fly on any of those over here?" Roger wondered.

"C'mon," Danny responded. "You oughta know by

now that the Marines always get the leftovers from the Army - we'll probably get those old H-34's. "You know," Danny added, "They sort of look like insects, too...kinda like grasshoppers. Maybe they're the mothers that gave birth to the ones sittin' over there."

"Cut the bull!" The Sergeant barked as he pointed the replacements in the direction of a waiting bus with wire mesh covering the windows.

"On behalf of the United States Marine Corps, I want to welcome you gentlemen to Disneyland east, better know as "the 'Nam." We hope that you will enjoy your stay and ride with us again when you return to the land of the big P.X." The driver did a Hollywood imitation of a tour guide as the Marines piled into the bus.

"Why the wire over the windows?" a black Marine who had plopped down behind the driver enquired.

"To keep the friendlies out," the driver replied matter-of-factly.

"To keep them out?" the black Marine questioned.

"Yeah," the driver added, "to keep the gooks from throwin' things into the bus."

Another Marine was curious. "What do they throw?"

"What... do I have to draw you a picture?" The driver responded. "They throw whatever they get their hands on - grenades, garbage...you name it! I was drivin' through the Dogpatch last week and some gook kid threw a dead rat at the windshield."

"Too much," the black Marine shook his head. "Man, if we gotta keep the friendlies out, what are the bad guys like?"

"BAD," the driver answered bluntly. "You guys are in for a real learnin' experience. If Mr. Charles doesn't get ya, the 'Nam will."

"What do you know, man?" a little Puerto Rican mouthed off. "The only action any of you REMFs taste is beer in the rear."

Several replacements snickered.

The smirk quickly disappeared from his face when the driver turned and glared at him with piercing, steel blue eyes which bore right through him. "I've got more time in the bush than you've got standin' in chow line playin' pocket pool...so I would advise you to shut your mouth or I'll be outta this seat faster than flies on a turd and shut it for you!" the driver growled.

"Welcome to Vietnam," Danny whispered to Roger through gritted teeth, as if to offer his own commentary on the encounter.

"Let's go," the Sergeant told the driver as he climbed into the bus, unaware of the confrontation he had just interrupted.

"Stupid cherries," the driver muttered to himself as he started up the bus and drove the replacements to a wooden receiving barracks.

The next day, they endured the drudgery of in-country processing. The ordeal left them feeling more like displaced refugees who had just stepped off the boat at Ellis Island than combat Marines.

After their orders were issued, their shot records double-checked, and they were given an orientation class on "do's & don'ts" while in the Republic of Vietnam, they were assigned to their units. Danny and Roger lucked out and got assigned to the same unit - 2nd Battalion, 1st Marine Regiment. They loaded their gear into open deuce-and-a-halfs and headed north over the steep switchbacks of Hai Van Pass to the Marine base at Phu Bai up the coast.

Besides a few Quonset huts, wooden barracks, and base paraphernalia, Roger hadn't seen much of Vietnam. The ride through Da Nang was filled with sights, sounds, and smells Roger had never experienced before. The road was choked with a throng of pedestrians and assorted vehicles. A steady stream of bicycles passed in both directions, carrying everything from old papa sans to young women wearing conical hats and long, elbow length gloves to protect them from the sun. Added to this steady procession was a mixture of three wheeled cycalos carrying passengers and produce to market, raucous sounding Vespas, jeeps, heavy trucks and crowded DeSoto buses loaded with Vietnamese and their belongings. Everyone appeared to be jostling for the right of way, including their driver who swore profusely and ground gears as he attempted to negotiate the congestion.

Along the sides of the road, shops and open air stalls sold everything under the sun - from exotic fruits to the latest stereo equipment from Japan. Old men repaired bicycle tires or mended shoes while Vietnamese women tended charcoal braziers and simmering pots cooking a variety of vegetables and fried dishes for sale - the Vietnamese sidewalk equivalent of "fast food."

By the time their convoy of trucks and jeeps had reached the old French fort at the top of Hai Van pass and started to snake their way down the mountainous road, the persistent cloud cover began to break. Their view of the coastal plain was breathtaking. It was one of the most beautiful panoramas Roger had ever seen. Golden beams of sunlight streaked to earth through bright blue rifts in the clouds, illuminating patches in the lush, green landscape stretching northward. To the east, the surface of the South China sea danced and sparkled like sunlit crystals in the sun's reflection. Gossamer veils of mist rose from the cool, green slopes, evaporating in the sun's warmth. Along the road, small waterfalls and ephemerals from recent rains plunged down cliffs and narrow gullies, creating little streams which wound their way out of the mountains to the emerald lowlands below. After the gray overcast and rains, the whole experience was exhilarating. The only ominous note was the solid wall of gun-metal gray clouds lingering to the west.

Roger turned to Danny, sitting next to him under the shelter of his poncho liner, and gestured toward the scenery below, as the driver downshifted into a narrow curve, "I don't think I've ever seen anything so beautiful."

"Then you haven't seen a black prairie night in Wyoming. It's so black, you can see a million stars sparklin'," Danny responded.

"Maybe not," Roger paused as their truck belched a sooty cloud of exhaust, "but that's still pretty righteous," pointing toward the scenery below.

After a couple of bumpy hours, inhaling exhaust fumes and being serenaded by the throaty cough of the diesel, the small convoy wound its way out of the mountains, past a picturesque fishing village and up the coast, before pulling into Phu Bai where the consignment of "new guys" was off-loaded. They checked in at battalion HQ for more processing, then they were directed to a large supply tent. The supply Sergeant issued them each an M-14, helmet liner and helmet with camouflaged cover, a poncho, two canteens, web gear, a cleaning kit for their rifle, a first aid pouch, extra magazines, ammo, a cartridge belt, a K-bar, a mess kit, an entrenching tool, two M-26 grenades, C-rations, Halazone tablets, salt tablets, and a little plastic bottle of bug juice. They were also given jungle utilities with extra large, baggy pockets on the thighs and canvas and leather jungle boots with several pairs of socks. When they had received their gear, they were both assigned to "F" Company as replacements.

They soon learned that Fox Trot Company had acquired the dubious distinction of being a hard luck company because of the high casualty rate it had suffered a couple weeks earlier on "Operation Harvest Moon." They had been cut to pieces when the company was air lifted into a hot LZ and dropped right in front of a regimental V.C. command post.

Over the next two weeks, the mulish mass of water logged grunts from "F" Company cursed their way through a sodden terrain, chasing an elusive enemy in running battles which further depleted their ranks. Marines endured the monsoon misery of soaked foxholes, dripping jungles, flooded rice paddies, swollen streams and boot sucking trails. They endured the constant cold of soaked fatigues clinging to their bodies, as they sloshed through a world better suited for amphibians or creatures with gills, than human beings. Nothing was dry in that drench - not paper, smokes, or socks.

The perpetual downpour and jungle wetness had taken their toll, especially on men's feet. The constant tidal flow through their vented jungle boots resulted in numerous cases of immersion foot, better known as "jungle rot". The constant wetness left feet crinkled and bleached like the pallid underbelly of a dead carp.

When untreated, they began to crack and bleed and gradually rot, with large chunks of flesh falling off.

When "F" Company was pulled back to Phu Bai, it was worn down and worn out - in need of fresh blood. Since its last operation, it was derisively referred to as "F _ _ _ _ Fox." Danny and Roger soon learned that "F" Company was the constant brunt of cat calls, crude jokes and gallows humor.

This was driven home the second day after Roger's arrival when he was hassled by a couple of grunts from Golf Company pulling latrine duty. He was heading for the latrine when he rounded the corner and ran into two Marines with their backs to him. They were stripped to their waists with bandannas tied around their heads. They were maneuvering a sawed off 55 gallon drum filled with feces and urine out of a compartment on the back of the latrine. Oily black smoke was billowing upwards from another drum burning behind them. Their sweat-slick bodies were coated with greasy, black soot. Roger rounded the corner just as the contents of one of the drums sloshed over the brim. It splattered the fatigues of one of the hapless Marines, who was wrestling the cumbersome container into the open.

The acrid stink of outhouse funk, burning diesel and sour sweat left him temporarily speechless. Roger just stood there watching the two struggling Marines.

" Aaaah, man, can you believe we're doing this? This is, what I call, a bummer!"

"Ew Wee, check out the smell of this one. Phew! This stuff would gag a maggot," the taller Marine noted with utter disgust, spitting out a wad of gunk.

"Pretty rank," the other one agreed, oblivious to Roger's presence. "I thought they banned this kind of stuff in the Geneva Convention?"

"If they did," his buddy noted, "somebody didn't get the word!"

"Look at your face." The smaller Marine doubled over in laughter.

Both of them looked like chimney sweeps at quitting time.

The taller Marine shot back, "My face? You oughta see yours!"

The smaller Marine responded with an animated shuck and jive routine, his left arm straight at his side with his palm opened backwards and his right hand reaching forward with the index finger pointing downward every other step, like he was gradually pulling himself forward with each stroke of his finger saying, "Listen, my man, I think its time us here honkies head on down ta the show'wahs an change dees funkie threads, if ya can digs what I'm sayin'?"

"I can dig it! I...Can...Dig...IT!" The taller Marine sounded out the words for effect.

Just then, the shorter Marine turned and noticed Roger observing their antics with an amused grin on his face. "What do you think you're lookin' at?" the smaller Marine scowled.

"What are you guys doing?" Roger asked innocently. He had never seen anything quite like it.

"What do you think we're doing?" The taller Marine chided. "What are you, one of those lame cheeries that just came in?" he asked, eyeing Roger's new jungle boots and fatigues.

"Ain't you never seen crappers being burned?" the other replied.

"Yea, we's the local sanitation department," the first Marine flashed Roger a toothy grin.

"How'd you guys score such a choice detail?" Roger tried to joke with the two filthy Marines.

"I wouldn't be doin' this if turd for brains hadn't fallen asleep on perimeter watch," gesturing sarcastically toward his partner. "The First Sergeant doesn't like us sleepin' on the job."

"You can stuff it, Rawlins. You were sleepin' too, remember?"

"You got that right, my man," the smaller guy chuckled. "I need my beauty sleep."

"Hey, what unit you with?" The taller Marine asked.

"Fox Trot," Roger replied, sensing the challenge in his voice.

"Now, that is a major bummer!" the shorter Marine responded.

"Yea.....Eat the apple and ....the Corps," Rawlins wisecracked. "That's one sooorryy outfit! And I can tell by lookin' at you that you ain't gonna improve it's image much."

Roger tensed at the put down. "I may be new, but I've got some news for you."

"Oh Yeah," Rawlins scowled. "And what could that be?"

"I'm not the one cookin' crap," Roger replied. He wasn't any "old salt," but he had enough sense to know that he wasn't a slacker or screw-up like these two. "I'm glad I'm in Fox Trot. At least they know where the real action is...not playin' with what they left behind."

"Well," Rawlins came back sarcastically, "there's just one thing I got to ask you before you go. When you get your legs blown off with old F_ _ _ _ _ Fox, can I have your boots?"

They both busted up and went back to stirring

their brew.

Roger couldn't shake the uneasy feeling in the pit of his stomach as he plodded back to his company area. Somehow, the encounter had struck a sensitive cord. Bar room boasts and untested bravado about being a tough Marine and killing gooks was cheap. He could cruise the sidewalks of Oceanside with his barracks buddies in their starched uniforms and spit-polished dress shoes with their marksmen badges and National Defense Ribbons, but he hadn't seen anything yet. He could knock down pop-up silhouettes on the firing range. He could crawl under barbed wire on simulated battlefields as explosions ripped around him and machine guns fired overhead. He could even beat some poor slob senseless during bayonet drill, but he was just playing Marine. He wasn't wise to the ways of combat.

Like a million men before him, Roger struggled with the same inner tug-of-war between cowardice and courage immortalized in Stephen Crane's, "Red Badge of Courage," which he remembered reading in high school. He was haunted with the same self doubts experienced by cowards and Medal-of-Honor winners alike.

He was still unproven, innocent and barely out of puberty. He didn't even know what it was like to sleep with a woman. He knew nothing about the naked perversities of war - what it was like to lay face down in the putrid muck of a rice paddy, paralyzed from the waist down, or to cradle a dying eighteen year old in his arms and watch him helplessly bleed to death, or to puke his insides out at the stench of decaying flesh.

As a teenager, he had thrilled at watching "The

Fighting Leathernecks" and Sergeant Striker in "The Sands of Iwo Jima". But, he wasn't naive enough to believe that the Hollywood portrayals of war romanticized by John Wayne and Randolf Scott were real. Even so, he was still fiercely proud to be a Marine - proud to belong to the Corps. Corny as it seemed, even to himself, he still got a lump in his throat when he heard the Marine Corps Hymn.

PFC Helle saw himself as a single strand in the proud tapestry of Marine Corps tradition - a glorious tradition immortalized in places like Chapultepec, Belleau Woods, Haiti, Shanghai, Guadalcanal, Tarawa, Mt. Suribachi, and Chosin Reservoir. He was only a tiny thread in a glorious legacy which wove its way from Tun Tavern to himself, and he was honored to be a part. He just hoped that he would do nothing to tarnish that tradition.

Chapter 2

The Company First Sergeant sent Roger and Danny to "weapons" platoon. They would fill the gaps left in 2nd Squad after Boals and Stukowsky snagged a booby trap on "Operation Harvest Moon" and finished their tour early.

Their reception was less than cordial. They were met with reserved nods and restrained handshakes from the "old guys." Those with "bush" time showed a certain leeriness - not because of cold indifference, but cautious skepticism. They were wary of any "new guys" because "new guys" were an unknown and unpredictable factor in the equation of a fire fight. It would take time for them to be accepted into their tight-knit family. Until they proved themselves, the rest of the squad would keep their distance.

Oddly enough, Roger understood the reasons for their aloofness and suspicion. He shared the same misgivings about himself.

It was less than a week since they'd been in country and they were going out on their first perimeter patrol. Roger and Danny were sitting on one of the sandbag bunkers along their section of the perimeter waiting for the order to move out. They were both keyed up with nervous anticipation. Danny took a deep drag from his cigarette, then ground out the butt on one of the rotting sandbags. Roger impatiently caressed the trigger guard of his M-14 with his index finger, as he stared across the perimeter. "Well...guess this is it," he stated.

"Yeah," Danny replied absently, lost in private thought.

They watched the expanse before them in quiet contemplation.

As the shadows lengthened, the mountains to the west faded from mottled greens to grays, to charcoal grey, then to blackness.

"Saddle up!" Sergeant Jeremiah Pope snapped as he emerged from the bunker with his radioman. His men simply referred to their squad leader as "Pope." Somehow, Jeremiah or Jeremy didn't fit. He was only twenty-one, but looked much older to Roger. Something about the way he carried himself showed that lifetimes separated them. One look at Pope's eyes, and you knew that he had the predatorial instinct of a killer shark. It wasn't the march of time that gave him that cold calculating look; it was gruelling months of pressure in the killing zone. Roger wondered if he'd ever have that look.

"Drake, you take point. Charlie Brown, you pull tail-end-charlie. Big Mike, you fall in behind the two new guys."

"Big Mike" nodded quietly as he stood there cradling his M-60 with brassy bandoliers of machine gun ammo draped over each shoulder, Pancho Villa style. Roger could tell by the way big Mike was fondling his pig that he had a special relationship with it.

"You two new guys will fall in behind me and Angel," Pope nodded towards Roger and Danny. "Just keep your eyes open and your mouths closed. All right, check your frags, make sure your tags are taped, and secure any loose gear. I don't want you clowns announcing our arrival to Mr. Charles. Each of you will maintain proper distance with the guy in front of you. I don't want any bunching up. We're going out a couple of klicks and set up an ambush site. Understood?" he asked. No one answered. "O.K. Lock and load!"

The squad headed through the darkness in single file towards a gate in the perimeter wire. "Hold it up!" Pope ordered the squad before sending the patrol through the gate.

Pope called in a commo check before stepping off, "Sidewinder One, This is Sidewinder Two, over."

"Sidewinder Two, we read you clear, over."

"We're moving out, Sidewinder One, will give sitreps as situation warrants.....We'll break squelch twice on the hour when in position, over." Pope released the button and listened to the familiar rush of static through the earpiece.

"Affirmative, Sidewinder Two, out."

"O.K., Drake, lead on. The rest of you keep cool and watch your butts."

A light drizzle began to fall as the men started out in staggered intervals, exiting through the barbed wire gate in the perimeter wire.

"Damn, I'm too short for this crap, Pope," a

stocky Marine with an M-79 whined as he shuffled past the squad leader.

"Knock it off, Blaine. I'm sick of your bitchin...in a month you'll be back home chasin' skirts. This is kid's stuff...just a little walk in the woods," Pope reminded him.

"Well, that's just outstanding...I feel better already!" Blaine vented his disgust. "Maybe you haven't heard, but war can be hazardous to your health!"

"That's old news, Blaine. Your belly achin' is gettin' old, too."

The squad filed silently through the gate as it headed into the night. Roger felt clumsy and slightly uncoordinated as he struggled to follow the vague outline of the radioman in front of him, and keep the proper distance in the darkness at the same time, without bumping into him. He wondered how Danny was doing behind him. Roger had no idea where they were going or where they were in the murky blackness. He concentrated on each step as he made his way down the sandy trail. The light drizzle subsided, leaving only the muffled sound of men moving through the damp night.

After about an hour of humping, Pope halted the squad and had them set up an ambush site at the intersection of two trails. One trail crossed an open field from north to south then disappeared into an island of secondary growth and banana trees on each side. The other trail led from a small village through their position to a graveyard about a hundred meters behind them. The squad was positioned along the low embankment of the old dike running north to south. It joined at right angles with the one coming from the village. They were in position to ambush anyone coming down the opposing trail from the cluster of huts west of them.

Word was that V.C. cadre were making their nocturnal rounds of the surrounding countryside. They were extorting taxes from the locals and threatening the villagers with reprisals if they cooperated with the American "imperialists" or their "reactionary puppet stooges" in the south.

Roger's night vision had improved a little, to the point where he could barely make out the dim outline of objects around him. The exact lay of the land was still a mystery. He just concentrated on keeping his eyes trained on the low brush covered trail in front of him.

Night vision, a sharpness of sight, an acuteness of hearing, peripheral vision, a keen sixth sense and a general instinct in the bush were some of the ambient skills one acquired in combat if he lived long enough. Roger had acquired none of these, as yet.

The night blackness played tricks with his eyes as he scanned the front. Bushes and shadows toyed with his senses, creating figments in his mind of enemy soldiers crawling towards them in the darkness. But, he wasn't about to freak out and start shooting at shadows that kept changing and make a fool of himself. After all, the rest of the squad wasn't shooting at anything. He felt awkward and stupid - like his first day in Junior High when he didn't know his way around.

The night weighed heavily upon him as he fought to keep alert and ignore the irritating puffs of mosquitoes which darted about his head in search of exposed patches of skin upon which to feed. He removed the small plastic bottle of bug juice from his helmet cover and squirted some of it onto his palm. He rubbed the oily fluid over his face and neck, but the local coalition of insects seemed oblivious to the repellent.

The minutes dragged by in slow-motion. He checked the radium dial of his wristwatch, then checked it again after what seemed like an hour and found that only seven minutes had passed. He yawned and blinked his eyes several times to ward off the weariness that was slowly enveloping him. *"This is getting old,"* he thought to himself as he shifted his body weight to prevent his right arm from falling asleep. Just then, Roger flinched at the unexpected boom of 105's back at Phu Bai sending out H & I fire. He was suddenly wide awake again. A second later, the loud, locomotive sound of "outgoing mail" rushed overhead. It was followed a few seconds later by the dull flash of impacting rounds in the distance. Moments later, the delayed "crunch" rolled through their position.

Roger was wide awake the rest of the night.

The men took turns on watch waiting for Charlie to come down the trail, but, except for the return of showers in the predawn darkness, the night was uneventful. With the unearthly half light of predawn, the squad began to stir and prepare to saddle up. They scarfed down some cold C-rats, took a few gulps from their canteens and headed back for their perimeter under dripping, toneless gray skies. It was the beginning of another melancholy morning in Vietnam near the close of the rainy season which was still wringing itself out.

Droplets of rain pattered on their helmets and poncho liners in a rhythmic cadence. The steady metronome amplified the contemplative mood of the men and drove them deeper into the solitude of their thoughts. Roger's reflections were on his first night in the bush as he plodded back through the headstones and grass covered mounds of the Vietnamese cemetery. He had learned his first lesson in 'Nam. Most duty involved long stretches of mind numbing monotony or backbreaking exhaustion. It was only occasionally interrupted by the electrifying terror of a fire fight, tripped booby trap or incoming fire. Another lesson was also driven home more powerfully than ever. He didn't like being green. He would rid himself of that stigma as fast as he could.

Over the next few weeks, Roger began to make good on his vow. Pope quickly sized Roger up and saw the potential in him to be a good squad leader in time. He took it upon himself to help tutor Roger in the finer points of being a grunt. Roger was soon pulling point under Pope's watchful eye - on security patrols around the perimeter at first, then on deeper daytime forays outside the wire. Roger's natural instincts were cultivated and gradually honed as he humped the sandy trails, open graveyards and little hills around Phu Bai. He didn't feel quite so green anymore, but he hadn't "seen the elephant" yet either. He hadn't even fired his weapon.

The local V.C. activity was light. Charles was laying low. Something was definitely up, but, other than the usual rumors and guesswork, nobody knew for sure. Roger hadn't even seen a V.C. yet - at least not one he was aware of. Pope had said that you couldn't trust any gook completely. Anyone of them could be the enemy - even a little kid holding a coke bottle or young village woman carrying a basketful of fruit. There might be ground glass in the coke or a grenade under the fruit. He could be everywhere and nowhere at the same time. You just didn't know for sure, so you never let down your guard. "When you do," Pope said, "that's when you've bought the farm!"

This was a war without fronts against an elusive and unpredictable enemy who often wore little more than black pajamas and Ho Chi Minh sandals. The pajama clad coolie quietly plowing his field by day behind his water buffalo could be just as quiet at night sneaking around the countryside planting booby traps which would take some Marine's legs off in the morning. For all we knew, he could be working behind the cash register at the base P.X., washing grunt's laundry, or shaving the exposed necks of Marines with a straight razor in some makeshift barber shop. The peasants seemed friendly enough when Roger's squad passed through the villes or handed out candy and cigarettes to smiling Vietnamese kids shouting, "G.I. Numbah One, G.I. Numbah One...V.Cee Beaucoup, Numbah Ten!" but you could never be certain what was really behind the look in their eyes.

And so it was, day after laborious day. Charlie would fire a few sniper shots, throw an occasional grenade or lob in a few poorly-aimed mortar rounds now and then. But, apart from the isolated harassment, it was quiet - almost too quiet.

About a month into his tour, the boredom was abruptly interrupted when Roger received his first exposure to the more sobering side of Vietnam. A low slung sun cast elongated shadows across the perimeter in its early morning glare as the men of 2nd Squad returned from their night patrol. They came through the gate hauling the body of one of their squad members in a poncho liner.

His entire squad had fallen asleep in the predawn

darkness when a squad of V.C. had come down the trail. He was the only one awake. When he stood up to warn the others, he took three rounds in the chest.

The dead Marine was laid on the ground and immediately drew a crowd of onlookers. What was almost a morbid sense of curiosity caused Roger to look at the partially draped body. Roger took one look and swallowed back a surge of warm bile which rose in his throat. The dead Marine was pale and gray from the loss of blood. His fatigue shirt was black and sticky from the hemorrhaging caused by ragged, fist-size holes blown through his rib cage. His matted blond hair was caked and greasy with sweat and dirt. A rim of dried blood coated his lips and the corners of his mouth.

Roger couldn't get over how young the dead Marine looked. He was struck even more by the faces of the squad members. Each was a study in emotions. He would never forget the look of weariness, frustration, and hatred etched on each of them.

24   Pointman

Chapter 3

It was early February, 1966, at the tail end of Tet and the beginning of the year of the Horse. Roger had been in-country for just over a month.

Five weeks to the day after his arrival, Fox Trot was assembled and trucked over to the airstrip with full combat gear. Their rucksacks were full and heavy with extra ammo. They were picked up by choppers and shuttled out to a helicopter assault ship laying offshore in the South China Sea. They would be the "reactionary force" for "Operation New York" which was scheduled to begin the following morning. Every man was ordered to remain fully dressed, in his jungle boots, with his combat gear packed. They were told to be ready to go in five minutes' notice. The call would come sometime after midnight.

The Marines of "F" Company were scattered

below decks in the mess hall and squad bays cleaning their weapons, killing time or writing letters home. The atmosphere was charged with the troubled misgivings of men poised on the brink of battle. Even their laughter and grab assin' was tinged with an edge of nervous tension.

Months of cumulative apprehension weighed heavily on the minds of many, especially the newer ones who had not yet been through their baptism of fire. Secret forebodings preyed upon private uncertainties - especially upon those who knew there were no certainties in combat.

Some sat stoically on their cots in fatalistic resignation to the fate which awaited them. The odds meant nothing to them. They had embraced that unique philosophy of war which holds that, "If the bullet has your name on it, there is nothing you can do about it. When your numbers up, its up!" It didn't matter if you were standing in front of a claymore or cringing in the deepest bunker. However, this belief was little consolation to those who hoped and prayed that through providence, prudence or prowess they could somehow beat the odds.

Danny was hunched over the edge of his cot, wiping down his M-14 with a can of Hoppes solvent. Roger was laying in the cot next to him with his hands behind his head, staring at the bulkhead in front of him.

Across from them, a small Marine with a Bronx accent was bragging about what a mean mother he was. "Tomorrow I'm goin' gook huntin'", the new replacement wisecracked as he ran the edge of his bayonet blade across a sharpening stone. "Gonna get me some gooks," he mouthed.

"You ain't gettin' diddily squat 'cept my boot up your ass if you don't quit beatin' your lips," Pope warned. "You got a big mouth for a little squirt... We'll all see how bad you are in the bush," Pope added, putting him in his place.

The cocky Marine said nothing, fearing that Pope would make good on his threat.

Roger sighed heavily.

"Something bothering you, Ol' buddy?" Danny asked.

"I'm going topside to get some fresh air," Roger replied as he rolled out of his cot.

He headed down a passageway deep in the bowels of the ship and up a series of stairways before entering a cavernous hanger bay below the flight deck. It was a beehive of activity as seamen fueled choppers and readied them for launch. Roger skirted the bay to a section of railing on the port side of the ship.

The night was coal black - so black that it was hard to discern any difference between the blackness of the sea and the sky. The only light in the inky expanse was from flickering pinpoints of starlight poking through holes in the clouds. Roger gripped the handrail and peered into the dark depths. The gentle rolling of the assault carrier did little to soothe Roger's nagging uneasiness. Specters of self-doubt gnawed at his mind. He still didn't have answers for those unresolved questions about his bravery, and he knew that the moment of truth was near.

He was standing there in the private inventory of his manhood when Danny found him.

"How's it goin,' Rog?" Danny asked, sensing that something was troubling his friend.

"Just thinking about tomorrow," Roger answered

glumly.

"Yeah, I've been doing some of that lately myself," Danny responded. "If you want to get something off your chest, just shoot, Buddy. I'm all ears."

Roger paused and cleared his throat, "I know that this may seem like a stupid question, but, do you ever get scared?"

"Do pigs fly?" Danny grunted. "No, seriously, sure...sure, I do. You'd have to be a fool, or three pickles short of a jar, not to be. It comes with the territory...Hey, I don't give a rat's ass about those gung ho types who are always shooting their mouths off about their killer instincts and how they're the baddest dudes that ever walked the earth. Its all bull - just a bunch of hot air!   Anyone with a lick of sense knows that.......Listen, for whatever its worth, I've watched you the last month and you've held your own. You'll do just fine."

Danny paused a moment before resuming. It was the most Roger had heard him talk at one stretch. "Roger why did you join the Corps?"

Roger hesitated. "I guess I had something to prove."

"Whaddaya mean?" Danny questioned. "Prove to who?"

"To myself, I guess," Roger responded. "Its like this, Danny, I grew up having almost nothin'. I mean my twin brother and I were real poor - dirt poor. I can't remember ever wearing new clothes. They were all hand-me-downs and thrift store bargains. Our real Dad skipped out on us when we were little kids and left my Mom with us and her drinking problem. She tried in her own way, but she was sick a lot and just plain worn out. My step dad had to work real hard, holding down two jobs, just to keep food on the table. There was no time for a family. The kids at school always teased us and poked fun at me and my brother, Ron, because of the old clothes we wore. They said we were low life and called us "welfare brats." We were moving around all the time - from one run down rental to the next cuz we couldn't afford to buy a house. We never felt like we fit in or belonged. Sometimes, my mom would get so frustrated with everything that she'd take it out on us kids. She'd yell at us and tell us we were never going to amount to anything, and I started believing it. I didn't have enough confidence to do anything right. It seemed like I was always screwing up and failing. I got lousy grades and failed at sports...Hell, I couldn't even get a date. I felt stupid -like a total loser. My life was going nowhere. But things started to change that day in high school when Ron and I decided to join the Corps on a whim. We walked into the recruiting office in Toledo and that Gunnery Sergeant shook our hands and said, 'What can I do for you, young men?' "

"The Corps gave me something that I can't put into words, Danny. She gave me back my self esteem and made me feel like I was somebody after all. The Corps made me believe in myself. I felt like I was doing something right for a change. For the first time in my life, I feel like I belong somewhere." Roger paused, struggling to find the right words to say. "And there's more, Danny; I never had a friend like you. I've never felt such a closeness as I've felt in the Corps. In some ways, the Corps has been more of a family to me than the one I had growing up. Don't get me wrong," Roger grinned, "There are some real jerks in the Crotch too," Roger chuckled. "But I wouldn't trade them for anything.....I guess what I'm sayin' is that I feel that I owe her for what she's given me. I've got to prove myself worthy - for her and for me. I just don't want to let her down.....It's kinda like when you and your brother had to prove you could make a go of it or lose the ranch. You did it because you owed it to your mom and dad. It's the same for me." Roger took a deep breath and slowly exhaled....." I don't know what else to say," he concluded.

"Its O.K. I understand." Danny assured him - and he did.

One of the most redeeming qualities of 'Nam was that unspoken bond of comradery forged in the crucible of combat. It was a sacred brotherhood birthed in the midst of mutually shared suffering and uncertainty. It was a covenant which compelled men, in some sublime way, to care for one another with such a depth of selfless love and loyalty that they would lay down their lives for one another in a firefight, drink from the same canteen or simply share the contents of a care package or letter from home. It was a brotherhood of men who were always there, when you needed to share some secret fear or naked dream. Whether they laughed or cried, cursed or complained, philosophized about the meaning of life, or simply sounded their running commentary on the daily discomforts around them, they had an understanding which often transcended the limitations of words and ran even deeper than the relationships they had left behind. Theirs was a special kinship of men seldom touched by others.

They stared into the darkness for several minutes before Danny opened up. "Now that you've gotten that off your chest," Danny said solemnly, "There's something I've got to tell you."

"Sure, Danny, what is it?" Roger asked.

"You're the only one that I can talk to about this, Roger." Danny wiped his hand over his face. "I don't feel right about going to Pope or askin' to see the chaplain, but it's really bothering me."

"You sure didn't seem like anything was eatin' you," Roger interjected.

"I just carry it different. Its the same dead weight. I've got this nagging feeling in my gut, Roger," Danny stumbled over his words. "Call it a premonition. I don't know what it is, but I know that I'm not going to make it tomorrow."

"Don't talk like that, Danny," Roger protested. "Didn't you hear what you just told me?" Roger pleaded.

"This is different, Roger. Don't ask me how I know, but I know that I'm not coming back from this operation."

"That's crazy, Danny! You...", Roger tried to argue with him, but Danny cut him off.

"I want you to make sure that my brother gets this letter," Danny said as he took a folded letter from his shirt pocket.

"But!.....," Roger attempted.

"Just promise me that you'll do it!.....O.K.?" Danny demanded.

"All right," Roger gave in, taking the letter and stuffing it in his breast pocket. "But I think you're on a wild one, Danny. You'll see," Roger tried to act reassuring.

"We better be headin' back. We've got a big day tomorrow," Danny quipped, trying to lighten the mood.

At 2:00 A.M., Gunnery Sergeant HeWitt charged into the sleeping bay and started rousting the groggy

Marines awake. "All right laddies, we got a hot date. Get outta those racks and get your rears in gear! Secure your equipment and move topside to your designated areas. Everyone will check their weapons to make sure no rounds are chambered. I don't want any of you clowns shootin' yourselves before Charlie gets a chance. Now move it!"

"Hey Danny, don't worry, Buddy!" Roger shouted as they ran to the waiting chopper in a crouch. "This is going to be a piece of cake," he assured him.

Danny tried to shout back, but the spinning blades were too loud.

The flight deck was crawling with activity. It was awash with the buffeting down draft of a dozen spinning rotors. Scores of Marines piled into the choppers for their ride to the waiting LZ. One by one, the H-34's trembled in nervous anticipation as each pilot throttled down and applied more torque to the engine. The men's bodies vibrated from the relentless hammering of the rotors. The wheels performed a delicate tap dance on the pitching deck of the carrier before the bug nose choppers tilted forward and climbed off into the blackness.

They didn't know it then, but they were going in to relieve an ARVN garrison which had nearly been wiped out by a crack battalion of hardcore V.C. The game plan was for "F" Company to be air assaulted to serve as a sweeping force while "Golf" Company would be choppered in west of them to serve as a blocking force.

Chapter 4

Men sat in silence, tightly clutching their weapons, as their chopper beat its way through the darkness. Except for the dim glow of the instrument panel and the red running lights, there was only pitch blackness - no stars, no moon. The fear on board was palpable. Marines sat riveted to their seats in straightjacket suspense. Men gritted their teeth or privately prayed as they assumed the various postures of those heading into the terrifying uncertainties of an LZ. Locked in the claustrophobic confines of a crowded chopper as it flew through the night was one of the most disconcerting experiences in Vietnam. You were seldom sure what you would jump into or what you would face when you hit the ground.

The chopper banked tightly to the left and made a spiral descent as it glided into the waiting LZ. Just above the din of the rotor blades, the crew chief shouted, "GET REEEADY!"

"Lock and Load! Selectors on semi!" Pope yelled.

Men tensed in anticipation.   Mouths were cardboard dry. Hearts were pounding from fresh doses of adrenalin. Fatigues were clammy from nervous sweat. "O.K., THIS IS IT!" the crew chief warned. Everything was happening so fast. The chopper was down!   They had landed in an open field in a long valley surrounded by convoluted hills. "LET'S GO!...MOVE IT!..GO! GO! GO!" Pope ordered. They were up and moving in the blackness, bumping into each other and groping for the exit. The sound of grunting, cursing Marines punctuated the chaos. The Marines stormed out into a swath of knee high Koani grass which was being battered back and forth in the down-draft of the whacking props. "SPREAD LEFT!....KEEP TOGETHER!" Pope yelled.

After the last chopper lifted off into the blackness, the platoons set up a hasty night perimeter. The insertion was relatively smooth, in spite of the potential hazards of a night air assault. Except for one broken ankle and a damaged PRC-25, the company was safely on the ground and intact.

"Listen up!" Pope instructed. "I want 2nd Squad deployed over there," pointing to a slight depression in the ground. "Mike, set your 60 up over there," indicating a position with a good field of fire. "The rest of you spread out in two man teams. Remember, keep alert, keep alive," he reminded them for the 15 millionth time.

He didn't have to worry about that; Everyone was wide awake and over-amped from the heavy dose of adrenalin. It was 0230 hours, but no one would be dozing off this night.

"Do you think Charlie knows we're here?" Danny asked.

"Well, if he doesn't, he must be hard of hearing. We're about as subtle as an earthquake," Roger responded.

Apart from the irritating whine of mosquitos and constant ratchetting of insects, the only sound was the hissing of parachute flares throughout the night. Every few moments, a flare would pop overhead, illuminating their position with an eerie green light. Roger and Danny lay in their prone position, mesmerized by the garish light show above them.

"Man, this is weird," Roger muttered. "I feel like I'm in a graveyard at midnight," he said, as he watched the hissing flares, haloed in a ghoulish greenish glow. Phosphorous globs dripped from the flares, as they swung back and forth under their tiny umbrellas and spiraled downward, trailing a corkscrew of smoke.

The eastern horizon began to blush with pink pastels and orange sherbets, before giving birth to a copper-colored sun. It was 0530 hours. The morning was calm. The sky was clean and blue. It was one of those brilliant Vietnam mornings after the rainy season which you both loved and hated. You loved it because it was absolutely resplendent with color; you hated it, because it was already hot and getting hotter.

Roger yawned and ran his hand over his face as he shook the night stiffness off. He couldn't believe how intense everything looked. The sky was the deepest blue he had ever seen. The surrounding hills were alive with a hundred hues of green.

By 0600 hours, the men had chowed down some cold C-rats, relieved themselves, applied the appropriate coating of repellent, chugged down a supply of water or Kool Aid and prepared to move out. Their corpsman passed through the squad dispensing pink salt and yellow dapsone tablets which helped guard against malaria but turned the skin a jaundiced hue.   Sergeant Pope returned from a huddle with Lieutenant Luery.   He informed the squad that the company had landed about a klick west of a village where an ARVN garrison that had gotten overrun the previous night by a force of V.C. of undetermined strength.   "F" Company was ordered to sweep west in pursuit of the V.C.

The temperature was in the mid-eighties and heating up as the men moved out across the valley. They were weighted down with 70 pound rucksacks, pregnant with extra ammo.   Roger was humping not only his normal load of gear, but was carrying extra magazines and three 60 mm mortar rounds.   Danny was lugging a can of linked M-60 ammo, which was awkwardly strapped to the back of his ruck.

As the sun climbed in the sky, so did the heat. By mid-morning, the temperature was pressing the 100 degree mark.   The humidity was keeping pace.   For several hours, the Marines swept through the valley. They moved over a varied terrain of low hills, fields of saw grass, occasional stands of bamboo, jungle outcroppings, and muddy rice paddies, pursuing Charlie.

Near noon, they passed through a small village. The only inhabitants were frightened women, children and old mama and papa sans.   Except for the conspicuous absence of young men, there were no signs of Charlie.   All they could get out of the villagers when they questioned them was, "No V.C.! No V.C.! V.C. Numbah 10!"

By early afternoon, the sun was blistering in its intensity.   Every movement was a labor in the sweltering heat and humidity.   Men gulped water from their

canteens, like they were dying of thirst. Sweat flowed
from bodies like water through a sieve. Rivulets of
perspiration coursed through oily repellent and jungle
grime, stinging eyes and blurring vision. Crotches,
armpits, chests, inner thighs and the smalls of backs were
soaked with sweat as the company struggled forward
through the merciless heat. Men's uniforms hung like
limp rags from beaten frames, wet and encrusted with
ringlets of salt. The sun's intensity stung shoulders
already rubbed raw from the weight of the shoulder
straps. Even the heat of their dog tags burned their
chests.

"Man this sucks!" Big Mike grunted. "This is a
real butt breaker!" he complained, as they pushed
themselves through a chest high maze of saw grass. The
thin blades sliced at mens' hands and arms, leaving razor
thin lacerations which stung and soon festered into red
pustules in the moist heat.

"Like I always say," Martinez quipped. "The earth
don't have any gravitational pull - it just sucks!"

"We gotta be crazy doin' this," Mike continued.
He pushed aside a clump of stiletto like shoots, slicing
his fingers and releasing a cloud of dust and pollen.

"Certifiable!" Blaine noted. "They don't call us
'Grunts' for nothin'."

"If you're an 0311, it comes with the territory,"
Pope commented. "Who else would spend thirteen
months in this armpit if he had any brains?" he added.

"No kiddin', Sherlock!" Hawkins agreed.

"Yeah, especially you, Blaine. You got a brain
like a BB rolling around inside an empty boxcar,"
Charlie Brown teased.

"Shut your lips, Brown. At least I'm not brain
dead like you and the rest of your tribe."

"Oooh! Jump back brother," Brown mocked. "This brother's shakin' in his boots."

"I'm tellin' you, Pope, this is too much!" Blaine protested. "I'm so short I could parachute off a dime! You know I've only got three weeks left. I shouldn't be out here, man! I've done my time."

"I know, Blaine," Pope agreed. "I talked to the 1st Sergeant and he said we were just too short of men as it was. I tried, Blaine, but the Sarge wasn't going to hear any of it."

"I don't believe this," Blaine gripped. "I've got to get out of this place!"

"Yeah! YeaH! YeAH! YEAH!......We got ta get outta this place, if it's the last thing we evah do!" Angel broke into a rendition of the Animals as the rest of the squad joined in, "WE GOTTA GET OUTTA THIS PLACE ....CUZ GIRL THERE'S A BETTER LIFE FOR ME AND YOU...You know its true babe", Angel finished off.

"You know you're a real butt face, Angel," Blaine sulked.

"Hey, I love you too, Ol' Blaine, buddy."

"All right, cool it," Pope cautioned.

The men labored on through the stifling heat. By early afternoon, the temperature had soared to 115 degrees in the open. It was a balmy one hundred in the shade. The air was so supercharged with humidity that it was almost suffocating to breathe - like sucking fluid through a straw. More than twenty men had collapsed from heat exhaustion, including the cocky Marine from the Bronx whose body temperature had soared over the 102 degree mark in the brain-baking heat.

By 1330 hours, the men were spent from six hours

of humping under the relentless pounding of the sun. No one spoke. They were too tired to waste the energy. Everything was still in the oppressive heat. The only thing that moved through that purgatorial landscape were grunts whose bodies protested every step. Each bore the wearied look of exhausted men, as they plodded ponderously onward in grim resignation, like burdened pack mules under the teamster's whip.

Even Danny was quieter than normal, but Roger was just too tired to try to talk to him.

They pushed through an area of "Gitcha Vines" which poked and snagged fatigues and equipment. They reached a checkerboard field of shallow rice paddies. Pope took point as the squad moved tentatively across, only too aware of how exposed they were. Crossing an open field in 'Nam was almost as nerve-wracking as flying into a hot LZ. They didn't like it. The men cursed to themselves at the strain of their predicament.

The muck squished in and out of the meshed portholes in their jungle boots, as they sloshed through the paddy.

"This place stinks!" Roger swore, as he struggled to pull his feet out of the boot-sucking gumbo.

"It just don't get much better than this," Blaine grumbled.

By 1400 hours, Pope had reached the embankment. He quietly sighed a breath of relief that Charlie wasn't waiting for them. He waved the men forward with his hand and waited for them to catch up before crossing the stream on the other side.

"Mike, set up your gun while the rest of the platoon catches up. I'm going to check things out. I'll be back in ten. If everything is clear, we'll cross. Understood?" Pope scanned the tired faces of his men.

"C'mon, Pope," Blaine complained. "When are we going to take a real break?"

"You never quit, do you Blaine?" Pope responded as he made his way down the muddy embankment, waded across the waist deep stream and disappeared into a curtain of bushes on the opposite bank.

Pope was back in five with word that it was all clear. No sooner had he gotten back than he got on the horn with the LT. for a status check.

"O.K., listen up! The Lieutenant says to cross but wants us to hold it up on the other side. We'll break for twenty before moving out. There's a large field about a klick across just on the other side of this wall of bushes," he said, pointing to the stand of secondary growth on the opposite bank. "We'll chow down and take a breather. Then we'll move out on line with the rest of the company across the field. The C.O. wants us to reach the ridge before sunset."

The squad filed down the gradual slope and waded through the mustard brown water.

"Awwh! This feels good," Roger sighed.

"Oh, man, what I wouldn't give for a tall, cool one," Blaine mused.

"A tall, cool what?" Charlie Brown asked.

"A tall, cool anything," Blaine wished.

"It do feel good," Big Mike reflected.

Several of the men dipped to their necks, before sloshing out of the creek and up the bank.

"Now that was refreshing! It's funny how the simplest pleasures can feel so good," Roger noted as he waded out of the muddy bottom, leaned his ruck against a steeper section of the sandy bank, and eased himself down.

The biting reek of sour sweat and unwashed feet

hung in the air as men tended to their personal hygiene. Big Mike had already stripped to the waist and was soaking his olive drab neck towel in the water. Several of the squad members had taken off their jungle boots and were putting on fresh pairs of socks. Blaine had just wrung out his old pair and hung them on the back of his ruck to dry.

"Boy, this sure do feel good!" Big Mike sighed as he squeezed his wrinkled toes in the cool mud.

Roger dropped his pack and stretched. He reached under his shirt to massage a sore spot on his lower back where the frame had rubbed him raw. "Gawd! What is that!", Roger grimaced as his fingers touched the slimy lump just above his waistline. "What is it, Danny?" Roger asked as he pulled off his fatigue shirt.

"Looks like a leach to me...thing's wicked lookin'," Pope replied matter-of-factly before Danny could respond. "Come over here and let me see it. It's a real beauty," Pope squinted in the glare of the sun as he carefully examined the creature. "Looks like a trophy winner. You been trolling again, Helle?" he joked as he admired the engorged four inch vampire, feeding on Roger's waist. "What I want to know is, who caught who?"

"Aw c'mon, Sergeant, get it off of me!" Roger pleaded.

"O.K. O.K. Hold still," Pope instructed as he lit up a cigarette and touched the glowing tip to the brownish-green slug. In a couple of moments, it released its grip and fell to the ground. Roger promptly drove his heel down on the blood sucker, splattering it in the mud. "I want the rest of you guys to check each other out for leeches," Pope ordered.

"That makes sixteen all together," Brown noted after the men had finished removing the last leech.

"O.K., everyone fill their canteens before we saddle up. No tellin' when we'll run into water again," Pope advised.

The surface gulped and bubbled, as the men submerged their empty canteens in the muddy water.

"I wish I had time to take a bath," Angel said.

"Yeah," Blaine jested, "We wish you had time, too!"

The men busted up at the timing of Blaine's humor.

"You scum sucking pigs aren't smellin' Ivory clean either," Angel laughed as he splashed Blaine with a handful of water.

"You better make sure you use Halazone tablets," Doc instructed. "Don't want any one gettin' the trots."

"Naw, we don't want any of that," Blaine said sarcastically. "Might have to get medevaced out of here. That would be a real tragedy."

After smashing their C-rat cans and policing their junk, the men downed more salt tablets, drank some precious water, and moved out.

The day was a major scorcher.

Chapter 5

All along the stream, Marines stood and began to move out. The men felt refreshed after their brief rest, but it was short-lived. In moments they were once again struggling under the weight of their packs and the heat of an unforgiving sun. Delicate wisps of steam rose from mens shoulders as sweat and river dunk evaporated in the sun's intensity. They were soon coated within a patina of sweaty grime and jungle funk.

They passed through the secondary growth and quickly entered a wide field about 1000 meters across. On the other side of the field was a wall of jungle green which sloped up to a ridgeline about 150 meters in height. Tentatively at first, the men of "F" Company started across the open field, which was covered with ankle-high grass and low scrub. The company was spread out in a staggered line as they swept forward.

About a hundred meters into the field, the

Marines came upon sharpened punji stakes, partially concealed in clumps of bushes and low grass. They were angled outward in an ominous gesture - a telltale warning sign that Charlie was close. The more seasoned men tensed and became more serious about the sweep.

"You guys be on your toes and keep alert. There's no telling where Charlie might pop up," Pope ordered.

As the Marines pressed deeper into the field, numerous mounds began to appear in the low grass. They were scattered in a haphazard manner for several hundred yards. The company had entered an enormous graveyard which appeared to have been abandoned and in a state of deterioration from neglect. Most of the graves were small, sandy mounds with plaster borders and headstones; although, some of them had low plaster crypts or cement casings. Many of the headstones were inscribed with names and inscriptions. A few bore metallic pictures of the deceased.

"Look at that!" Danny noted with surprise. "I didn't know there were Nazis in Vietnam," he said, as he gestured with his M-14 toward a toppled headstone with a swastika marking.

"That's a Buddhist symbol," Pope stated. "The Navajos use the same symbol backwards," he added.

A cautious hush had fallen upon the men as they moved through the cemetery, closing on the treeline which shimmered in the wavering heat vapors of the afternoon sun.

Roger could hear the steady drone of a spotter plane overhead as it passed over the ridge ahead of them.

"Viper One, This is Bird Dog, over," the little O-1E spotter plane radioed the Company Commander.

"Roger, Bird Dog, read you five by five. What do you have?" Captain Jacobs requested, as he crouched behind a cluster of tombstones with his radioman.

"I see some movement along the ridge, Viper One."

"Roger that, Bird Dog. Are in pursuit. Keep in visual contact, over."

"Will do, Viper One. Out."

The company pressed on. Time seemed to slow as the men calculated the distance to the lush curtain of vegetation and coconut palms before them.

Roger's squad was seventy-five meters in front of the 810th Viet Cong Battalion which was concealed in the treeline. These were not peasant farmers sneaking around the jungle in black pajamas, wearing tire tread sandals and carrying vintage French rifles. They were main force regulars, well equipped with web gear, heavy machine guns, new Chinese assault rifles and rocket propelled grenades. They were also dug in and waiting.

"Thooomp, Thooomp....Thooomp!" The hollow, metallic cough of mortars drifted from the jungle.

Roger shot a quick glance at Danny only to see the same look of wide eyed terror reflected in his face.

"BOOM! BOOM! BOOM! BOOM! BOOM!" A Chinese .51 caliber machine gun opened up, sweeping the staggered line of grunts.

The men flinched in stunned silence for a split second at the realization of what was happening. Roger turned to Pope just as a .51 cal round hit him under the lip of his liner, blowing his helmet ten feet into the air and disintegrating the top of his head in a shower of brains and bone. Instantly, a hailstorm of AK's opened up, raking the company with a deadly fusillade of fire.

Everything was happening in a slow motion choreography.

Roger gasped for air as a tremendous surge of adrenalin rushed through his veins. Things were out of control. *"Danny!"* he thought. He turned to his left just as another .51 caliber round slammed into Danny's chest, lifting him off the ground and hurling him backwards. The impact jerked Danny's M-14 out of his hands, throwing it into the air, end over end, before it embedded itself barrel-first in the sand.

Roger was in shock, but he fought to react in time.   **"Karummph!   KarumMPH!...KaRUMMPH!"** Deadly grey-black blossoms of 61 mm mortar rounds exploded across the field. *"What do I do now?"* Roger fought to maintain control, struggling to think, calling upon everything he had been taught as he dove into the sand and started firing into the tree-line. Oddly, the only thing that shot through his mind were the words of his Drill Instructor back at the rifle range:

"All ready on the left;
"All ready on the right;
"All ready on the firing line;
"Watch your targets;
"Targets!......"

"FIRE WHEN READY!"

"This is crazy," he thought, as he snapped off rounds.

Marines were dropping around him as they took hits or scurried for cover. Others were frantically scooping out firing holes in the loose sand with their rifle butts and helmets.

"GUNS UP!" Lieutenant Leury screamed. "GET THOSE GUNS UP!"

Big Mike was already on the ground with his 60 on bipods, firing measured bursts into the treeline. "Tatow tow tow Tow....TaTow Ta Tow Tow Tow!" he swept the jungle as his "baby" spit out a brassy stream of 7.62 casings.

The confused cacophony of AK's, M-14's, .51's and M-60's reached a deafening pitch, as each side tried to gain fire superiority.

Roger squeezed off rounds as fast as he could pull the trigger, firing blindly at the muzzle flashes which blinked from the foliage. As the last casing spewed out of the ejection port, he grabbed another magazine and reinserted it. It was gone in seconds. "Damn!" he yelled as he crammed another magazine into his rifle and flipped the selector to fully automatic. A random burst stitched the soil in front of him, kicking up geysers of sand and dirt.

The insane staccato of automatic weapons sounded like a gigantic popcorn machine gone berserk.

"Corpsman! Up!" someone screamed, and then another, as men cried out in panic.

"Danny!" He thought. *"Pope!"* He wanted to cry but he couldn't. There was no time for that now. The hate cleared his mind and gave him fresh purpose.

"Sssss zzzzz whoooo," an RPG streaked from the curtain of greens and landed behind Big Mike. "KawRUNCH!" the grenade exploded in a orange cloud pelting Mike with dirt and bowling him over from the concussion.

A second RPG shot from the foliage and exploded thirty feet behind Roger, causing the ground to lurch from the impact.

"Corpsman!" Mike bellowed. A fountain of blood squirted out of his gunner's neck from a severed Carotid artery. Charlie Brown was writhing on the ground, grasping his neck as arterial blood pumped out of the jagged laceration.

Blaine swore to himself, but rose up and ran toward Mike to feed the gun. "Ammo! Ammo!" another gunner screamed. Blaine scrambled over to Danny's body and grabbed the can of machine gun ammo he was carrying. He ran to Mike, in a zigzag pattern, half stumbling in the loose sand as the crack of AK rounds bullwhipped around him. Mike was behind a headstone stuttering away with his 60, oblivious to the rounds blowing pockmarks in the plaster headstone and ricochetting off the surrounding graves. **"AMMO! UP! DAMN IT!"** Mike bellowed as his last belt fed through the 60.

"I'm coming!" Blaine shouted, as he closed the gap with Mike. "Aeahh!" Blaine screamed as an AK round hit him below the knee, knocking his leg out from under him and spinning him around as a crimson stream of blood sprayed from his leg. Mike scurried in a low crawl to retrieve the can to feed his gun. Blaine was screaming in pain as he doubled up squeezing his knee. "It'll be O.K." Mike tried to assure him as he grabbed the can and scampered back to his gun. He quickly slammed in the fresh belt and started hosing down the treeline.

"Bird Dog! Need marking rounds in treeline, over!" Captain Jacobs yelled.

"Roger, Viper One." The FAC pilot responded coolly as he swooped down low, dipping his nose toward the front edge of the treeline. "Whoosh..whoosh!" the marking rounds streaked from the rocket tubes. The phosphorous rounds impacted just inside the treeline, blossoming into graceful umbrellas of molten white streamers.

"Got gunships on line, Viper One. Will stay on station, Over." The FAC pilot radioed.

"Roger that, Bird Dog. May need fast movers. Do you copy, over?" Captain Jacobs instructed as he looked over his terrain map and double checked the grid coordinates.

"Will do, Viper One," the FAC Pilot confirmed.

Just then, the sound of gunships making a low pass hammered in overhead, followed by the "whoosh, whoosh, whoosh!" of 2.25 rockets streaking from their pods. A string of orange-black explosions ripped through the treeline, splintering trees and bamboo, snapping off palms, and throwing up clouds of dirt and foliage.

The two choppers banked tightly to the right as they pulled up from their first pass. The Heuys circled back and came in parallel with the treeline. Their door gunners were chattering away with their swivel-mounted 60's, slashing through the undergrowth with thousands of rounds. The choppers climbed sharply to the left, spilling a glimmering stream of shell casings which tumbled from the banking gunships in a golden shower. The choppers came in again for one final pass, shredding the vegetation like it was in an enormous blender.

Charlie seemed temporarily stunned by the fury of the gunships.

"DROP YOUR RUCKS!" The word echoed down the line. "Lay down suppressing fire!" Word was passed to M-60 and 'Blooper' men. The 60's opened up again amid the "blooping" sound of grenades lobbing into the treeline. "Up and at Em! ... LET'S ROCK & ROLL!" The Marines rose and started running toward the enemy, firing fully automatic bursts as they ran. "Uuunh!" a Marine next to Roger grunted as he crumpled to a heap. The dull "thud!" of a high-velocity impact somersaulted Martinez headfirst from a hit. Roger ran forward, screaming at the top of his lungs. He was firing from the hip. Others went down. Men were screaming as the jungle exploded with a wall of return fire. Roger wasn't thinking. He was on fully automatic himself as he rushed the muzzle flashes. It was pure instinct which ruled him now.

He leaped over a dead Marine. **"KAROOOM!"** He was in mid-stride when a loud explosion erupted in front of him blowing him backwards in a shower of sand and rocks. He was on the ground spitting sand and firing again. Roger reached for another magazine when he noticed that the front of his fatigue shirt was wet with blood. *"I'm hit!"* he thought as a wave of panic shot through him. He rolled to his back and frantically began to tear at buttons to check his chest. He didn't feel anything. He was laying on something. In the chaos, he thought it was a log or something blown out of the jungle. He was squirming and swearing, feverishly ripping open the front of his shirt. He ran his hands over his chest but found no bleeding. He rolled back to a prone position when he realized what he was laying on. It was a leg amputated below the hip with the jagged tip of the femur still protruding. The blood splattered him when the leg was blown off by the explosion.

"Oh, God, I can't stay here," Roger thought, as he gagged back the hot puke in his throat.

"Got to get up and move!" he thought. He was up

and running again. Squad leaders were yelling "Move! Move! Move!" The men broke into the treeline in hot pursuit of the V.C. who were withdrawing through the jungle, dragging their wounded and dead and firing their AK's as they retreated.

In a frenzied stampede, Marines assaulted the treeline, rushing through broken limbs and tattered foliage which sprang back, snagging weapons and grabbing gear.....Rounds slapped through the moist vegetation, ripping through stalks and broad leaves, ferns and trees, clothing and men. The muffled "crunch" of grenades punctuated the chaos...They were firing wildly, rushing forward in a panicked rampage - stumbling, cursing, tripping, yelling, firing blindly at fleeting shadows which darted in and out of the dappled greens. Marines insane with adrenalin, insane with hate, panting, coughing, screaming as they tore through the tangle, firing wildly - it was five minutes of sustained heart attack, a grand mal seizure, a head on collision, a fall from a twenty-story building, a point-blank bullet in the face - the wildest roller coaster ride of their lives - then the firefight was over.

"F" Company pushed only about a hundred meters into the forest when the men were ordered to break off contact. Golf company would cut them off with gunship support.

Chapter 6

Roger straggled back through the jungle in a state of dazed exhaustion. Sporadic shots tapered off. Moans filtered through the curtains of green. Marines lay crumpled and sprawled in awkward dead poses. The acrid smell of burnt Cordite floated in the dense air. Rays of sunlight filtered through holes blown in the jungle canopy, illuminating a mantle of smoke and haze which hung in the thick vegetation, creating a mesmerizing display as the sunlight danced through the shadows. The jungle floor was trampled and torn - littered with the scattered remains of battle - a pith helmet here, blood trails there, a crater gouged in the earth with delicate wisps of smoke still clinging to the freshly turned dirt.

Shadows were already lengthening as the sun arced into Laos. It was still hot and steamy from the day's sauna but the intensity was backing off. Marines trudged wearily out of the dense vegetation, dragging their wounded or shouldering them in a fireman's carry. Their faces were dirty and grim, their eyes dark and hollow -the forever saddened faces of battle weary grunts. The grisly task of gathering the broken shards of "F" Company had begun in earnest.   Corpsmen had established a makeshift triage area in a shallow depression surrounded by headstones and mounds.

Roger made his way across the field to the first aid area. The ground was littered with soiled dressings, gauze patches, medical kits, empty syringes, canteens, discarded clothing, helmets, and saline bottles hung from rifles stuck in the sand.   Marines were sprawled on poncho liners with a variety of wounds. The sickening, salty sweet smell of fresh blood hung in the air. One Marine was laying with his back propped against a headstone with his shirt open and his flakjacket pulled back. He was chalky white from shock. He sat there with a blank, absent look on his face. His chest was smeared with dried blood as if some preschooler had finger painted his chest with reds and browns. Blood was seeping from the corner of his mouth, as a Corpsman tried to stop a sucking chest wound which was wheezing and frothing with tiny pink bubbles.

Another Marine had a mound of blood soaked compresses wrapped around his head from a round which had removed part of his jaw.

"Get me more compresses! More morphine! Tie this one off. Hold him !...Hold him down; he's going into convulsions. This one needs a trach! Hand me one of those salines. Put him over there." The various chants of Corpsmen sounded around the area as they worked with cool resolve to stabilize the wounded.

"Gaawyah," Roger turned to see a brown Marine

with a gaping stomach wound heave a warm belly full of blood and bile onto the lap of a tending Corpsman.

"Water...water," the low, plaintive moans of thirsty Marines drifted through the air.

Roger was emotionally paralyzed by the carnage he saw. "Danny," he remembered again. "Just a piece of cake..." The words stabbed at his conscience like hot pokers. "F" Company was only a shattered remnant. Forty percent of them were killed or wounded in action. Two more would die before they made it back to Da Nang. The whole battle had lasted less than an hour, but the repercussions would endure for lifetimes.

The resonant slap-thumping of incoming slicks sounded in the distance, as dust-offs began to arrive. The first had a large Red Cross stenciled on a white background on its nose. Roger shielded his eyes from the glare of the sun as he watched the Heuy hover in. Seconds later, it glided in with its underbelly flared up and its tube skids rocking back and forth, as it churned up a cloud of loose debris before setting down about twenty feet from the wounded.

Roger turned his back toward the chopper to protect himself from the turbulence of the prop blast. He squinted his eyes to avoid the dust, only to grimace at a row of dead Marines partially covered with poncho liners. The loose liners were flapping back and forth from the flurry of the downdraft, flashing on and off the gruesome reminders of death. Roger was pained by the sight of dirt encrusted jungle boots protruding from the flapping liners. Some were new. Others were cracked and sun-bleached from other days such as this.

The last of the medevac choppers readied to depart with its cargo of wounded. The co-pilot gave a thumbs up and the porters backed away in a crouch as the pilot throttled down. The spinning blades slapped faster and faster as the Heuy lifted up, canted its nose forward, and climbed off across the field.

The sinking sun was splashing a collage of pastels on the horizon as Roger and a detachment of new guys were volunteered to gather the dead to be loaded onto the next wave of choppers which would take them back to the morgue unit at Da Nang. They scoured the cemetery and treeline for bodies. Roger and a small black Marine found Pope laying in the trampled grass, splattered with blood and grey matter. He was laying in the grass looking straight up as if he was looking at something far away.

The black Marine took one look at Pope's head and retched his guts out uncontrollably. Roger choked back the puke as he fastened Pope's helmet to what was left of his head to keep it from falling apart. They rolled Pope over into one of the body bags the chopper had dropped off. Roger zipped it shut and hauled the faceless bag over to a waiting pile stacked like cord wood.

Roger found Danny sprawled on his back, spread eagle, with his arms extended back like he was reaching for something. His skin was taunt and pasty - the color of pale wax. "Man, this guy is one messed up muthah!" the black kid grimaced.

"Shut up!" Roger snapped.

"You know this guy?" The black marine asked.

"Yeah, he was my best friend," Roger answered.

"Oh, man, I'm sorry...I'm really sorry." The black marine apologized.

"Danny," Roger groaned within himself. *"Just a piece of cake."* The words haunted him. Danny's face was frozen in a look of surprise. His mouth was opened

wide in a grotesque expression of terror, like he wanted to scream. His eyes had a vacant look, like nobody was home. He was looking up at Roger, but it seemed like he was looking right through him.

Roger took a swig from his canteen, swished the water around in his mouth to wash the sour taste of bile away, then spit it out. The black marine swatted away a cloud of flies which had already begun to congregate on Danny's chest, then they rolled him over onto the body bag. Roger gagged again and swallowed back the urge to vomit at the sight of an enormous cavity in Danny's back which had been blown completely through the plates in his flakjacket.

"You all right?" The black Marine asked.

"Just leave me alone," Roger muttered. "Let's just get this over with!"

They grabbed the ends of the rubber bag and lugged the lifeless form over to a waiting chopper. They heaved the dead weight onto the blood smeared floor of the chopper, like a sack of potatoes. The door-gunner dragged the bag across the slippery floor and pushed it up against a growing stack of bodies.

After the last of the dead was hauled off, Roger staggered over to a cluster of mounds and slumped down with his back against one of the plaster crypts. *"Danny. Why?"* He asked himself. Roger had never felt so alone in all his life, as the mournful sound of the last chopper receded in the distance with Danny's corpse. Pope was gone. Danny was dead. Charlie Brown died of shock from a traumatic loss of blood. Martinez would spend two months in a hospital outside Tokyo. Blaine finally got his ticket home early - the long way.

Roger sat with his elbows on his knees staring at the field, now bathed in a strange orange glow. It was the first time someone really close to him had died. He knew something had died inside of himself, as well. It was more than just that universal delusion of immortality entertained by adolescent men. It was his youthful innocence.

"Never again," he swore to himself. *"Never again."* Troubled questions pricked his mind. *"Why Danny? Why? Why not me?...Why Pope? Why didn't I get it instead of you?"*

The choppers had carried off the dead and wounded, but had left behind men with more subtle wounds - not wounds of the flesh, but of the heart and soul.

"I'm not letting anyone get that close again," Roger vowed.

The hardening process had begun - a process fueled by hurt and hate - a process which would soon turn a heart as cold as case hardened steel. The bloodletting and carnage had triggered that subtle defense mechanism which learns to shut off feelings before they can awaken painful emotions. Roger had quietly put on an emotional flakjacket in the twilight greys of that forsaken cemetery.

"Never again," he promised himself, as he buried his head in his hands and held back the tears.

Chapter 7

An orange-grey glow was all that remained on the western horizon, as the last of "F" Company loaded onto choppers and headed back to the Iwo Jima in the blackness of the South China Sea.

Roger returned to the assault carrier with his emotional flakjacket firmly in place. He also returned with a festering abscess of hate eating at his insides. He could shut out the feelings of others, but he couldn't shut out the hate. He seethed with an insatiable lust for payback - and that with interest. *"The gooks are gonna pay,"* Roger vowed. *"I owe you, Danny,"* he swore, *"And Pope and the rest."*

The enemy had become an even more obscene abstraction in the aftermath of the blood bath he had just witnessed. They weren't human beings any longer; they were gooks, gooners, dinks, slants, slopes, zipper-heads. They were animals which needed to be exterminated, and he was going to waste as many as he could for Danny, for Pope, for himself.

That night, in the carrier squad bay, was the loneliest night of his life. His friends were gone and he wasn't about to let anyone get that close again. The Corps was still his family, but he had distanced himself emotionally - not because he didn't care, but because he cared too much.

Roger was tormented by the empty bunks which surrounded him in the dim confines of the bay. Less than a day before they had been filled with Marines laughing, talking, kidding, reading letters, passing around pictures of their girlfriends and wives and dreaming about that hot car they were going to buy off the showroom floor when they got home.

He slumped down onto his cot and started to unbutton his filthy utility shirt which was soaked with dried sweat, dirt and blood. That's when he felt Danny's letter in his breast pocket. He reached inside his pocket and pulled out a crumpled letter. It was soiled and stained from the day's battle. He looked at it for a moment and turned it over. It was addressed to Danny's brother in Wyoming. He slowly peeled back the sticky flap and extracted a single sheet of paper. The conspicuous gold eagle, globe and anchor of the Marine Corps emblem was embossed on a blood red background at the top of the page. It was dated the day before. It was neatly printed with the words:

Dear Paul,

By the time you receive this letter, you will know that I'm not coming home. It's very hard for me to write this to you or explain what it's like being over here. I don't know if you would understand, but I still feel like I did the right thing. I mean that, Paul and I want you to know that for sure. Please don't question that or let anyone back home try to tell you different. I know we haven't talked a lot since mom and dad died, but for whatever its worth, I know that they would have been real proud of how you took care of me and the ranch. You've done real good. Please don't cry for me. Just think to yourself when you see all those stars shining in the heavens at night that your little brother's somewhere up there looking down on you. I want you to know that I will miss you and the ranch and all the good times we shared, even if it was hard at times. I've never told you this, Paul, but I love you. You've been more than a brother to me - you've been my friend.

Your Brother, Danny

He finished reading the letter and returned it to its envelope. He wanted to cry, but the tears wouldn't come. He fell back into his cot and tried to sleep, but the sleep wouldn't come, either.

He lay there in the dull light of the sleeping bay tossing and turning on his bunk. Anguished reflections flashed through his mind. He was physically wiped out and psychologically shattered. His mind was racing out of control. It was falling over itself with agitated thoughts, like he'd just come off a three day run of crank, like he had just finished his fifteenth cup of coffee at 3:00 A.M in an all night diner, like he was on the last twenty mile stretch of a long haul run from Amarillo to

L.A. It was the most restless night of his life. His mind screamed at him with unanswered questions and disjointed thoughts, playing over and over like a stuck phonograph needle: *"What if , what if, what if...If I hadn't, if I only had...Why am I alive?...Why did Danny? Why did you have to die?"* They were problems he couldn't solve, questions he couldn't answer, thoughts which kept sticking up their ugly heads, even though he desperately fought to push them back down and silence them forever.

The sheer toll of exhaustion finally drove him into a fitful sleep, which was broken an hour later by a terrifying nightmare of the day's events. He bolted awake in a cold sweat from the brutal replays of the firefight. He was there again looking at Pope's head explode. He turned to see the terror in Danny's eyes as the round picked him up and threw him backwards like a rag doll. *"Why Danny?"* Roger grieved in silence.

"I've got to get it together," he knew. *"I'm blowin' it and I'm going to get myself wasted if I don't pull myself together,"* he concluded, *"Can't wimp out now - I owe Danny too much."*

The following morning, the residue of "F" Company choppered back to Phu Bai to be replenished and resume the monotonous routine of perimeter security around the base. The monotony was even more tedious than ever - the routine even more predictable.

The dry season had hit with a vengeance, quickly evaporating any remembrance of the monsoon deluge. One dull day blended into another in the blur of a blistering sun - Death Valley days which parched everything desert dry. The air was so hot it hurt the lungs to breathe. The country which had been drowning for months soon sweated itself free of billions of gallons of moisture it had absorbed during the monsoon rains, drying up alluvial fields, bunkers, and men. The mud bog which had been the company's compound quickly baked and dehydrated in the heat, turning into hardpan, then to dust. Like its rainy counterpart, everything was soon coated, but this time with a powdery layer of orange-red dust, the consistency of fine flour.

Perimeter duty got old real fast under the relentless heat and opaque glare of a dry season sun. Roger had regained his composure, but one all consuming passion still simmered beneath the surface - a lust for payback. He was numbed with boredom and fed up with Romper Room patrols along an uneventful perimeter. He was tired of squinting in the glare, tired of do-nothin' duty, tired of watching sandbags deteriorate in the scorching heat, tired of sitting in his musty bunker smelling mildew and killing bunker rats.

Three weeks into his drudgery, word trickled down that a new unit was being formed to work in rural villages alongside of the Vietnamese. It was part of President Johnson's "Pacification Program". The units would be composed of companies broken down into small, squad size units of Marines who would live in the villages and work with men recruited from the local peasant societies where the Marines were assigned. This program would integrate the Marines and Vietnamese into a unified fighting force which could coordinate operations and build a sense of rapport and cooperation. The Marines would benefit from the militia's familiarity with the area, local customs, language, and people. The Vietnamese would benefit from the Marine's military training and expertise. These special units were designated as C.A.C. companies or "Combined Action

Companies". The name was quickly changed to CAP units or "Combined Action Platoons" because the previous acronym, under certain pronunciations, formed an obscenity in Vietnamese.

The goal of this program was to station a squad of fourteen Marines and a navy corpsman in a strategic village to train and work with a unit of Vietnamese Popular Forces or "PF's" who were often sarcastically referred to as "Ruff Puff's". Their mission was to secure the tactical area of responsibility (TAOR) from Viet Cong infiltration and gradually win back the countryside.

Because these units offered an opportunity to meet the V.C. in face to face confrontations, Roger jumped at the chance to volunteer. Roger was attached to a CAP squad and sent to the village of Loc Ap about three klicks south of Phu Bai. The village of Loc Ap straddled a macadam stretch of Highway One near a small river emptying into the South China Sea. It was your typical roadside village, consisting of a cluster of plastered buildings, open stalls, and ticky-tacky shanties constructed out of bamboo, discarded C-rat boxes, ammunition crates, cardboard, and corrugated tin. Roger's squad had the responsibility of guarding two nearby bridges - one, a squat concrete span and the other, a rusty rivet and girder railway bridge built thirty years earlier by the French.

Except for the routine I.D. checks and the distraction of occasional convoys rumbling down Highway One, Roger's two weeks in Loc Ap were as boring as perimeter duty at Phu Bai. The handful of PF's they were attached to were listless and lazy and preferred to spend most of their time squatting on their haunches playing cards, smoking cigarettes or taking siestas.

The tedium was finally broken on his twentieth day in Loc Ap when Corporal McClure received word that a CAP squad in a village five klicks north of Phu Bai had been wiped out on a night patrol when they walked into claymores strung in the trees. The following day, a deuce-and-half picked up the squad and trucked them north to the village of Gia Le to replace the previous unit.

The situation north of Phu Bai was much more intense. They could sense it in the air and see it written on the faces of the locals. The surrounding countryside was a mosaic of paddy lands, untilled fields, congested jungle outcroppings and sandy hills. It was also a no-man's-land which the Viet Cong stalked by night, planting homemade booby traps and command detonated mines on Highway One leading north to Hue.

The squad established their compound in the courtyard of a quaint little French hospital made of white plastered brick and red-tiled roof. The compound was enclosed by a four foot wall of white stucco which had weathered a yellowish-orange from successive seasons of sun and red mud. The wall was speckled with dabs of fresh white plaster where patched pockmarks from previous battles had left their signature.

The situation at Gia Le was substantially "beefed up" with a larger force of Ruff Puffs, two armored personnel carriers, and a track mounted with a 106mm recoilless rifle.

Their primary mission was to patrol the surrounding hamlets and farm lands, to secure the northern fringes of the Phu Bai airstrip from guerilla activity and deny Charlie control of the area. Roger's squad was attached to a thirty-five man platoon of Ruff Puffs who were poorly motivated and ill-trained. They were a ragged collection of disheveled peasants and teenage conscripts. They stood there in bare feet and their mismatched uniforms with an odd assortment of vintage M-1's, World War II Thompson sub-machine guns and .30 caliber carbines, looking more like a gang of Mexican revolutionaries than a competent fighting force. The squad took one look at them and could see that they had their work cut out for them.

Corporal McClure and the other squad members quickly got down to the business of reshaping the rag-tag militia they had inherited.   Each squad member concentrated on imparting their skills. Outdoor classes were set up to teach them how to clean, disassemble, re-assemble, load their weapons, and sight and fire. They were given basic first aid lessons, taught how to check I.D.'s, take possession of prisoners, and use the radio. They were taken out in the field where they were taught small-unit tactics, how to pull a patrol, how to give proper hand signals, how to set up various ambushes and how to lay down grazing and suppressing fire. Doc did MedCAPs in the surrounding villages. He made weekly rounds with his medical bag, cleaning sores, passing out pills, giving injections and instructing the villagers in basic sanitation, preventative medicine, and personal hygiene. Doc even delivered a baby in a nearby village. Other medical personal supplemented Doc's medical care by providing basic dental care with DentCAPS. Construction materials, tools and machinery were brought in for community building projects such as school construction.   CAP units even provided instruction in animal husbandry, pest control, trash removal and water purification.

The initial lethargy and lack of motivation was quickly replaced by a new eagerness and esprit de corps.

The platoon of P.F.'s began to evolve into a credible fighting unit. During those first few weeks, the members of the squad slowly befriended the local villagers of Gia Le, although Roger still guarded his emotions from getting too close with the rest of the squad members. He wasn't cold, but he maintained a measured distance emotionally. They shared the villager's meals, their lifestyles and their simple needs and joys. It was a time of refrain - an almost tranquil time which seemed oddly removed from the war which was raping the people of both sides. These were not gooks to the Marines. They were simple people who seemed to share many of the same hopes and dreams which they had. The men got a kick out of eating the local food, playing with the village kids and trying out their smattering of Vietnamese phrases with the villagers, especially the shy young women who would giggle and blush when the Marines would say, *"Chau Co - Chau Chi"* (Hello, miss).

During this time, Roger concentrated on sharpening his skills walking point. He was driven to excel, so he volunteered to pull point as much as he could.   He was also driven by more subtle considerations. Though he seemed calm and collected on the outside, he had a simmering hatred within which drove him to be the best he could be - not just to survive, but to even the score.   So, he grew tough, lean and hard as ten penny nails.

Roger gradually learned the fine art of staying alive. He began to master the ambient skills of surviving on the lethal edge - of surviving on point. His mind began to function smoother. His thoughts were more lucid, his reflexes more adroit. On point, his system was charged with ample doses of adrenalin, which accentuated his senses. Walking point was a naked game of survival whose outcome depended upon every muscle, every sinew, every nerve ending being alert and poised for fight or flight. Roger soon adjusted to its unique disciplines.

He got good at what he did - very good - and he knew it. He drew a certain satisfaction and personal pride in the knowledge of his proficiency, but deep inside, he knew he would never be satisfied until he settled the debt he felt he owed Danny and the rest.

With the proficiency of the P.F.'s significantly improved, the patrols began to step up their frequency as Corporal McClure sought to put the pressure on Victor Charles. As the CAP activities increased, so did those of the V.C. as well. The men started picking up rumors of nocturnal tax collection, rice confiscations, and propaganda harassment. The tension was soon reflected in a new nervousness among the villagers which the squad couldn't help but detect.

Chapter 8

Corporal McClure assembled the squad in the morning to discuss the details of the patrol they were going to pull that night.

"Battalion wants the CAP squads to step up their patrols around Phu Bai. They want us to do a security sweep through this pocket of paddy lands about five klicks west of us," pointing to a valley on the terrain map spread out in front of the men. "Helle, since your pulling point, I want you to plot the patrol route, so we can call in our reference points in case we need artie." Corporal McClure paused a moment to let the thought sink in. "Got any suggestions?"

Roger scanned the map for a moment before responding; "I think we should take the patrol through these small villages," Roger suggested. He pointed to several dots on the map indicating the location of *Son Toi I, Son Toi II* and *An Nghia* village. "Sergeant Nhiem

(The P.F.'s Platoon Sergeant), has an uncle in *Son Toi I* who passed him word that V.C. tax collectors are making their rounds of the valley."

"Yeah, I heard the same from little Pham Phung...that cute little Vietnamese gal with the baby," a stocky Marine named Paterson added.

"Well, that lines up with intell reports," McClure concluded. "Your suggestion sounds right on to me, Helle. Let's map it out."

The rest of the squad watched and occasionally offered suggestions as Roger plotted a circular route which would take them through the three neighboring villages. When they had agreed on the patrol route, an overlay was traced and sent to Phu Bai with the predetermined check points and grid locations in case they ran into any trouble and needed artillery support.

"Any other suggestions?" McClure asked.

"No, Corporal." Roger answered.

"O.K., Let's do it!" McClure exclaimed.

At 1500 hours, the squad loaded up with light packs and weapons, called in their routine commo check and headed out into the countryside with two additional squads of P.F.'s. It was another searing day in the 'Nam. The heat was so intense, they felt like they were slowly barbecuing on a rotisserie. They made their way in a looping route across Highway One and down a series of interlacing dikes which took them about four klicks west to a small ville identified on the map as *Son Toi 1*. It was an island in a lime green sea of freshly planted rice paddies. The village consisted of a dozen bamboo and thatch hootches surrounded by hedgerows and windbreaks of eucalyptus and spindly fir trees.

It was early sunset when they reached the outskirts of the village. Corporal McClure and Sergeant

Nhiem halted the squads and prepared to enter the ville. Except for a lone water buffalo wallowing in a muddy bog alongside of one of the dikes, everything was quiet. The dumb brute eyed the approaching Marines warily and gave them a disgruntled snort to signal his annoyance at their intrusion.

"You better quit lookin' at me like that you stupid cow or I'll put a bullet between those big brown eyes of yours!" Scroggins sneered. The mud-caked buffalo shook his head to drive off a cloud of flies, then nonchalantly rolled over into the sour smelling muck to resume the pleasures of his late afternoon mud-bath.

"Stupid cow," Scroggins grumbled

"He's not a cow, you idiot. You ain't got the brains God gave a piss ant, Scroggins," a tall, lanky Marine nick-named 'Stick' kidded. He was a bean pole from somewhere in Nebraska with a pimply face and a mouth crowded with too many teeth. "Scroggins, I'll bet you never got out of the city till you joined the Crotch. Did'ya? Am I right, or am I right?" Stick teased as he spit a brown stream of tobacco juice out one side of his mouth. "You wouldn't know a cow from a wart hog."

"Aw, you don't know everything, Stick. I don't care what you say. It still looks like a dumb cow to me," Scroggins protested. "Maybe you know cows and pigs and stuff like that, but you'd be lost where I come from. Back in Detroit, I knew my way around the streets....Man, I knew where the action was...If you can dig what I'm sayin'? And Leonard Washington Scroggins the II knew his way around the women too!.... Man had all the right moves!"

"Oh, gimme a break," Stick groaned. "You're so full of it, Scroggins your face is brown. Your street smarts didn't keep you outta the Crotch, did they?" Stick mocked.

"Boy's just jealous cuz he ain't got the moves with the ladies. Maybe you know your way around a cow paddy, Stick, but you're 'bout as lame as they come around the chicks!"

"Well, you're still one dumb dude, Scroggins."

"Yeah, and your one ugly, skinny suckah!" Scroggins sneered as he slapped Stick playfully on the back.

"Alright, you two, give it a rest. We've got business to take care of," McClure shook his head in disbelief. "You two are worse than my little brothers."

"O.K., Panella, I want the gun set up over there to cover us when we go in," pointing to a dike which ran parallel to the ville and offered a clear sweep of the entire village. "Thumper, you stay behind me. I'll follow Helle in. The rest of the squad keep your intervals and be alert. Alright, Helle, you lead off...lets move out," Corporal McClure ordered as they began their sweep of the village.

Roger crept cautiously forward down the dike. It was paved with bamboo reinforcing which crunched slightly under each step. He reached a footpath skirting a wall of trees and clotted brush bordering the village, then moved down the dirt path. He was moving with a catlike grace -pausing every few paces to look and listen. Except for an almost imperceptible breeze which gently sighed in the branches overhead, everything was still. He reached an intersecting corridor which trailed down a hedge lined footpath about five feet across. He could just make out a saffron colored hootch through the congested greens of the hedge. Roger turned to McClure and touched his index finger to his lips to emphasize silence. He then hand- signaled them to follow him slowly as he entered the main path leading into the village. The labyrinth-like maze of hedgerows and footpaths gave Roger the creeps. It wasn't open like most villages. Its congested corridors and concealed hootches were unnerving. It gave him a foreboding feeling, like he was walking into a trap.

He was moving with agile, fluid movements down the footpath, his eyes darting purposefully back and forth, straining to maximize his peripheral vision, analyzing every contour for irregularities in symmetry of the vegetation, any abnormalities in the hedge-lined path before continuing forward.

He didn't know what it was, but something was wrong - something subtle, something which hadn't caught his eye, something which hadn't registered in his brain - but he sensed it was there in the back of his head. Nothing was out of place that he could discern, but something told him differently. The only thing he could smell was a faint whiff of nouc-mam floating in the warm air.

Thirty meters down the path, Roger reached another intersecting lane lined by tall trees and brush on one side and a thick hedgerow on his left. He hand-signaled for the squad to hold up while he paused to take his breath and listen. He cocked his head in various angles trying to pick up sounds. There weren't even the normal village noises. Even the local coalition of mosquitos had withdrawn for their night assault. His ear suddenly pricked from the sound of a bird trilling overhead. *"Man, I'm tense,"* Roger calmed himself as he looked up to see if he could catch sight of the bird. Up in the branches, eucalyptus leaves fluttered in the gentle breeze, reflecting the setting sun like a thousand tiny mirrors.

Roger ran his hand over his face to steady himself, then started down the adjoining path. His brain sifted every shred of stimuli for potential danger as he inched into the village. Every few paces, he paused to look and listen before resuming his advance. Each footfall was measured - the delicate placement of each step, toe first, delicately, carefully measuring each stride, cautiously scrutinizing every inch of ground for trip wires trailing off through the dirt and leaves, listening for the muffled rustling of leaves, the sound of voices, the crack of a twig, alert for the slightest trace of movement.

About twenty meters down the path, he suddenly tensed at the sight of a man partially concealed behind the shrubbery of the ten foot hedge. He motioned Corporal McClure, who was just rounding the intersection, to hold it up. The man was squatting on his haunches in what appeared to be an entrance through the hedge. He was looking down the path in the opposite direction, unaware of Roger's approach. It seemed like the man was lost in the beauty of the pastel sunset which had begun to burnish the countryside with golden highlights. Roger crept closer without alerting the man and nudged him on the back of his shoulder with the tip of his rifle. *"Cho toi xem the can cuoc cua anh"* (give me your identification card). The Vietnamese peasant flinched in alarm from the tap of the rifle.

The man startled and sprang to his feet, wearing a conical straw hat, old black trousers and a dull green fatigue shirt which was hanging loose around his waist. He was middle-aged, with a weathered brown face and deep black eyes which clearly mirrored the fear on his face.

Colors were fading in the approaching dusk.

"Xin loi, toi khong hieu ong muon gi," (sorry, I do

not understand) the man replied nervously, feigning humility.

"The can cuoc! Dua the can cuoc cua anh day!" (give me your I.D. card, now!), Roger ordered. They hadn't patrolled this area of villages recently so it was customary to check for identification cards which the South Vietnamese government issued with the person's name, picture and statistics printed on a laminated plastic card. If you were caught without a government I.D., you were suspected of being a V.C. and hauled in for questioning.

The Vietnamese shook his head as if confused.

"The can cuoc! Dua the can cuoc cua anh day!" Roger demanded.

"Toi khong hieu ong muon gi!" the man pleaded.

"Sau lam, Sau lam." (not good, not good) Roger shook his head, as if to say, "that's just too bad!"

Roger caught movement out of the corner of his eye coming from the open area on the other side of the hedge. He heard the distinctive singsong chatter of Vietnamese men in the courtyard. Roger stepped closer to the entrance to get a clearer look at the courtyard. Two khaki-clad soldiers with web-gear were coming out of a hootch set back in the enclosed compound. They were laughing and talking to each other with their A.K.'s slung over their shoulders, unaware of Roger's presence. He turned for just a second, when the first man jumped back and reached into his pants to pull something out.

"Dung lai!" (don't move), Roger hissed between clenched teeth.

Roger's chest tightened. A deep breath caught in his throat as he stepped back to see the wooden handle of a Chi-com grenade halfway out of the man's trousers. The V.C. was struggling to pull the potato masher from his waistband.

Everything was happening in a split-second blur. Roger sprung to action. He lunged forward grabbing the man firmly by the collar and slammed his body to the ground. Adrenalin overwhelmed him with strength and reflex. The V.C. was desperately trying to get the grenade out of his pants. His face was a portrait of wide-eyed terror. Roger looked up. The two approaching soldiers saw movement and were unslinging their assault rifles. Roger looked down in time to see the man on the ground trying to pull the detonator string of the grenade. Everything had shifted to slow-motion as images clicked by. Roger drove his boot down on the wrist to keep him from pulling the cord. Everything was unraveling. *"No time left,"* Roger reacted. He jabbed the barrel of his M-14 into the chest of the squirming V.C. and squeezed off three quick rounds, which imploded the man's heart and rib cage and jerked upwards from the recoil, blowing off the man's jaw in a cloud of blood and bone. Without thinking, Roger dropped to one knee and aimed through the opening at the two frightened soldiers who were each bringing their weapons up in response to the gunfire. Corporal McClure was down with the rest of the squad in anticipation. Roger flicked the selector to fully automatic and cut lose a fifteen round burst which stitched the first soldier in a diagonal line across his stomach and carried over to the other soldier across his upper torso, ripping open his chest and spinning them both backwards like tops.

Suddenly the village exploded with a flurry of activity as V.C. sprang to action, spilling out of hooches and scrambling to escape.

"LAI DAI!...LAI DAI!" The P.F. squad leaders shouted.

It was like someone had kicked over an ant's nest. The popcorn popping sound of small weapons opened up as the force of Marines and P.F.'s opened up on the village. Rounds were zipping through the foliage and hootches, cracking through the brittle bamboo siding and snapping through leaves and branches as the V.C. raced through the hedges and footpaths to flee out the opposite side of the village.

McClure scurried to Roger who was laying in a prone position firing into the hootch from which the two soldiers had exited. In a couple of minutes the order was passed down the line to cease fire. A squad of V.C. tax collectors had melted back into the countryside.

Corporal McClure took one look at the V.C. bodies sprawled in front of Roger's position and shook his head. "Damn, Helle, you gonna win the war all by yourself? You're some piece of work!" McClure patted Roger on the back. A wave of satisfaction swept over him unlike anything he had ever experienced. Roger was beaming from ear to ear. He wasn't that kid back in Toledo who was always screwing up anymore.

"Whoa! Check this out!" Scroggins exclaimed as he admired one of the mint condition AK-47's the uniform soldiers were carrying.

"It's the first one I've seen any regular V.C.'s issued around Phu Bai," McClure added.

"Hey, if you think that's far out, check out the damage our man Helle has done!" Thumper pointed at the three bodies. "Looks like he single handedly waxed some of Uncle Ho's finest...Just a little payback - huh, Helle?" he added, patting Roger on the back.

Several of his squad members had jogged over to his position, only to be amazed by the dead V.C. "How did you get the jump on all three, Helle?" Paterson asked in amazement. It wasn't often you saw whom you were shooting at in the blind anonymity of a firefight, let alone get three confirmed kills in a face to face shoot out.

"I just walked up on this one before he knew I was there," Roger replied casually, gesturing with the barrel of his rifle toward the first body.

"That's too much!.....You just walked up on him and he didn't even hear you?" Stick asked in disbelief.

"There it is," Roger replied matter-of-factly.

"Well, I guess they didn't get the message," Thumper joked, as he surveyed the scene of the shoot-out.

"What's that?" Roger enquired.

"War can be hazardous to your health."

The curtain of darkness was falling fast, enveloping the village in shades of grey as the patrol finished their search. Besides the two V.C. weapons and the grenade, they only found a couple blood trails and several abandoned web belts that had been left behind when the V.C. cut out.

"Looks like the gooks diddi-maud out of Dodge," McClure noted. "Let's saddle up and make it back, before Charlie decides to give us some surprises of his own." They secured the bodies and weapons and headed back to their compound before the V.C. could double back and catch them in an ambush.

Roger was basking in the euphoria of his first kill as they walked back to their CAP compound. P.F.'s carried the bodies of the dead V.C. through the velvet blackness suspended from bamboo poles like big game trophies between the porters. The column resembled a safari returning from a successful hunt.

Lost in the solitude of the march, Roger savored the knowledge that he'd passed some supreme test. He'd survived his first exposure to the terrors of combat. He'd done it like a Marine and now he'd proven to himself that he could pull the trigger when that moment of "him or me" arrived. His rite of passage from boot to first blood to first kill was complete.

Minor benchmarks in a person's life back in the sanctuary of America could be fraught with their own unique fears and insecurities - passing that first driver's test, learning to cross the swimming pool on your own, that first solo ride on your bike without training wheels, that first date, graduating from high school, or your first job interview. But they were all trivial in comparison to the tests he had just passed. None of those challenges was as disconcerting as the unique sacraments of war - a man's baptism of fire and his first kill.

Roger had passed both and finally put to rest the troubled questions of his personal courage or cowardice which had dogged him for months. He'd "seen the elephant" and lived to tell about it. He'd looked the monster in the face and hadn't backed down. In some small way, he had validated his manhood. He had also broken the curse he had carried for years - *"you'll never amount to anything. You're just going to be a bum!"* Until the Corps, it had been a self fulfilling prophecy. He'd failed at everything he'd ever attempted. He'd messed up his wood shop project, was uncoordinated at sports, never fit in with the "in" crowd back in high school, and barely graduated. But that brief firefight in *Son Toi 1* had changed all of that. He'd finished off that sense of inferiority just as decisively as he had those three enemy soldiers. He had what it took. He hadn't choked. He'd done it with a cool, detached proficiency.

He hadn't dishonored the Corps. What is more, he thought, as he plodded across the paddy lands west of Phu Bai, he had also settled part of the score for Danny and Pope.

Later that evening, Roger came down from the massive adrenalin run he had been on. The effects of the self-induced high had worn off. The adrenalin had boosted his strength and given him an artificial high which had blocked out much of the realization of what had happened. Like a painkiller, it had temporarily numbed his mind from the terrors of the ordeal. It had bolstered his instincts for survival and charged his system with an almost superhuman ability to face the challenge. It was like the mild mannered accountant who is transformed after a few stiff drinks into a belligerent brawler, with the fearless nerve to take on a whole bar full of Hell's Angels. But it is in the aftermath, when your body comes down off the run, when one has time to calm down and consider what has happened, or could have happened, that you pay the price for the fix you were on.

Roger couldn't stop shaking. His fingers were twitching nervously. He was shaking so bad with tremors that he could barely stand up. He couldn't stop the replays of the shoot out either. He had reacted with trained precision under fire, but now he was paying the price. All the thoughts of "what could have happened" careened through his mind like a run-away train.

He headed over to the shower in the blackness of the compound to try to sooth away the intensity of the come down. The shower was a jury-rigged affair made out of a 55-gallon drum filled with water and makeshift shower head. The lukewarm water felt good as it ran down his body, washing away the sweat and grime from the day's patrol. Washing away the delayed reaction wasn't that easy. It would take hours before that subsided.

In the light of the morning sun, they searched the bodies of the three Viet Cong soldiers they had carried back to the compound. One of the two uniformed soldiers was a V.C. Lieutenant. The man he had found squatting at the entrance of the hedge was a local cadre officer. He was carrying an old B.A.R. pouch with documents. The other two weren't carrying much of value - a couple balls of glutinous rice wrapped in bamboo leaves, a small bag of tobacco, a comb, a few coins and paper script, and a propaganda leaflet. But Roger found something in the Lieutenant's pocket which further tempered the euphoria of his accomplishment. It was a water stained letter which was worn and yellowed like it had been read many times. Folded inside the letter was a dog-eared picture of a young Vietnamese woman with two little girls. Roger knew it was a picture of the man's family he had left somewhere to mourn over his disappearance - never to know what happened to her husband, to their father. The hate had been there with a vengeance, but it was suddenly softened by that tattered scrap of paper and simple photo. It had been subdued by the impact of taking another man's life. Somehow, at that moment, the old "kill or be killed" logic didn't quite cut it. This wasn't a dog or a gook sprawled in front of him with his chest ripped open. It was a human being - a man who had loved and laughed and dreamed of life.

That first kill had changed Roger in many ways.

Those thick callouses which had safely shielded his heart and soul were no longer so thick.

Chapter 9

"Attention!" The Gunnery Sergeant called the CAP formation to attention. A Brigadier General from the 3rd Marine Amphibious Force stepped forward with the Battalion Sergeant Major and began to read from a piece of paper:

> *PFC Helle, for conspicuous heroism in saving your squad from a possible enemy ambush while on patrol in the village of Son Toi 1 on March 16, 1966, and with complete disregard for your personal safety, said actions resulting in the death of three enemy soldiers and the capture of weapons and important documents, I hereby award you the Vietnamese Cross of Gallantry with Gold Star*

The Officer finished reading the prepared citation and pinned the medal on Roger's chest. "Well done,

Helle. Outstanding job!" The General shook Roger's hand firmly then stepped back and saluted.

"Thank you, Sir!" Roger responded, giving a sharp salute in return.

It was the proudest moment in Roger's life. Over the next three days, he spent a lot of time in the solitude of his bunker fondling his medal and re-reading the words of the citation; *"...for conspicuous heroism in saving your squad..."*. He sat in the bunker staring at the scrap of paper like it was a winning lottery ticket for ten million dollars. *"I did this?"* Roger wondered in amazement. He had trouble believing that it had really even happened. But there it was in black and white.

He carefully sealed the medal and citation in a padded envelope and mailed it home. He didn't understand the emotional crosscurrents tugging at his heart, but he knew he needed to make a point. The wounded little boy inside of him was still crying out for approval. The kid who had never done anything right was screaming out, *"Look here!...I did something right!...Am I somebody now?...Am I worth something now?"*

Two days later he got word from Battalion headquarters that he was being promoted to Lance Corporal. McClure, who was promoted to Sergeant, appointed Roger as assistant squad leader.

He still wasn't comfortable with all the questions about what he had done, but he was convinced he had done the right thing. The Corps had said he did good. His team members were proud of him, and he was proud of himself.

The warm acceptance of his team members dispelled much of the emotional distance Roger had fought to maintain. The new found respect brought him

that special sense of belonging and closeness he had
longed for. He had tried to encase his heart in
hardness, to insulate his feelings, but his attempts went
against everything in his nature. He had joined the
Corps to belong more than he had realized.

The camaraderie and kinship with his brothers in
arms was emotionally disarming. He stopped the quiet
retreat inside of himself and started to let down his
shield. The mask of seriousness he had hidden behind
gradually came off as he started to lighten up. He even
started horsing around with his teammates and joining in
with their playful banter.

"I's been givin' it a lot of thought, Helle,"
Scroggins toyed.

"Yeah, you'd have to work that brain of yours
overtime to get anything figured out." Stick commented
sarcastically.

"Shut up, Stick, I'm doin' the talkin'. Helle, I'm
gonna start callin' you 'Spook', cuz you're real quiet like
a ghost."

"That so?" Roger winked at Stick and Panella
who were listening to Scroggins. "Who's calling who
Spook? I may be quiet, but the brothers are the best
night fighters around. They just naturally blend into the
night. Charlie never sees 'em till it's too late!"

"What are you talkin' 'bout, Helle?" Panella
chimed in. "You ever seen Scroggins smile at night?
Man, his teeth are so white, it looks like Times Square
on New Year's Eve!"

"Oooh...He got ya on that one, Scrog!" Thumper
teased.

"Hey...you white boys are just jealous cuz black is
so beautiful. My Mamma always use to say, 'The darker
the berry, the sweeter the juice!'."

"Well, I do have to give you that one...You do have the Stick beat in the looks department," Panella added.

"Like I told you before," Scroggins preened as he glided the tips of his fingers along the side of his head. "Black is beautiful, cuz black don't crack!"

"That is what I call unmitigated bovine excrement, Scroggins. C'mon you guys, don't feed his ego anymore than you have to. He's already so full of it we're gonna have to start carrying shovels around just to be with him," Stick pleaded. "Listen, Scrog may have the looks and maybe some moves with the women, but I've been with this sorry sucker since Parris Island and I'm tellin' you that all his cool don't make up for what he's missin' in the brains department. Most of the time, he can't find his rear end with both hands."

"Yeah!" Scroggins challenged, "And you're still the ugliest red-neck, honkie hick I've ever met. I'll bet you were so ugly when you were little, Stick, your mamma had to tie a bone around your neck just so the dogs would play with you!"

Roger and Panella busted up. "What a royal put down!" Panella roared.

"You just wait," Stick sulked, "Time'll prove I'm right!"

The next night, Roger, Stick, Scroggins and Herrera were watching the perimeter around their compound, trying to catch Charlie at his game. Some of the locals had been infiltrating their perimeter defenses at night and turning around the command detonated claymores. If somebody on watch squeezed the "clicker", 700 steel ball bearings would blow in the wrong direction and take out anyone with his head above ground. A couple Marines in another CAP squad had been severely wounded by the same tactic. The squad had found several claymores that morning which had been turned the previous night.

McClure was really ticked off and determined to nail the culprits. The game of hide-and-seek had become a personal obsession with McClure - they were messin' around on his turf. At first, the Marines painted the backside of the claymores white so they could tell if Charlie was tampering with them, but Charlie wasn't stupid. He painted the front side with whitewash so the Marines couldn't tell if they had been turned or not. It was a cat-and-mouse game with the mouse trying to outsmart the cat. McClure was determined to build a better mousetrap. He had the squad rig the claymores with buried trip flares.

They got their first mouse the next night when a V.C. playing with a claymore set off the flare. The green flare arced into the sky, bathing the hapless gook in a green floodlight. He was just standing out in the open in the quivering light of the flare holding the claymore in his hands with a terrified look on his face like he knew he was going to meet his ancestors.

"Gotcha this time!" McClure triumphed as he detonated the explosive charge, disintegrating the hapless V.C. in a crimson plume which didn't leave enough of him to put in a band-aid box. "Strike one gook! Marines one, gooks zip," McClure gloated.

The next night, Roger, Scroggins and Stick were on watch when Roger heard the cans tinkling in the concertina wire strung around the perimeter outside their compound. The others were peering into the darkness to see if they could see anything, but it was pitch black.

"Plink....Plink, plink!" the pebble-filled cans rattled

in the wire.

"I think somebody's trying to come through the wire," Stick whispered.

"Scroggins," Roger hissed, "I want you to throw an illumination grenade out there so I can see what it is. I'll get ready to shoot," Roger said as he put his M-14 on fully automatic and aimed towards the sounds.

"Ping!"   Roger could hear the sound of the grenade spoon flying free.

Roger was standing in the blackness with his back against the stucco wall of the clinic. He was poised to fire as soon as the grenade went off. He flinched at the sound of a dull thud behind him.

"Oops!" Scroggins moaned.

The grenade ignited behind Roger like a gigantic flashbulb, lighting up the whole courtyard and clearly silhouetting Roger in the open. The V.C. immediately opened up. Roger dove to the ground and grab-crawled around the corner of the building in a panic as green tracers streaked overhead gouging pockmarks out of the plaster wall and ricocheting into the blackness like popping sparks.

Roger scampered back out of the open, only to find the others doubled up with laughter. Scroggins and Stick were laughing so hard they could barely breathe.

"Scroggins!" Roger swore, "I'm going to...!"

"What did I tell you, Spook? Is he one dumb dork, or is he one dumb dork?" Stick busted up.

"You should see the look on your face, Spook!" Scroggins bellowed.

Roger couldn't resist the humor of the moment and started laughing as well.

The squad settled into the predictable routines of

CAP duty at Gia Le. They even adopted a stray mutt they named "Elephant" because of its oversized head. Elephant was a mangy black dog with bowed legs and a smashed-looking face, which looked like he'd run into a wall too many times. He was kind of a cross between an Australian Dingo and an English Bulldog. Elephant was always wheezing and snorting like he had acute sinus problems - no doubt a side effect of his exaggerated pug-nose. He wasn't exactly Ol' Yeller' or 'Rin Tin Tin', but he had ingratiated himself with the squad and become their unofficial mascot.

Elephant's all-consuming passion in life was to follow the Marines around the compound with his tail wagging in hopes of securing some scraps of food. He was a hustler, like many of the Vietnamese these Marines had encountered. Most Americans never really got to know the Vietnamese people beyond the pimps, panderers, and prostitutes who seemed to want only what the Americans could give them. Elephant wanted food, and he wasn't the least bit picky. Elephant was like a garbage disposal on four legs. He would eat anything, including the more notorious types of C-rats which Marines had a universal loathing for - ham & lima beans, fudge brick, date nut pudding, crackers and cheese spread - items even the Vietnamese refused to eat. Sometimes the kids would even throw the cans back at the Marines who gave them to them.

Herrera once gave him a cracker with cheese spread and a liberal coating of extra-hot tabasco sauce he had gotten in a care package from home. "Come here, Elephant. Come here, boy," Herrera coaxed Elephant into his trap. The dog approached warily. "I've got a little surprise for you." Elephant wagged his tail back and forth as he eyed the cracker in Herrera's hand. "C'mon, Elephant. Here you go." Elephant grabbed the cracker and greedily devoured it, only to be shocked by the instant burning sensation filling his mouth. Elephant started licking his chops hysterically, running around in circles like he was a wild bronco, trying to shake something off. "Outta sight! Check out this dog, man." Herrera laughed sadistically. "Man, that's one hot dog!" He howled. Herrera doubled over with tears in his eyes from laughing so hard. Elephant was licking his chops like he was in a race to lick something off. "Crazy dog!" Herrera laughed.

"Herrera, you jerk, why did you have to do that?" McClure asked. "How would you like me to pour that bottle down your throat?"

"Man, it's just a gook dog." Herrera protested lamely.

"Yeah, and you're just a stupid grunt, Herrera."

From that point on, Elephant shied away from Hererra. He only took something offered from him after carefully smelling it first. He was ugly, but nobody said he was stupid.

In late April, Roger came down with a bad case of diarrhea - otherwise known as the "Saigon Shuffle" or "Ho Chi Minh's revenge." It was probably from too much village food. Roger had the "trots" so bad that he had to slit open the crotch of his pants with his K-bar. No one in the bush wore underwear anyway because they would ride up your leg on a hot hump and rub your inner thigh and butt raw in the heat and humidity. Opening your trousers was just another trick of the trade in case of an emergency.

"O.K., let's saddle up." McClure ordered.

"C'mon, Sarge, I've got the runs too bad to be going out on patrol - how 'bout cutting me some slack?"

Roger asked.

"Nothin' doin', Helle! A little loose bowels never hurt any Marine. You ain't sick are ya? You got the fever?" McClure asked.

"Naw," Roger replied reluctantly, "But I've had the runs for three days. I think I'm getting dysentery."

"As long as there's no fever, you're going on patrol. Have Doc give you some Lomotal or something," McClure responded.

"I did, and it's not working." Roger pleaded.

"Well, that's tough!" McClure said, finishing the conversation.

The sky was flushing with rose red pastels as the squad lined up in the compound. They were going to some foothills about five klicks west, overlooking a small village. They had word that a V.C. patrol was coming through that night.

The squad members were waiting for McClure's signal to move out, fidgeting and smoking their last cigarettes for the night. Elephant was sniffing around the men in hopes of following them out on patrol.

"Get outta here, Elephant!" Herrera growled at the dog. "Dog's not lookin so good lately. His nose has been runnin' ever since he ate that hot sauce. I think those C-rats are killin' him, man."

"C'mon, Elephant," Roger gently shooed the little mutt away with his boot. "You can't go with us, boy." Roger's intestines suddenly cramped. "SplusShh!" Roger could hold it no longer. A watery gush of loose stool burst from Roger's bowels, running down the insides of his pants and soaking his legs in the warm fluid. "Crap!" Roger groaned.

"You got that right, man!...Oh, that's crude dude! Ain't you never been pottie trained?" Herrera grimaced.

"You smell like somethin' crawled up inside of you and died, Spook!" Scroggins pinched his nose. "Man, that is funKIE!"

"Helle, I hate to have to be the one to tell you, but you need to see your mortician. I think he needs to change your embalming fluid," Stick shook his head in disgust.

"C'mon, McClure, do we have to put up with this?" The other squad members complained.

"I said he's goin' and that settles it! He'll just have to stay down wind," McClure turned around to hide his grin. "You take Tail-end-charlie, Helle." It took everything in his power to keep from busting up.

"Gimme a break," Roger responded.

"Charlie don't have to worry about the Spook sneakin' up on 'em tonight. They can smell him coming a mile away," Herrera chuckled.

"Yeah," Thumper added, "about as subtle as a fart in a crowded elevator. I don't think we've got to worry about gettin' hit tonight - not unless ol' Charles wants to die from chemical warfare."

Everyone busted up, including McClure.

"Hey! I can't help it," Roger moaned.

"O.K., let's move!" McClure ordered, silencing the men's banter as they filed out of the compound and into the night. Elephant gave a few sniffs, crimped his noise, and decided not to follow.

After two hours of humping, they wound their way up a kidney shaped hill about sixty meters high with gradual sloping sides. It overlooked a well-used trail leading into a village at its base. The hill was covered with scattered scrub and old fighting holes dug by other marines who had been there before.

"Psst!...Helle, I want you on the opposite side of

the hill to cover our rear." Sergeant McClure instructed.
"I think he better guard his own rear," Panella
snickered.

"Helle, your password is 'Watchdog'. Got it?"

"Yeah, Yeah," Roger answered as he moved
across the hill.

It was 2200 hours. Roger lay in the darkness for
several hours watching the opposite slope. He'd never
felt so miserable in his life, laying there shivering in the
clammy funk of his soiled fatigues. The sour stink of his
own feces was almost unbearable. He wanted to be on
the other side of the hill with the rest of the squad, but
he knew they didn't share his desire. He had to admit
that he wouldn't want something smelling as bad as he
did laying next to him either. About 0130 hours, he
realized that it was past the time his squad was supposed
to signal him to join up so they could move out.

Roger re-checked the radium dial of his watch.
It was 0145. Something was wrong. Someone should
have come for him by now even if he did smell like an
outhouse in August. He rose out of his fighting hole and
started to cross the top of the hill in a low crouch,
carefully negotiating the loose rocks and shallow fighting
holes.

"Psst!...Psst!...It's watchdog," Roger whispered.
"It's me, Helle...I'm comin' in....Psst, are you guys there?"
There was only silence. Roger crept forward quietly, in
case they were asleep and woke with a start. "Hey,
where are you guys?" Nothing. "Oh, great!" Roger
murmured. "They stick me on the far side of the hill by
myself and then they pull out without me."

He calculated the squad had about a two hour
head-start. He started down the sloping trail above the
village, acutely aware of how vulnerable he felt moving

through enemy territory at night. The heavens were ebony black and sprinkled with tiny lights which blinked off and on, like someone was trying to send coded messages from a distant galaxy.

He was halfway down the hill when he heard a commotion coming from the village. He ducked down and listened carefully. There were voices - the high pitched jabbering of Vietnamese arguing. His ears pricked as he tried to discern the source of the voices. He inched closer to the edge of the village to get a closer look. It was 0250 hours. From a congested clump of large broad leaves, Roger could see the light from a single kerosene lantern burning in one of the hootches. In the faint yellow light, he could barely make out the outline of several V.C. soldiers standing outside of the hootch. He figured it was the V.C. tax collectors rousting the village chief to pay up. He knelt there in a low crouch listening to the shakedown, less than thirty meters away. He stayed there for over two hours watching and listening and trying to decide what to do.

In the violet half-light of early dawn, he could make out about ten V.C. coming and going. They were hauling sacks of rice which they piled up in front of the hootch. *"What do I do?"* he thought to himself. He had ten magazines and four frags. *"I know I can get at least half of them if they bunch up,"* he calculated. *"It would be suicide, but a definite Congressional Medal of Honor,"* Roger mused. *"Posthumously...,"* he dismissed the fleeting fantasy. *"What would Vic Morrow do?"* He chuckled to himself. *"Probably get the hell outta here!"* he concluded.

He counseled himself on the merits of a strategic withdrawal. He backed out of the thicket and headed back to Gia Le. About 0830, he straggled into the compound with a look on his face that could kill.

"Hey! There's Spook!" Scroggins beamed. "Where you been, man? We been worried about ya."

"Where do you think I've been, you meathead?" Roger snapped. "You jerks left me back on that hill!" He was grasping his M-14 like he wanted to administer a vertical butt stroke to someone.

"Whoa! Calm down, Spook. We was just gettin' ready to come out and get ya. Right, Stick?" Scroggins offered diplomatically.

"There it is, Spook, just like the man said. I guess we were all so shook up by your accident last night that we weren't quite thinkin' straight," Stick gave an infectious wink.

"I don't believe you clowns," Roger shook his head. He turned around to hide the tight smile slowly spreading across his face. "I'm goin' to the shower to clean myself off," Roger grunted. "You guys are just too much!" He mumbled as he plodded across the compound.

That night, Sergeant Nhiem and the village chief invited the squad to a Vietnamese meal to celebrate Roger's safe return. Sergeant Nhiem seated the squad on woven mats around heaping bowls of steaming rice, pieces of fish, leafy vegetables and warm bottles of 33 Beer. They could tell that he'd gone to some expense to make the dinner special because of the generous mounds of food in front of them and a bowl containing roasted chunks of meat. They had eaten a lot of meals in the village, but they had never had any red meat - maybe a rubbery chicken or some river fish, but never red meat.

Scroggins helped himself to a chunk with his fingers and plopped it into his mouth. "Umm!...This is pretty good!"   Scroggins purred as he savored the delicacy, "Just like home cookin'."

"Hey, gimme a piece," Stick responded.

"A little chewy, but real good," Roger noted.

"Beats ham and lima beans," Panella said.

"Garbage beats ham and lima beans," Herrera added. "I only know one living creature who will eat it."

"What kinda meat is this?" McClure asked the chief.

"El Phant," the chief answered.

"Elephant?" McClure responded.

"Yes. El Phant," Nhiem confirmed.

"Where do they buy elephant meat around here?" McClure was curious.

"No, No!...El Phant, El Phant....Woof,Woof!...El Phant," Nhiem emphasized.

"Elephant?" Roger responded in disbelief as he turned to McClure.

"You gotta be kiddin' me!" Scroggins turned to Stick with a wide-eyed look.

Stick was turning shades of green.

No one finished the meal. One by one, they politely excused themselves to make emergency trips to the wire.

Chapter 10

The CAP squad kept up their regular pattern of patrols through the surrounding villages, paddy lands and rolling foothills. They also continued their "in the field" training of the P.F. platoon they had inherited.

Herrera ended his tour and rotated back to the world in May. He was replaced by another Mexican-American kid who had been in-country about six weeks. His name was Rudy Fernandez.

Rudy was a likeable kid with jet black hair and olive brown complexion. He was a second generation Mexican American who had joined the Corps just after his seventeenth birthday. His dad had enthusiastically signed his enlistment papers. Rudy's old man had started out twenty years before working the fields of Central California as a migrant worker, picking peaches and cherries in the San Juaquin Valley, tomatoes in the Sacramento and artichokes and lettuce in the Salinas.

He had worked as a seasonal farm laborer, performing the backbreaking toil of stooped labor through the forties, sending money home to his family back in Juarez and stashing away as much as he could save. He dreamed of making a better life for his family in America and didn't plan on being a wet-back forever. He wanted better things for his children. In '51, he brought his wife, three kids and his mother across the border. They settled in Stockton, where he opened a roadside fruit and vegetable stand, and eventually a Mexican restaurant, where his wife and mother did the cooking and the kids helped out serving the patrons. By the early sixties, Rudy's dad owned two small restaurants and had saved enough put a down payment on a modest home.

In spite of his struggles to adapt to life in America and overcome the racial barriers, Rudy's father loved America as much as any immigrant from the old world ever had. He loved it because of the opportunities it had given his family. It had taken them out of the rural squalor of Mexico and given them a hope for tomorrow - something he always thought symbolized the American dream.

His dad was proud to live in America and prouder still when he received his citizenship. It was a feeling he never ceased to instill in his kids. Rudy grew up in a patriotic home, steeped in his dad's love of country. A picture of John F. Kennedy hung on the wall next to one of Jesus praying in the Garden of Gethsemane and another of the Blessed Virgin. When he heard Kennedy's inaugural call; "Ask not what your country can do for you, ask, what you can do for your country?...," he was moved with pangs of patriotism and a duty-bound sense of obligation. To Rudy, those words were a solemn summons which called him to repay the country which had done so much for his family. When the Marine Corps recruiter came to his high school during his senior year, he made up his mind. It was like all the tumblers suddenly lined up in his head. *"This is it!"* he thought. *"Ask...what you can do for your country. This is how I'll do it...Pop will be so proud!"* A week later, he was on a bus, heading for the Marine Corps Recruit Depot in San Diego.

When Rudy arrived, Roger took an immediate liking to the energetic young kid. Maybe it was because he saw a lot of himself in him. He was just a kid to Roger even though Roger wasn't even nineteen years old himself. Rudy was still months short of his eighteenth birthday, but it wasn't time which made Rudy seem so much younger to Roger, it was the hardening process acquired in combat.

Roger felt compassion for the new Marine - maybe because he had been in his boots himself not so long before and knew that Rudy's innocence would soon be lost as well. And oddly, Roger felt a tinge of guilt, too - maybe because he knew that he would play an inevitable roll in Rudy's passage from youth.

Rudy was eager to learn and urged Roger to teach him the delicate art of walking point. Like Pope before him, Roger took Rudy under his wing and started schooling him in the finer points on short patrols around Gia Le - teaching him how to move with a slow feline grace, how to sift sounds and interpret subtle impressions, how to move your eyes and detect minute hints that could indicate danger. He taught Rudy how to become the hunter and not the hunted. Rudy caught on fast.

It was Rudy's fourth patrol and the squad was

heading back to their compound. They were a couple of klicks south of Huong Thuy. They were coming back around noon across a paddy dike which ran perpendicular to the highway. They were sweating profusely under the opaque glare of the noon day heat. They were about two hundred yards from the stretch of roadway, shimmering from heat waves rising off its surface. A powdered blue Lambrette was sputtering down the road loaded with about six Vietnamese piled on top. A deuce-and-a-half was coughing northward on a collision course with the Lambrette.

"Check out the truck. Looks like the guy's gonna hit the Lambrette!" Panella noted. "Honk!...HonK!" The driver of the truck laid into his horn but the Lambrette just kept coming on.

"Man I think that crazy gook wants ta play chicken with deuce!" Scroggins responded.

"Wanna bet who's gonna win?" Stick replied.

"HoooonnK!...HONK!" At the last moment, the Lambrette swerved off the roadway onto the dirt shoulder in a cloud of dust as the truck roared past. "BOOM!" An enormous explosion hurled twisted scraps of the Lambrette a hundred feet into the air and scattered body parts all over the roadway.

"Oh, Jesus!" McClure shouted, as the squad picked up its pace. The deuce-and-a-half didn't stop as it receded in the distance.

"Keep your eyes open. Looks like a command detonated mine," McClure panted as the squad double timed to the slaughter. A faint plume of smoke drifted lazily across the opposite field. Body parts and red ooze covered the roadway, looking like an eighteen wheeler had run over a pack of jackrabbits.

When Roger reached the roadway, he looked

down the stretch but nothing was coming in either direction.

"Sick, man, really sick," Panella grimaced in disgust.

"Sangre de Christo!" Rudy groaned as he doubled over and barfed his guts out.

"Welcome to V-i-e-t-n-a-m, Poncho!" Stick stretched out the word to emphasize his point as he smacked away on a wad of gum.

Three nights later, Roger took Rudy on his first big patrol. They had received some rumors that the V.C. who had planted the mine might belong to a village east of them on a river emptying into an inland bay. The squad saddled up around 2200 hours and headed out with Sergeant Nhiem's platoon of P.F.'s They cut across farm land and paddies until they reached the river about a hundred yards north of the village. The river was too deep to wade across, so Roger suggested to McClure that he would swim across with a light line, then pull across a heavier rope. The rest of the patrol could hold on to it as they crossed. McClure agreed.

"O.K. you guys, hang tight till I get across...and for God's sake, cover me. I don't want to be out in the middle of the river if Charlie decides to open up," Roger said.

He waded through some reeds and water grass until he was about waist deep, then eased into the slow moving water and started to breaststroke across the hundred meter wide river. A three-quarter moon shown through a scudding overcast, illuminating the countryside and glinting off the water's surface. The current was flowing slightly upstream, giving the water a salty taste from the tidal flow of the South China Sea. Roger was halfway across when he was startled by light in the water around him. *"What the...?"* he thought. With each stroke of his arms through the water, a liquid light show of phosphorescent bubbles exploded around him. Then it dawned on him that it was something in the salt water illuminated by the moonlight.

Everything was still except for the quiet swishing sound of Roger moving slowly through the water. He reached the opposite bank and squished across the spongy mud bottom. When he was up the bank, he tugged on the line to signal, then started pulling the heavier nylon rope across. When he got it, he tied it to a nearby tree and waited for the platoon to pull themselves across. *"The PF's are getting good,"* he thought to himself as he sat watching the PF's cross. *"A couple of months ago they would have sounded like an old truck on a bad road."* When the patrol had reassembled, McClure, Sergeant Nhiem, Roger and the P.F. squad leaders finalized their plans. They would move downstream and encircle the village. They would wait until dawn before springing the trap.

It was about 0500 hours and the eastern horizon was showing the first hints of light. The patrol was set up with fire teams in place and three 60's with clear fields of fire covering the village. The only thing moving was a single hog rooting in a pen and a few chickens scratching around one of the huts.

"Nghe Day!...Nghe Day!" (Attention! Attention!) Sergeant Nhiem's voice interrupted the morning stillness. *"Hoi moi nguoi trong lang!"* The bullhorn blared. *"Cac nguoi da bi bao vay. Khong loi nao thoat duoc!"* (You are surrounded. There is no escape!) *"Tat ca cong quan hay bo vu khi va dau hang!"* (All V.C. must lay down their weapons and come out!) Sergeant Nhiem

demanded. *"Hay lap tuc thi hanh!"* (Immediately!) He ordered.

The men scanned the village for movement in the pale morning light as they nervously fingered their triggers. Nothing moved.

"Toi lap lai, tat ca cong quan phai bo vu khi va dau hang." Sergeant Nhiem repeated his surrender warning. *"Cac anh khong the thoat duoc dau!"* (You cannot escape!) *"Ai tron chay la bi ban lap tuc!"* (Anyone trying to escape will be shot!) Nhiem paused for a few moments then turned to Sergeant McClure for instructions.

"Tell them to gather in the center of the village, and tell them to do it now!"

Nhiem nodded with his lips pursed in determination. *"Moi nguoi phai tu hop o giua lang...NGAY BAY GIO!"*

A leaden silence hung in the morning air as the patrol anxiously waited for something to happen. Sergeant Nhiem looked to McClure, but McClure indicated with facial expression to wait. A minute passed, then, one by one, the villagers started to come out of their hootches and gather in the middle of the village. Nhiem's men moved forward with their carbines at ready while a squad circled around the village from behind and came up from the river bank. When Nhiem's men had cordoned off the village, he began to interrogate the villagers. There were no young men present, only women, children, old men and haggard looking mama sans with their teeth stained a pomegranate red from chewing betel nut.

"This is what we're up against a lot of the time, Rudy," Roger instructed. "See the defiance in their faces? You can bet they're either hiding some V.C. or weapons or some of the village men are working for Uncle Ho."

"I can dig it." Rudy replied. "You'd have to be blind not to see the hate in their eyes for us."

"You got that right, Man." Scroggins noted. "This is definitely a V.C. ville."

"Either we woke them up too early in the morning and they haven't had their coffee yet, or they just don't like our friendly little bed checks," Stick added.

"Viet Cong O dau?" (Where are the V.C.?) Sergeant Nhiem asked the villagers. *"Ho dang O dau?"* (Where are they hiding?). The people glared at him in silence.

"Cac anh dang giau ho O dau?" (Where are you hiding them?), Nhiem shouted at the huddled mass.

"Khong co Viet Cong O day!...Viet Cong khong tot dau!" (No V.C. here...V.C. no good!) A feisty young woman spit out the words.

"Cho toi biet ho O dau!" (Tell me where they are!). Nhiem demanded again. *"Co dang giau ho O dau!"* Sergeant Nhiem eyed the woman.

Nhiem was getting nowhere with his questions. The villagers were playing dumb.

The rest of Nhiem's men were poking around the village and searching the huts when two of them ran up to Nhiem with a B.A.R. belt and some-web gear. It had some ammo pouches and a Chinese grenade attached.

The countenance of the women who had told the Sergeant there were no V.C. in the village suddenly dropped at the sight of the evidence.

"O.K.   Lets turn this place upside down!" McClure ordered.

The men were rooting through the hootches, looking for weapons and hiding places when Rudy shouted, "Over here! Look at this!" He had found a tunnel entrance in one of the hootches under a woven mat covered with a large basket of rice.

"Hay di ra voi hai tay gio len!...Neu khong chung toi se quang luu dan vao ham!" (Come out with your hands on your head...Or we'll throw a grenade in your hole!)   Sergeant Nhiem shouted into the tunnel entrance.

Three V.C. emerged wearing black pajamas and sandals. The woman who had been shouting at Nhiem started to cry. One of the P.F.'s went into the tunnel and pulled out a cache of weapons - an old Chinese burp gun, a Soviet sniper rifle with scope and several SK's wrapped in rice paper and cosmoline.

After a thorough search, the V.C. were blindfolded and marched back to Phu Bai for questioning.

"Good work, Rudy," Roger congratulated the kid for uncovering the tunnel entrance. "I think your gettin' the hang of it."

"All in a day's work, Amigo," Rudy responded with a grin. "I've got a pretty good teacher, for a gringo!"

A couple of days later, the squad headed out on a night patrol to set up an ambush north of Gia Le. It was a full moon above a partially cloudy sky - not the best of nights for patrolling. Roger had Rudy beside him as they walked point together. The squad had just skirted past a village on a path which threaded through a tangled stretch of overhanging jungle. Only the faintest trace of moonlight penetrated the canopy. An apprehensive stillness hung in the air like an ominous refrain. There were no jungle sounds of birds or frogs or monkeys, only the soft pitch of wind sobbing and sighing through the double tier canopy overhead.

"Roofh!..Roofh!, Roofh!" the sound of a village dog pierced the night, but the men moved on without saying a word.

Roger and Rudy passed by the village on their right and broke out of the tangle into an open stretch of field which was brightly illuminated in the moon's glow. It was very dangerous moving in the open under such conditions. They continued down a trail which wrapped around the village until they came to a small dirt road coming from the cluster of hootches behind them.

Psst!" Roger motioned for Rudy to take the right side of the road.

The squad cautiously followed the pointmen, as the pair made their way down the one lane road. They were spread out the maximum distance because of their visibility in the moonlight. McClure didn't want them to get bunched up and cut down if something opened up.

About 200 meters down the lane, Roger reached a brush covered bank with a narrow concrete bridge crossing a sluggish stream about thirty meters across. In the moon light, he could see the details of the opposite bank. It sloped up to a cluster of trees on the left hand side of the road and a waist high stand of brush and hedgerows on the right. The road crossed the bridge and ran through the middle.

Roger scanned the opposite bank for a long time before speaking. "I don't like it," He whispered to Rudy.

"Why?" Rudy wanted to know.

"Something's just not right. It's too quiet. I can feel it in my bones," Roger muttered. His stomach muscles knotted. "Lets hang loose and wait awhile." He wasn't sure what was tugging at his senses, but some refined instinct told him that something was wrong.

"Roger, what's up?" Sergeant McClure asked as he slid up next to Roger laying in a prone position watching the river crossing.

"I don't know, but I got this bad feeling inside. I don't like this crossing or the look of things on the other side of the bridge. We're just too out in the open and this is a perfect night for Charlie to bag some grunts."

"Your leadin' the show on this one, Helle," McClure deferred to Roger's instincts.

"What say Rudy and I double back and cross farther upstream? We'll circle back to see if we can scare something up just in case someone is over there waitin' for us."

"Sounds good to me," McClure agreed. "We'll set up the gun on this side and cover you."

Roger and Rudy back-tracked down the trail about 150 meters until they reached a treeline bordering the left side of the lane. They veered left through the front edge of the treeline for a hundred meters then headed back to the stream. When they reached the bank, they settled on their haunches for a few moments to watch and listen.

It was very quiet. Silent waves of clouds drifted overhead - their luminescent outlines highlighted by the moon's reflection.

"Look's O.K.," Roger concluded after a few minutes of silence. "You ready to cross?"

"After you, Amigo," Rudy grinned.

They walked down the bank through some slick mud, then stepped quietly into the silt choked water. The warm swampy smell of muddy water filled their nostrils as they waded across the waist-deep stream.

Both were tense and ready. Moving through the moonlight in the open was an unnerving feeling which blurred the distinction between the hunter and the hunted.

They made their way up the slope and disappeared into a shadowy clump of trees. About twenty meters into the trees, they reached the edge. Before them was a large field bathed in the bluish glow of moon light. The field was a patchwork of untilled paddies, criss-crossed with narrow dikes.

"We'll head West then loop back and come up behind the bridge crossing to see if anybody is in position for an ambush," Roger instructed.

"Gotcha," Rudy acknowledged.

They gradually worked their way across the field until they were about forty meters from the back edge of the bushes at the bridge approach.

Roger tapped Rudy on the shoulder and motioned him to drop. In front of them were eight V.C. covering the bridge. *"I knew it!"* He thought to himself. He leaned over and quietly whispered in Rudy's ear. "O.K. this is it...You take the three on the right. I'll get the others on the left. We go fully automatic. I'll throw a grenade, then you start firing. O.K?" Rudy nodded.

Roger took an M-26 grenade from his flak jacket and bobbed it up and down in his palm a couple times like a big league pitcher getting ready to toss the winning pitch. The thin skinned jacket of the M-26 covered a tightly coiled steel spring which was designed to fragment into hundreds of shreds of shrapnel. It could be lethal up to a five meter diameter. Roger straightened the pin and took one look at Rudy before throwing it. He held the grenade to his chest with his left hand and grabbed the ring with his right index finger. He took a deep breath, pulled the pin, letting the spoon fly free then lobbed it into the V.C. position. **"BAM,BAM,BAM,BAM,BAM....!"** Rudy opened up with his M-14, followed immediately by Roger's. **"KaBOOM!"** The frag exploded in a cloud of leaves and dirt. Several V.C. went down. They both slammed in fresh magazines and kept pouring volleys into the V.C. ambush. A couple of carbines blinked back in return. "Crack, Crack, Crack...!" A sudden chain-reaction opened up to their left, lashing the air around them. Rounds thudded into the dirt. "Let's move!" Roger shouted. "There's more of them on our right flank!" The V.C. muzzle flashes looked like strobe lights firing on and off in quick succession. Roger and Rudy started running back to the stream as bullets lashed the air around them. The chatter of automatic weapons was deafening. Tracers lasered across the field, scratching fluorescent green streaks in the darkness. "Aawwh!" Rudy screamed as he tumbled into the dirt from a hit. "I'm hit Roger!" He screamed in panic.

Roger turned and ran back. He was a few feet away when his right leg was knocked out from under him. He didn't feel much, just a dull numbing sensation in his right calf. He picked himself up and ran over to Rudy. "Got me in the thigh," Rudy winced in pain. Roger slapped another magazine into his rifle and fired a sustained burst into the opposing flank. He picked up Rudy in a fireman's carry and started lugging him back across the field.

"Tatow...tow, tow, tow, two, TaTow!" the comforting sound of Panella's M-60 opened up in the distance, spraying the V.C. position. M-14's joined into the rising crescendo of fire as they poured volleys into the V.C. ambush.

Roger reached the stream and crossed with Rudy on his back. He was breathing hard from the exertion and his leg was burning from the filthy water seeping into his open wound. When he reached the opposite bank, he lowered Rudy to the ground and helped him as they both limped and hobbled until the rest of the squad found them.

Doc sprinkled some powder on their wounds and tied them off with field dressings. Rudy was bleeding pretty bad, so Doc gave him some blood expander and a transfusion of dextrose to keep him from going into shock. He also gave them both a shot of morphine to dull the pain.

A half hour later, they were both on a medevac back to Da Nang. Roger's was just a superficial leg wound. He was patched up, given a few hundred thousand units of procaine penicillin, some streptomycin and a handful of Darvons and sent back to his unit two days later. Rudy ended up with complications and was medevaced to Japan. Roger never saw the kid again.

Such was one of the more painful ironies of 'Nam - men could touch the most intimate of relationships and be torn apart in moments, never to see each other again.

A week later, Roger was awarded his second Cross of Gallantry and first Purple Heart.

Chapter 11

Trying to sweep the surrounding countryside clear of V.C. infiltration was a never ending battle. It was often as frustrating as trying to force the ocean back with a push broom. It was a constant struggle to win the hearts and minds of the people. They were often little more than helpless victims caught in the middle of a conflict they didn't understand, much less want.

For the average Vietnamese peasant, political ideology meant little. Apart from the ancient cycles of the rice harvest, he could have cared less about Thieu's corrupt regime in the South or Ho Chi Minh's great patriotic struggle in the North. He just wanted to be left alone to his time-honored rhythms - left alone to plant and till and harvest his life-giving rice - left alone to live his simple life in peace.

But, like it or not, he was often the victim of a struggle from which he couldn't escape - a struggle which often forced him to take sides, for better or worse.

Viet Cong activity around the villages of Gia Le had tapered off to nocturnal operations. If they couldn't convert the people through propagandistic tirades against the "lackey, running dogs" in Saigon or Communist slogans praising the heroic freedom fighters liberating the people from the yoke of U.S. imperialism, they would resort to coercion, intimidation and outright terrorism.

Due to the Marine presence, the V.C. political cadre, tax collectors and hit squads were threatening the villagers with harsh reprisals if they cooperated with the Americans. It was the CAP squad's responsibility to win over the people by living among them and encouraging them that the Marines would protect them if they resisted the Viet Cong.

A chief from a village about three klicks south of Huong Thuy sent word to McClure's squad that he wanted to cooperate with them but was fearful of the V.C. death threats. He sent a message through a village elder requesting the Marines to come to his village to discuss the matter further. The elder stressed that the chief was an honorable man who hated the Viet Cong and their tactics, but had a family and didn't want them to be harmed. He said that the chief was fed up with the harassment, forced conscription of the young men, bullying, rice confiscations, and propaganda. He just wanted his village left alone.

Roger had been through his village several times on periodic patrols. On one of these patrols, the chief's daughter had caught his eye. *Do Thi Xuan Mai* was seventeen and the most beautiful woman Roger had ever seen. She was an exotic mixture of Vietnamese and French from her mother's side. Her grandmother had gotten pregnant by a French trader in Hue during a brief but passionate liaison. Mai also had the blood of Vietnamese Emperors running through her veins. Successive emperors had scoured the countryside for generations, searching for the most beautiful women in Cochin China to stock their stables of concubines in Hue. The women of Hue were famed for their exceptional beauty and physical appeal.

Mai was taller than most Vietnamese women. She had soft, amber colored skin with delicate facial features and perfect lips - not too full yet not too thin. Her hair was silky black and hung to her waist. Mai was lovely in every way. She had a shapely figure that men would kill for, especially Marines.

Roger was immediately attracted to her, and any idiot could tell that Mai was infatuated with Roger. To her, the handsome young Marine from a distant place beyond the ocean was just as exotic and appealing. Mai carried herself with a feminine grace which accentuated her loveliness. At seventeen, she was very much a woman, but with just a sparkle of girlishness in her warm, almond eyes. She was shy, but had an alluring hint of sensuousness which could arouse any man. In the midst of the filth and rampant squalor of Vietnam, Mai was like a delicate water lily in a pond of green slime. Roger was captivated by her beauty, but also by her modesty and innocence - virtues which seemed so pure and refreshing in a land polluted with violence.

Mai's father had been sending her to a small secondary school in Gia Le. She was planning on entering the university in Hue to become a nurse the following year. Roger had first seen Mai while passing through her village on patrol, but began to take interest in her coming and going each day from school. Like a love sick puppy, Roger would hang out on Mai's way home from school, whenever he got the chance, in hopes of seeing her. He tried to be cool, but his actions were obvious to everyone.

At first, Roger would just smile at her as she passed by in her white *Ao Dai* and greet her with a simple, *"Chau Co, Mai."* She would blush and turn away while her girlfriends giggled and teased her playfully. After a while, she would come by herself and stop to talk with Roger or walk with him a bit. They would share small talk and flirtatious conversations with each other, teaching each other phrases and asking each other simple questions.

"Neu co noi chuyen voi mot nghuoi linh my, cha co phan doi gi khong?" (Does your father mind if you talk to an American solder?) Roger asked sheepishly.

Mai smiled and shook her head like a little girl.

"Mai, Co bao nhieu tuoi vay?" (Mai, how old are you?) Roger asked.

"I am seventeen, Raw-jeur" (she had difficulty pronouncing the "g" in his name)

"Neu co vui long, toi rat han hanh duoc tiep chuyen voi co. Toi muon hoc them tieng viet voi co." (If you would like, I would like to spend time with you. I'd like to learn more Vietnamese from you.) Roger suggested.

"I would like that Raw'jeur. It is very different in America where you come from...no?" She had a soft melodic voice. Roger couldn't help but grin when she talked. Her voice sounded so cute, with her halting English.

"Yes, it gets very cold sometimes. It is very different from Vietnam." Roger spoke slowly so he would not run his words together. "Do you know what snow is, Mai?"

"Yes, Raw'jeur. It is cold and white and very pretty. No?"

"Yes, Mai...pretty like you." Mai blushed and looked down in embarrassment.

"No...I am ugly." She smiled coyly.

"No, you are very beautiful, Mai."

"You talk with tiger eyes, Raw'jeur.....eyes like you are hunting." Mai giggled.

"What am I hunting, Mai?" Roger played along.

"You know, Raw'jeur." Mai looked him in the eyes.

Mai was silent for a moment before speaking. "Raw'jeur, I am very afraid for my father and my village. My father does not tell me everything but I can see it in my mother's face. I know that the V.C. come to our village and talk to my father."

"Don't worry, Mai. We will protect your village. Roger touched the back of her hand gently. Mai looked up with her eyes filling with tears. *"Cha co da tung giup do chung toi rat nhieu."* (Your father has been very helpful to us.) *"Toi rat quan tam den su an toan cua co va gia dinh...Chung toi muon bao ve dan lang duoc an ninh tu Viet Cong."* (I'm very concerned about you and your family's safety...We want to try to protect your village from the Viet Cong)....Roger paused a moment before continuing, "I will protect you, Mai," he assured her.

"Co rat dep. Toi nghi ve co rat nhiem." (You are very beautiful. I care very much for you.) Roger added.

"I am very happy, Raw'jeur. I like very much to talk with you!"

"I like talking to you too, Mai. Can I walk with you for a little while?"

"Yes, Raw'jeur. I would like that."

"I Can't Wait Forever, Even Though..You want Me...To...I Can't Wait Forever, Even Though..You Want Me   To!.....TIME WON'T LET ME..*Oh No!*...TIME WON'T LET ME..*Oh NO!*....TIME WON'T LET Meeeeeeeeee E...Wait That Long!"

"Turn that radio down, Panella. I can't hear myself think." McClure told him.

"O.K., O.K., Sarge, don't blow a fuse! You sound like my parents. I'm just groovin' on the sounds," Panella responded as he turned down the volume of his transistor radio.

"Whatdaya think, Spook? Got any guesses about Mai's father? Think he's serious 'bout cooperating with us?" McClure asked Roger as the squad chowed down before moving out to Mai's village.

"We've talked a lot about it," Roger said, "And..."

"Yeah", Stick cut him off, "Much time as you've spent moonin' over Mai, it looks like you've been doin' a lot of talkin'."

Roger's face turned red.

"Guy's got it bad," Scroggins added. "Kinda turns ya on, huh, Spook?" He chuckled.

"Cool it!" McClure snapped.

"Aw, c'mon, Sarge, you gotta admit that she's one righteous lookin' lady," Stick grinned.

"No lie, Dude," Scroggins responded. "Wish they grew round eyes like that, back in the World!"

"Why don't you meat-heads quit runnin' your mouths?" Roger was embarrassed.

"All I can say, she's real scared about what's comin' down," Roger responded to McClure's inquiry. "She says her father really hates the Cong and wants to do something about it, but he's real worried about his family."

"Well, nothin' ventured, nothin' gained," McClure concluded. "We're just going to have to have a little powwow with Mai's old man."

"As I write this letter, Woo o o Ooo...Send my love to you...You know I want you to remember that I'll always...Be in love with you.....Treasure these few words while we're together...keep all my love forever....P.S....I Love You....Yoouuu you you" One of your favorites this morning on Armed Forces Radio. Its currently 95 degrees in Saigon under clear skies...Here's a few Motown memories from Aretha Franklin and a little *R.E.S.P.E.C.T...."*
"Alright, Panella, turn it off. We're movin' out. Let's do it! Saddle up!" McClure ordered.

It was your typical thermal day of suffocating heat as the squad moved through the muggy paddy lands south of Mai's village. Roger hadn't seen her for a couple of days and hoped he would see her in the village. Just the thought of her face caused Roger's heart to jump. He plodded through the steam bath dripping wet in his soaked fatigues, oblivious to the discomfort of the morning sun.
Mai's village was a lush oasis cradled in a picturesque valley of emerald paddy lands, fruit trees and vegetable gardens. The village was a klick west of Highway One north of Gia Le. Roger led point down the well used path leading out to the village. The cluster of saffron colored hooches were sheltered in groves of coconut trees and banana palms about 200 meters in front of him. He paused to take in the picture postcard beauty of Mai's little paradise and fantasized what it would be like just to chuck everything and live

with her in such a peaceful setting.

He wiped a slick sheen of sweat from his face and dabbed the hollow of his neck with his towel where perspiration had pooled, then scanned the fields on either side of the dike. *"It's strange,"* he thought absently. *"There are no villagers working in them."* Usually there would be women and men with their conical hats and their pants rolled up planting seedlings or weeding in the shallow paddy water. There were no teams of water buffalo plowing the paddies with farmers gently swishing the buffalo's rumps with a long stick. The fields were deserted. There were no sounds either - no dogs barking, no sounds of children playing, nothing. Nothing was moving. Roger suddenly snapped out of his day-dreaming and tensed with alertness. Something was wrong with the picture.

He halted the squad of Marines with the wave of his hand. They promptly settled into a squat or stepped to the sides of the dike. Panella was walking with his M-60 laid across his neck, but with Roger's signal, he brought the gun down to his waist in anticipation.

"What is it, Helle?" McClure enquired.

"You don't see it?" Roger asked.

"See what?" McClure responded.

"That's what I mean, Sarge..nothin'."

"Yeah, I see what ya mean now," McClure agreed as he panned the empty fields.

"Something's up. Don't know what, but we better watch our step."

Roger looked up briefly to check the sun's position. It was almost overhead. Other than the bright yellow ball glaring at them, the only other presence in the sky was a lone contrail dissipating in the jet stream.

"I'll flank to the left and check things out," Roger

suggested.

"We'll spread out and follow," McClure added. Roger crossed the paddy to his left down an intersecting dike and approached the village on a well used foot path leading in from the fields. That's when he first smelled it. The sickening stench of death drifted from the village. An icy tingle shot down his spine. His heart started to beat faster as he neared the edge of the village. He suddenly froze in his tracks, paralyzed by the grisly spectacle in front of him. A large bamboo pole was driven into the ground with the decapitated head of the village chief impaled upon it. Blind rage rushed through him. *"Mai!"* He feared, as a near claustrophobic bolt of terror seized him.

Time seemed distorted, as if everything was suspended in some strange warp. How much time had passed wasn't clear, but, McClure's words brought him back.

"Those dirty murdering Son of a B.....'s!" McClure swore.

"Sweet Jesus! Holy Mother of God!" Panella gripped his M-60 like he wanted to squeeze it to death.

His eyes were glazed over. They had that fish-eyed look of death. He was unfazed by the cloud of flies landing on his face. The V.C. had brutally tortured him. They had cut off his testicles and stuffed them in his mouth as a supreme gesture of humiliation.

The squad maneuvered leerily into the village not knowing what to expect.

"Bizzzzzz!...BizzzZZZ!" A horde of black flies swarmed all over the body of a woman. About twenty meters past the first hootch, they found the chief's wife laying in a pool of blood and urine soaked soil. The pungent ammonia stench of urine and sour excrement was overwhelming.

"Oh God! Oh God! Oh God!..." Paterson doubled over at the sight and vomited out a mouthful of puke. "Bastards!" He gagged. "I'd rather shoot a V.C. gook than a rabid dog," he retched.

Even the hardest members of the squad had to fight back the urge to throw up. The V.C. had left her where they had killed her. She had been seven months pregnant when they began to torture her. The V.C. had bayonetted and disemboweled her, killing the baby.

As the squad spread out to check the village, a few terrified villagers filtered out of their hiding places. They began to relate what had happened the night before. Roger was choking back the tears as he listened to their tale of horror. The V.C had taken Mai and her nine year old sister and gang raped them in front of their father and mother, while they forced them to watch the indignity. Then an officer shot them both in the back of their heads with his pistol.

After raping the two daughters, they staked the mother to the ground and disemboweled her. They stuck a filthy rag in her mouth to choke off her screams. Several V.C. then unfastened their pants and urinated into her open abdominal cavity, laughing as she writhed in agony and slowly died in excruciating pain. They then tortured the village chief by slowly pealing off strips of flesh from his body. When they had finished flaying him alive, they castrated him in front of the villagers and chopped off his head with a machete.

After asking the villagers about Mai, he found her laying in a ditch outside the village where the V.C. had dumped her and her sister's body when they finished abusing them.

All of this was done as a brutal object lesson to

the villagers of what would happen if they cooperated
with the Americans.

Later that day, the Marines headed back to Gia
Le, numbed and dejected beyond reason by the mindless
carnage and bestial insanity they had witnessed.

Roger was too numbed with shock to do much of
anything but remember how innocent Mai had been and
how senseless it all seemed.

Chapter 12

V.C. activity began to intensify from Phu Bai to Hue. Battalion headquarters ordered the CAP squads to increase their patrols to counter the threat. Night ambushes began to bag more Viet Cong who were moving in greater numbers than ever before. Intelligence information gleaned from recon patrols, captured V.C., village sympathizers and informants started pouring in. Rumors of Viet Cong activities amplified, indicating that the enemy was preparing for something big. Even the villagers at Gia Le were nervous.

A week after the atrocities at Mai's village, Roger was leading the squad back from a patrol when he stepped out of a pocket of jungle into a small clearing at the same moment a V.C. pointman stepped out on the opposite side. Both were pumped with adrenalin and poised for action. They saw each other at the same instant and rushed to outdraw the other. The V.C. was bringing his AK into firing position when Roger cut loose with a semi-automatic burst which drove the point man backwards in a grotesque dance of death, before depositing him in a crumpled heap at the jungle edge. The rest of his patrol retreated back into the sanctuary of the jungle.

"Will ya look at this!" McClure was amazed as he nudged the lifeless form with the toe of his boot. "Too much, just too much!" He shook his head in disbelief. "Can ya believe this? It's our barber? Guy cut my hair back in Gia Le just two days ago."

"Check it out, Stick! It's Mr. Hai." Scroggins noted. "He was always such a nice guy...jokin' with us all the time. Use to call me, 'Misser Leonard.' "

"Well, he's a nice, dead guy now!" Panella commented matter-of-factly, as he smacked on a piece of chewing gum.

"Man, this is gettin' scary, Spook. The Cong is up to somethin'. I think the deal's about to go down." Scroggins responded.

"Yeah, Hai does kinda look like he knows more than he's tellin' us," Paterson noted.

The Viet Cong had moved some hardcore units into the area to reinforce the locals. They were determined to frustrate the pacification efforts of the CAP squads. The small mobile units were gradually denying the countryside to Charlie and this was an intolerable situation for the Viet Cong, if they hoped to exist.

From information they pieced together, Intelligence calculated that the V.C. were using an area east of Gia Le as a staging area. The area contained a fishing village along a tributary of the Perfume River flowing south from Hue into *Cau Hai* Lagoon. This stretch of coastal lands was a jade colored mosaic of paddy lands and lattice work dikes bordering the South China Sea.

Roger's squad was ordered to take out a patrol to the small fishing village and set up an ambush, in hopes of catching a V.C. unit moving through the village at night. CAP headquarters was increasingly concerned about Viet Cong deployment and unit strength in the area. The village was reached by a long dike which crossed an enormous rice paddy between Gia Le and the fishing village. None of the men liked going out to this particular village because they always took pot-shots or sniper fire. They were always some distance away when they took fire, but they knew that the place was as riddled with V.C. as a rotten foundation with termites.

Every time they entered the village, they asked where the V.C. were , but all they could get out of the villagers was the predictable "No V.C! No V.C....V.C beau coup numbah 10!" The Marine's anger was only tempered by the expressions of fear and frustration on the faces of the villagers. They knew what intimidation and terror could do to simple people.

That night, they headed down the mile-long dike under a heavy cloud cover which darkened the landscape. Roger liked it that way. He was tense and uptight because of the mounting frustration and anger he felt since Mai's death. He was trying not to let his pent-up emotions dull his cutting edge on point. He knew that the rest of the squad was depending on him not to let them down. In spite of a distinct tautness in the air, the patrol was uneventful and returned to Gia Le without incident.

The next afternoon, Roger found McClure sitting at a table in their quarters brooding over a cup of coffee, like he was meditating upon its contents. "Something wrong, Sarge?" Roger asked.

"You could say that," McClure responded glumly.

"What's the matter?" Roger asked with concern in his voice.

"Headquarters wants us to go back to the fishing village we staked out last night. Intelligence says we need to find out what Charlie's up to. I think they're trying to dangle us over their noses like a piece of bait!"

"They what?" Roger asked with disbelief in his voice. "They can't do that! Nobody runs a patrol on the same route two nights in a row. That's askin' for trouble!"

Just then, several squad members came in, laughing about something.

"Hey..how come you guys look so happy?" Panella asked.

McClure looked up from his cup of coffee. "You're not going to believe this, but Headquarters wants us to go back tonight and set up an ambush near the fishing village we visited last night."

"You're kiddin', right?" Panella asked.

"I wish I was, but I'm serious," McClure answered.

"Serious as a heart attack," Roger added.

"I don't like this one little bit!" Stick spit out a wad of tobacco juice. "Unh uh!...I don't like this at all!"

"It stinks...I know, but Marine Intelligence needs more info and they want us to get it. They want us to find out what Charlie's up to." McClure tried to calm their tempers.

"Intelligence!" Paterson grumbled. "Now that's

a crock of...What a contradiction in terms!...Military Intelligence," he spit out the words. "Why don't they go out and find out for themselves?"

McClure pulled hard on his cigarette before speaking. "What's really bothering me about this whole thing is that I'm scheduled to leave for R & R. this afternoon, so I can't be with you guys. I wanted Helle to take the squad, but Phu Bai wants a replacement NCO to take my place while I'm gone...Don't ask me why."

"Hey, we'll be alright, Sarge. You just have a blast in Bangkok and don't worry about us. We're big boys, now. We can take care of ourselves," Roger told him.

"Yeah, that's right, Sarge. Just have fun. You know we would if we were in your shoes," Stick smiled.

Later that afternoon, a jeep pulled into the compound from Phu Bai with the replacement squad leader and picked up McClure to take him back to Phu Bai to catch a chopper to Da Nang for his flight to Bangkok.

McClure conferred with the replacement for a couple minutes off to the side, then said his good-byes to the squad.

"You guys take care," McClure said with a slight edge to his voice. He threw his utility bag into the back of the jeep and swung into the passenger seat. "I'll be back in a week with some real stories to tell!" He tried to be upbeat.

"Hey, don't do anything we wouldn't do, Sarge!" Panella joked.

"Hey, I'm gonna do that and a whole bunch more!" McClure gave a mischievous grin. "You guys watch your step...O.K.?" The men could see a protective look of concern on his face.

"Don't worry, Sarge. We got it under control!" Roger tried to assure him.

"Yeah, I'll take good care of them," the new squad leader said. "Don't worry."

"See you guys," McClure shouted as the jeep headed off in a cloud of dust.

"I'm Sergeant, Terry, the replacement Sergeant introduced himself to the squad.

"Corporal Helle...assistant squad leader," Roger shook Terry's hand.

"Helle, let's see...It's 1530 now," Terry checked his watch. "I'm gonna get my gear squared away...Say we meet around 1800 hours to go over the patrol route for tonight..O.K.?" Sergeant Terry responded.

"Sounds good to me," Roger replied.

The rest of the men drifted off, leaving Roger by himself under the shade of a tree overhanging the entrance to the compound. "Those stupid desk jockeys in Phu Bai are going to get us all killed!" Roger grumbled. "Oh well, at least McClure's gonna have a good time."

At 1800 hours, Roger found Sergeant Terry, sitting at a table in their dining area with a map spread out in front of him.

"Pull up a chair, Corporal. I understand that it's your turn off tonight. Is that right?"

"Yes, Sergeant, we rotate every two weeks and let one guy off for that night. But with Sergeant McClure gone, I wouldn't feel right staying behind and watching Geckos climb the walls. I know this AO better than anyone in the squad and I think it's best if I pull point tonight."

Terry hesitated. "I don't think so, Helle. If you want to go out with the squad, that's up to you, but you're not gonna pull point tonight. I may be new to you guys, but I've done my time in the bush too. It might sound corny, but if I'm gonna win any confidence with the men while I'm here, I think it's only right that I start out by pulling point. I can't be askin' them to do what I am unwilling to do myself. Can I?"

"Just the same, Sergeant, I would feel a whole lot better if you let me walk point. I know the trail and this village and, no offense, Sergeant, but you don't," Roger stated flatly.

"Look, Helle, I don't want to have to pull rank and get off to a bad start with you, but I'm pullin' point and that's the way it's gonna be! Do I make myself clear?" Terry said firmly.

"You're callin' the shots, Sergeant." Roger knew the argument was over and got down to the task of mapping out the route.

The squad filed out into the darkness around midnight with Terry walking point. Roger was in the eleventh position behind Paterson. He didn't like it one bit, not because Terry was taking his position, but because the guy was a little too unreasonable for his own good.

The squad moved quickly through the night. The black vault was sprinkled with thousands of shining stars. They headed north on a path which ran adjacent to Highway One until they came to an old French fort which a garrison of ARVN's had taken over. After reporting in their patrol route so no trigger happy ARVN's would open up on them by mistake, they headed east. In a few minutes, they reached the wide dike leading out to the fishing village.

Malevolent swarms of hungry bugs batted about their heads, in obvious oblivion to the thick coating of oily repellent smeared on their faces and necks. Terry led the squad in a brisk pace down the path past several intersecting dikes and occasional stands of trees.

Roger didn't like the unfamiliar feeling of being so far back in the pack. He was accustomed to walking point. He was keyed up and edgy as he kept pace with the column of men. *"They're going too fast,",* he took a mental note. *"Terry is pushing the squad too fast...He's in too much of a hurry."* Terry's pace agitated him.

The squad was a couple hundred meters from the outskirts of the village. Roger had a vague, ominous feeling in back of his mind. *"He's got to slow this race down and take his time."* He wanted to say something, but hesitated. The only noise was the gentle swishing sound of men moving along the dike.

His concerns were nagging him. Then he sensed it. Some inner instinct triggered a premonition of impending danger. His body was suddenly electrified by a strange prickly sensation crawling up his spine. *"I've got to warn them!"* The thought shot through his mind as the squad stepped into the killing zone of an L shaped ambush.

"KaBLAAMM!"

A violent flashbulb explosion erupted behind the squad hurling the last three men into the paddy water like rag dolls. Roger's entire life flashed through his mind in instant replay. "Splash!" He landed on his back in the paddy water. His ears were ringing, but, otherwise, he was unhurt.

The curtain of blackness was rent by flashes as Marines screamed from hits.

"Tat tat tat tat tat...pop pop pop...Bruuuup!...tat
tat tat...pop pop...bruuuup! bruuump! tat tat tat tat!"
Rifles crackled and stuttered in a chaotic
cacophony which grew in intensity until it reached a
maniacal clap.

"Zzzzzzssst Thuo!....KRUNCH!" A B-40 rocket
opened up the dike a few meters away pelting the
surrounding paddy water with thousands of geysers from
falling mud.

"Auugh!.....Ugh!" men groaned as rounds thudded
into their bodies.

"Where's my rifle?" Roger freaked as he groped
along the muddy bottom with his hands. He couldn't
find it. He half-crawled, half-swam through the muck to
the edge of the dike and dug his hands into the mud to
secure himself.

Green and red tracers scratched fluorescent lines
across the field in a perverse Morse Code. A captured
60 raked the dike with angry bursts. Bullets spit into the
bank, kicking up clods of dirt which fell around him.
Roger was submerged in the paddy with his head just
above water, half buried among the shoots.

The hailstorm of fire sputtered off, then stopped.

"Guurrgle..gurgle..." He could hear the gasping
sound of a Marine struggling for air. "Help me....help
me," the faint whimper floated in the air. Roger was
terrified and trembling. He was wet and shivering from
cold.

"Oooh...oh," a new guy a few feet from him was
moaning softly. "It hurts," he cried.

"Ssssh," Roger whispered.

"Oh, God, it hurts bad..."

Roger canted his head slightly, straining to listen.

He could hear the muffled sounds of men approaching. They were speaking in clipped Vietnamese phrases. He pulled himself along the side of the dike through the stagnant water and cupped the wounded Marine's mouth with his hand. There were two of them laying next to each other. They had been behind him when the command detonated mine went off, blowing them off the dike also. Both were bleeding profusely from multiple shrapnel wounds. Their eardrums were ruptured and leaking blood from the concussion.

The sounds were getting closer. *"Lam kha lam, Van."* (Nice work, Van) He heard one of them say. *"Coi lai cac xac chet...Gom tu nhung gi minh co the dung,"* (Check the bodies...gather anything we can use.) another instructed.

"Oh, God, I don't want them to find me!" he shuddered as an avalanche of panic overwhelmed him. He hurriedly covered the heads of the two wounded Marines with some rice shoots, then pushed himself back from the bank as far as he could reach and still hold on. Through the rice shoots, he could just make out the ghoulish silhouettes of V.C. scavengers moving along the dike, stopping to kick a body or stooping to gather weapons.

"Nguoi nay con song, Trung si Tran!" (This one's still alive, Sergeant Tran) *"Minh se lam gi voi nhung nguoi bi thuong?"* (What do we do with the wounded?) One of the soldiers asked.

"May biet minh se lam gi ma, dung thang kho!" (You know what to do with them, fool!) another snapped.

"Auughh..." He heard the anguished rush of air from a wounded Marine as one of the V.C. finished him off.

"Chung ta phai lam nhanh len truoc khi truc thang den!" (We must hurry...before the helicopters come!) One of them ordered. *"Nhanh len, cac anh em!"* (Quickly, Comrades!)

The V.C. were talking and laughing softly as they hurriedly went about the grisly business of stripping the bodies of personal effects - watches, wedding rings, wallets.

"Trung, dong ho do coi dep a," (Nice watch Trung) he heard one of them say.

"Stick...." Roger thought he heard the plaintive voice of Scroggins, pleading in the darkness.

There was a pistol shot and then another as they systematically stilled the twitching bodies.

"Dung la linh cuop!" (Filthy Marine dogs!) One of them scowled.

Agonizing moments passed in terror filled suspense - then the ghostly apparitions moved off into the night. A worried silence followed in the wake of their departure. The night was tomb quiet as Roger waited and listened, afraid to move. "God, it burns so much!" One of the wounded muttered.

"It'll be O.K. Just hang in there," Roger urged.

"I'm so tired," the other spoke.

"Stay awake! Don't fall asleep!... Listen to me! You've got to try to stay awake!" Roger pleaded with him. Both were losing blood fast and slipping into shock. He couldn't lay there clinging to the dike forever or they would die. He had to chance it. He took a deep breath and mustered enough resolve to pull himself up out of the slop to check out the squad.

Ten men were sprawled along the dike with their limbs splayed in grotesque angles. He checked each one for signs of life, but they were all dead - riddled by bullets and shrapnel wounds. Several had their throats slit. He found Sergeant Terry half-naked with his boots off and his fatigue shirt removed. His chalk white chest was smeared with blood from some of the twenty-seven rounds which hit him.

Miraculously, Roger found the radio still intact. It was under the body of Paterson who was slumped over it backwards on the slope of the dike with his head partially submerged under paddy water. He turned him over and pulled his body up onto the dike. He then removed the radio pack, adjusted the squelch knob and keyed the handmike. His hand was shaking badly and his voice quivering, but somehow, he managed to call in.

"Zebra One, this is Zebra Two, over." The reassuring rasp of the radio broke the silence.

"Zebra Two, this is Zebra One, read you clear, go."

"We need an immediate dust-off! We've walked into an ambush," Roger requested, as he gave his position. "Need a back up team now, do you copy, over?"

"Roger, Zebra Two. What's your status, over?"

"We have two W.I.A.'s - serious!" Roger choked, "Ten K.I.A.'s, over."

"We copy, Zebra Two...hang on. Help is on the way, out."

After calling in the dust-off, he carefully pulled the two wounded Marines out of the paddy water and laid them on the dike. There wasn't much he could do except encourage them to hold on. He took several shirts from the dead and covered the wounded to keep them warm. In fifteen minutes, a platoon of ARVN's rumbled up in a couple of armored personnel carriers and deployed into a defensive perimeter. In the distance, Roger could hear the muffled whacking sound of a Heuy coming toward them. In moments, it floated in, picked up the two wounded survivors and carried them off. Both died of their wounds before they reached Da Nang. They loaded the dead onto the two "tracks", then the grim procession made its way back to the ARVN compound.

Roger was reeling from aftershock and emotional exhaustion as he headed back. *"Terry shouldn't have been pulling point,"* he thought to himself as he sat hunched over in the track. *I should have stood my ground."* He told himself. *"They were my responsibility! If only I had warned them."*

He spent a fitful night rehearsing the lightning events which had wiped out his squad in the blink of an eye.

The following morning, he returned to Gia Le - back to the painful reminders of his friends laying where they had left them. He had come back, but they hadn't and that knowledge haunted him.

In the loneliness of their compound, his emotions caved in around him, burying him under an oppressive burden of guilt. It clawed at his mind, gnawed at his heart, set heavy in his throat, like something pushing down hard on his chest - guilt because he had made it and they hadn't, guilt that he hadn't reacted faster, guilt that he hadn't said something...guilt because he was relieved to be alive even though his buddies were dead. It was a heaviness from which he couldn't escape. It dogged his every move, filling every space like a seditious presence. He couldn't shake the anguish of knowing that he was alive and his friends weren't coming back.

A replacement squad arrived later that afternoon

from Phu Bai. Roger was placed in command and ordered to take out a third patrol the following night. He hadn't even had time to decompress from the previous night. He was so rattled with fear that he was nearly paranoid, though he tried not to show it to the new squad. That night, they headed out around 2200 hours. Roger was psyched out of his gourd with dread as he led the patrol out on point. His palms were wet and clammy as he gripped the stock of his M-14 with sweaty hands. His body was soaked with nervous sweat. He was tense and jumpy - too jumpy!

The tension in the air was so thick you could cut it with a knife. About five hundred meters from the compound, he passed a bamboo hootch when he heard a sudden banging sound coming from inside. He spooked in panic and cut loose with a fully automatic burst, splintering the brittle siding. He dropped to one knee, rammed in another magazine and emptied another twenty rounds.

The sounds of animals grunting and thrashing drifted from the hootches. Roger inserted a fresh magazine and approached the hootch warily, not knowing what to expect. His mind had cleared from the rush of adrenalin but he was still rattled. Several labored grunts punctuated the stillness. He looked inside the first hootch and found several water buffalo laying on the dirt floor.

The squad rushed up, only to discover what had happened. Roger had managed to waste seven water buffalo in his freak out.

"Wow, Far out! What a body count!" One Marine wisecracked. "Count 'em...One, four, five...no, seven V.C. water buffalo." The rest of the squad broke into laughter.

Their laughter helped ease the tension, but only temporarily. He had survived again, but something deep inside had withered and died. His friends were gone and he was left with his self-imposed burden of guilt and blame.

Chapter 13

Roger resumed his routine duties at Gia Le, breaking in the new squad. McClure came back a week later from R & R. His return was met with mutually shared shock at the loss of their friends. McClure's reaction was one of stunned silence. He said little over the next few weeks and kept to himself. Like Roger, he tried to suppress the guilt and quietly retreat into his own private hell of grief and self-incrimination. The atmosphere between them was strained by an unspoken understanding of the heaviness they shared, but couldn't bring themselves to talk about.

Roger spent those few weeks at Gia Le on automatic pilot - simply going through the motions of assistant squad leader in a detached, zombie-like state. Neither his nor McClure's hearts were in it any more since the loss of their squad. A part of each of them had died that night in the paddy. They both knew inside that it was time for a change.

About a month after the squad was wiped out, Roger was awarded his third Cross of Gallantry for his actions on the night of the ambush, but the award was hollow. It was little consolation for the loss of his men. Roger didn't even want the stupid thing. In his mind, it was like getting rewarded for letting his men down. As far as he was concerned, the best award would have been for him to be with his friends.

Roger was offered a temporary reprieve from the pressures of CAP duty when headquarters asked him if he wanted to take the position of personal driver and body guard for the Battalion CO. Reports of Roger's uncanny instincts and consummate skills on point had reached headquarters and caught the attention of Lt. Colonel "Blackjack" Weston, who was in command of the security Battalion protecting the perimeter of Phu Bai.

Weston was a living legend - a bona fide "Leatherneck" from the "Old Corps". He'd won the Navy Cross and a chest full of other medals for heroism under fire. He'd paid his dues in the South Pacific at places like Guadalcanal, Tarawa, Peleliu and Iwo, and in Korea with the "Frozen Chosin." Weston was a Marine's Marine - fearless, tough, proud. He was a crusty salt - a "kick butt and take names", "never give ground", "no guts, no glory" kind of commander who was more at home with the common grunt in the field than hanging around with some rear-area lifers. Colonel Weston was a Chesty Puller sort of Marine who was more in his element braving bullets than sitting behind a desk.

In the Colonel's mind, a young, battle seasoned Marine like Helle was a perfect choice - not so much because he needed a personal body guard (Weston could

Roger and Ron at China Beach (March '70)

Captured weapons from "Operation New York"

Roger after his first kill while at Gia Le

Marines on a typical village patrol through the paddy lands west of Phu Bai

NVA were not the only dangers along the DMZ

Marines on a search and destroy mission in heavy brush

A Marine examines a homemade booby-trap while searching a hostile ville

Roger's bunker at the Rockpile before it got hit

Roger's squad on a sweep at the beginning of "Operation Prairie"

A former NVA demonstrating a sapper crawling through the wire

Some of the NVA bodies after the sapper attack on Camp Carroll

Roger as a D.I. back at Parris Island

Sergeant Tre

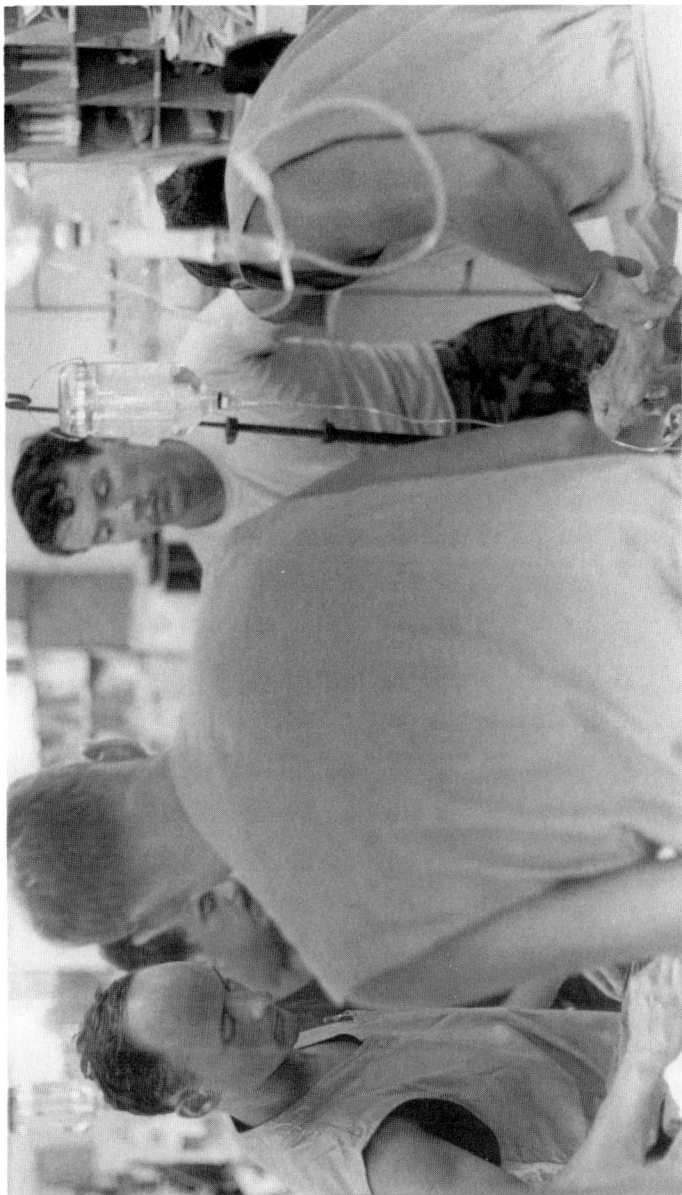

A flurry of activity to help a wounded Marine at the 95th "Evac" Hospital in Da Nang where Roger was medevaced to

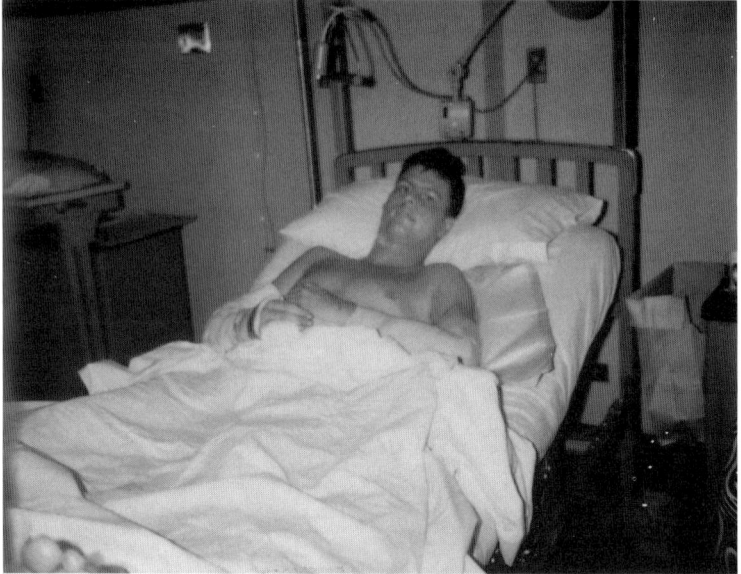

Roger at Great Lakes Naval Hospital 4½ months after getting hit

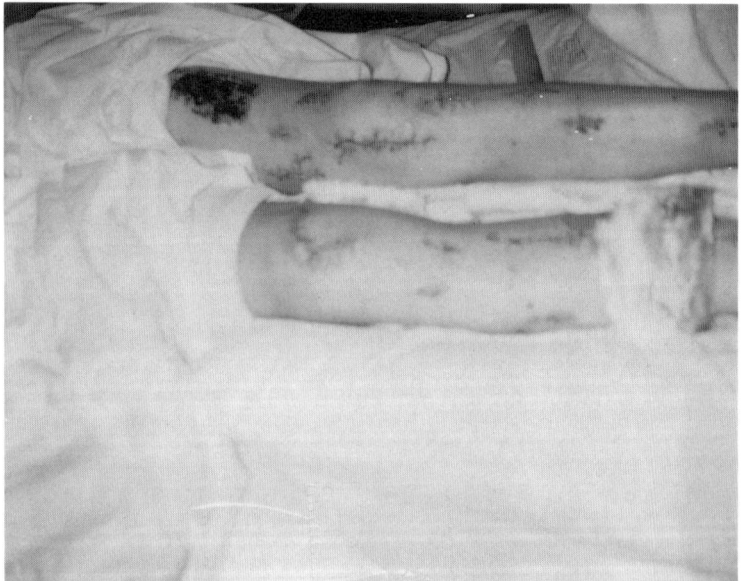

The Vietnamese people also suffered from the tyranny of war

*The trail leading to the fishing village where his squad
was ambushed - 1966 and 23 years later*

Roger, Shirley and Jamie kneeling at the spot where his squad was wiped out

Josh and Jamie with a little Vietnamese girl

Roger holding one of the Polio Orphans he supports through the humanitarian efforts of "Vets With A Mission"

take care of himself), but because it helped enhance his fighting image.

Roger was drained from his duty in Gia Le and needed a change - a time to start over and put some of the pain behind him. The guilt was still there, but there was little he could do about it except push it down deeper inside and move on. He would just have to live with it.

"Corporal, Helle," Weston, confided, "You know what they're starting to call us around here?"

"No, sir," Roger responded, even though he knew what the Colonel was driving at.

"They call us the 'Phu Bai National Guard!'....National Guard for C'rise Sakes! I've had enough of this rat hole...Just between you and me, son, if I don't get back into action soon, I'm turning this friggin' command over to you!" Weston snorted.

"You know, Helle, you remind me a lot of myself, when I was a young Marine back in the big one. You're a good Marine, son. Stick with me and some day you'll make officer grade the same way I did - not behind some typewriter, but by showing what it takes in combat!" Weston smiled approvingly.

On August 13th, Weston got his wish when Battalion was ordered north to Dong Ha in preparation for "Operation Praire." MACV was planning to launch a major operation to stem the tide of NVA men and materials flowing down the Ho Chi Minh trail through Laos. Intelligence reports indicated a major buildup just north of the DMZ. The NVA had moved the 304th and 341st divisions into the area in preparation to infiltrate south.

Little did Roger know when he volunteered to be Weston's body guard that he would be "jumping out of the frying pan into the fire." He also had no idea what to expect of duty in the DMZ. From what he had heard through scuttlebutt, it was the last stop for Marines - the far side of the moon.

The Battalion was assembled in short order and moved by chopper and armored convoys up Highway One, passed Hue to Dong Ha. Dong Ha straddled the intersection of Highway One and Route Nine, which snaked West through Cam Lo and the treacherous mountains to Khe Sanh, and then eventually through *Aideo Pass* into Laos.

The Battalion regrouped during a brief lay-over in Dong Ha, then moved up Route Nine past Cam Lo in a convoy of deuce-and-halves, APC's, and M-48 tanks. They headed up the road several klicks, then dismounted and force-marched overland through lose scrub and elephant grass with tank escorts. It was a torrid day of oven broiling heat, as the men were moved over the rolling terrain as fast as possible to avoid an ambush. They were moving into NVA territory infested with hardcore units. The pace was gruelling and the heat unbearable. Many of the men fainted from heat exhaustion and heat stroke, before the Battalion reached a place called "The Rockpile", where they formed a Battalion perimeter.

The "Rockpile" was situated on a plateau, a klick west of Route Nine. It had a sheer, 700 foot rock outcropping jutting above the Marine position on its northern fringe - hence the name "Rockpile". In short order, the green hill top was marred with ugly brown scars from trenches, fighting holes, and sandbag bunkers. It was a forsaken looking place, cluttered with coils of concertina wire, gun emplacements and reinforced bunkers, giving the impression of some World War I trench scene on the western front.

The main responsibility of the Battalion was sending out patrols to ambush and interdict the steady flow of NVA moving down the Ho Chi Minh trail. Their secondary mission was to engage the enemy and draw them out into the open so artillery and air support could annihilate them.

The North Vietnamese Army had other ideas. They didn't like their hated arch enemies trespassing in their backyard. From the first day, the Marines became the target of daily mortar and rocket attacks. Eighty-two and 120 millimeter mortars and Katusha rockets became a regular occurrence.

"Thoomp...Thoomp,Thoomp!"   "INCOMING!" Shouts echoed across the fortified outcropping. The hollow cough of mortars started the stopwatch running as men scurried across the hill like frightened rats, seeking shelter in holes and bunkers. "One, one thousand...two, One thousand...Three..." some silently counted off in the back of their minds, while others tried to second guess the pattern of impact or cringed in their bunkers as the death angel stalked the hill top.

"Weeeee!"   The falsetto shriek of incoming mortars was followed by the obnoxious **"Karumph! KaruMPH! KaRUMPHF!"** of rounds walking across the hill. Men waited and tensed at the obscene wail of shrapnel flying through the air from exploding rounds, praying that the next impact didn't land in their hip pocket. The barrages would last a few minutes, then the enemy would break down their mortars and scrambled back into their tunnels or the sanctuary of the mountain jungles.

Except for occasional direct hits and shrapnel wounds, they generally accomplished little more than rearranging the rust colored dirt.

Their arrival at the Rockpile was at the beginning of the monsoon season. The temperature began to drop, causing men to shiver in the dank chill at night. The toneless gray clouds began to return as the first rains started falling. The rains were intermittent at first, almost tentative. Then they hit with a vengeance. In short order, the barren hilltop was transformed into a muddy mess of drenched everything. Almost daily, towering, blue-black thunderheads massed over the mountains of Laos before they began their march to the sea - pregnant cloudbursts which released torrential sheets of rain. At times, the Marines were soaked in gray mists of drizzle and fog. At other times, millions of incoming droplets hit the ground like miniature bomb bursts, churning the dirt into a muddy red soup. Nothing escaped the near constant drumming - sandbags, bunkers, poncho liners, canvas, men. Relentless lines pelted cans strung along the perimeter wire and corrugated roofing until it reached a noisome crescendo which sounded like a thousand snare drums. Every depression, every rut soon pooled with water, turning the hilltop into a mini-Minnesota. Eventually, everything started to rot and mildew from the constant damp - even men's nerves. It was a miserable time for muddy grunts, huddled in the leaking holes of their rat infested bunkers.

The incoming barrages seldom let up. The only difference with the advent of the rainy season was that, instead of rearranging the dirt and coating everything with a red dust, the explosions splattered mud everywhere.

It was becoming increasingly difficult for the Marine observers to determine the NVA firing positions so the gun crews could counter-fire. The mist and gray blankets of rain concealed the muzzle flashes and distorted the direction of sound. Colonel Weston didn't like sitting on top of that hill and taking the daily harassment from the enemy. The constant bombardments were wearing on everyone. The steady pounding reached a point where many of the Marines began to feel a dull, sustained throbbing in their heads like a low grade migraine. Nerves were frayed and men were getting more uptight by the day. The NVA had moved recoilless rifles into position and small artillery which they were hiding in caves concealed along the "Razorback" - a sharp ridgeline about a thousand meters northwest of them. They would roll out the guns, fire a few salvos, then pull them back into the safety of their caves dug into the sides of the mountains. They had the Rockpile zeroed in and had little difficulty hitting their mark in spite of the weather. In fact, the incoming was becoming more and more accurate as the NVA gunners fine-tuned their targeting.

Colonel Weston decided he'd had enough. He had observed the craggy outcropping of the Rockpile through binoculars and had a hunch that the NVA might have some forward observers concealed in the rocky crevices and caves directing fire. He decided to send a recon squad up the Rockpile to root out any spotters hiding in the rocks. Roger volunteered.

"Corporal, Helle, I want you and your squad to scout out those cliffs." Colonel Weston pointed to the mist shrouded ridge a few hundred meters away. "I've got a sneaking suspicion that the enemy might have some spotters dug in up there," he said, as he scanned the face of the ridge with his binoculars. "If they're up there, I want you to get 'em out. Is that clear?"

"Yes, Sir," Roger affirmed.

A light drizzle was falling as the squad started up the slope, negotiating boulders and loose rocks and grabbing brush for hand holds to pull themselves up the steep grade. They were nearing the summit when Roger noticed the openings of two caves above them to their right. They were dark and frightening looking, giving the crude impression of darkened sockets in a skull.

"O.K., let's take it slow now," Roger cautioned the men as they huddled under a rocky overhang. "Baker and Howorth, you come with me. We're going to check out the first cave. The rest of you cover us," Roger instructed the squad.

The three men moved cautiously along the face of the ridge. About twenty feet from the mouth of the first cave, Roger halted the others and looked back down the slope to see if the rest of the squad was in position. Everything was set. He inched his way up to the edge of the cave and paused with his back against a large boulder to listen for sounds. The sinister black opening was only a few inches from his head. He decided against throwing in some grenades. Prisoners would be more valuable at that point, though getting them posed a far greater risk. Roger raised his hand above his head and pointed to the opening to indicate to the men below that they were going in. Through the mist, he could just make out the ugly brown scab of their firebase several hundred meters below. He touched his finger to his lips to stress silence. The other two nodded.

His heart was pounding so hard, he thought it was trying to break out of his chest as he slowly rounded the edge of the cave and started in. The tunnel was nearly black as they entered. The suspense was nerve wracking as they pushed themselves up against the wall and listened. Nothing could be heard. The tunnel was damp and reeked of defecation and urine. They waited a moment for their eyes to adjust to the darkness, then pushed themselves deeper inside. The men were only dim shapes in the darkness of the cave. Roger was only a few feet inside when he thought he heard movement coming from deeper within the cavern. The men were freaked and nearly hyper-ventilating from the fresh rush of adrenalin.

They were trying to control their breathing when something came flying out of the cave and clattered into some rocks in front of them.

"Grenade!" Baker yelled. "Aaaaaah...," they screamed in panic as they dove into the rock strewn floor and opened up on fully auto. "Pow pow pow pow, Pow powpow!" M-14's exploded inside the echo-chamber. Muzzle flashes illuminated the darkness like strobe lights. "Ping! Cha-Whooo....K'eeeee!" The sharp crack of bullets was deafening as rounds tore into walls, splintering stone and ricocheting erratically inside the cave.

Bloodcurdling screams mingled with the noise of firing - inhuman wails of pain which sent chills through their bodies.

"Hold your fire!" Roger shouted.

"What was that?" Howorth asked.

"We better check it out." Roger rose to his feet and crept deeper into the tunnel. The screaming had stopped. Roger flicked on a flashlight and panned the beam along the walls, probing the recesses. The small spotlight sniffed among the shadows, like the probing nose of a bloodhound trying to locate the source of the screams.

"Not again! This is too much! " Roger uttered in disbelief as the beam locked onto a family of Rock apes sprawled among the boulders at the rear of the cave where they had been cut down. They had thrown a rock at the Marines to get them to leave their cave, but they were trying to evict the wrong people.

"Man, you're in trouble now!" Baker mocked.

"We can't take him anywhere," Howorth nudged Baker with an impish grin on his face.

"I think we're gonna have to report you to the Humane Department for cruelty to animals, Corporal. Let's see, that makes seven water buffalo and seven apes as far as I can figure it. Looks like seven's your lucky number!" Baker teased as the three of them busted up.

"They what?" Colonel Weston couldn't believe his ears.

"That's right, Sir, the radio report said they wiped out a squad of Rock apes but there were no signs of NVA. They're coming down now, Sir." A messenger from the commo bunker relayed the report to the Colonel.

"Well, at least they didn't come back empty handed," Weston chuckled to himself.

"Should I call in a body count, Colonel?" a young aid suggested.

"No, I think the Battalion's not that hard up, Captain. We'll be getting enough of the real thing, soon enough," Weston responded.

The daily barrages kept up with annoying regularity, exacting a steady toll from direct hits or serrated bits of shrapnel whizzing across the hill top. It was a nerve shattering time for the entire Battalion. Men dug deeper and stacked sandbags higher to shield themselves from the fire. The barrages of incoming would occur two or three times a day.

Roger emerged from the musky smelling interior of his bunker and headed across the perimeter to see some guys he had befriended in one of the 4.2 mortar pits. The mortar was ringed by rows of green sandbags stacked five to six layers high around stacks of wooden ammo crates.

"Hey, Bobby, Little Guy, Jimmie D," Roger shouted as he approached the mortar pit. "What's up?" Roger greeted the guys.

The three Marines were sitting on the rim of their sandbag emplacement, smoking cigarettes and shooting the breeze. They were wearing their field jackets and steel pots with sun bleached liners scrawled with graffiti.

"Same O, same O," Bobby responded as he squinted his eyes behind some thick black framed glasses. "The gooks fire some in; we fire some out." He sounded bored.

"We heard you wasted some gook apes up on the Rockpile yesterday, Roger. Word has it that ol' "Blackjack" himself done put you in for the Silver Star. On behalf of our mortar team, let me be the first to congratulate you," Jimmie D teased.

"Yeah, all we want to know is if those monkeys put up a tough fight?" he added with a mock seriousness in his voice.

"You guys cut it out. I'm never gonna live that one down," Roger replied.

"Thoomp, Thoomp Thoomp!" the hiccuping sound of mortar rounds exiting their tubes sent the crew racing to return fire.

"Catch you dudes later, I'm outta here," Roger said as he scurried off across the compound for the safety of his bunker. He was running full out when the first round impacted off to his left. **"Karumph!"** A blizzard of flying shrapnel whined around him. **"KaRUMPH!"** the second round hit forty yards behind him. *"They're coming my way,"* Roger guessed as he closed on his bunker. It was a race to beat the next impact. He could hear the shrill howl of a large 120 millimeter mortar screaming in behind him as he slopped across the mud.

"KARUMPH!....BAM!...KABAM..BLOOM!" The 4.2 mortar pit took a direct hit from the 120, setting off a chain reaction from the stockpile of ammo crates. The shock wave slammed him in the back like a truck hitting him from behind. He splatted into the slippery mud and slid a few feet then pushed himself up to look back. An enormous orange fireball spitting black and white streamers was rising a hundred feet into the air over the mortar pit. "KaBlam!" His body shuddered from another concussion as he shielded his eyes and cocked his body slightly to buffet himself against the heat waves rippling across the hill top.

He waited until the explosions stopped, then he made his way back to the pit. What used to be the pit was a blackened crater with the charred remains of the mortar crew scattered indiscriminately in a thirty meter radius. Roger passed a boot with the top of an ankle still protruding, a dented helmet with the words, "Mean Marine Killing Machine" scrawled on its side, and fragments of clothing and globs of crimson gore. There wasn't enough left of the men even to tell who they were.

Soon after, Roger launched a major rebuilding project on his own bunker to reinforce it. He worked for days with an obsession to dig it deeper and reinforce it stronger. There were no other bunkers like it on the hill.

"Hey, Case, rumor has it that Helle is startin' to turn into a mole," the stubby Marine chuckled. "Where ya goin' with that hole, Helle? Are you planning to dig to China?" Wiggins asked, as Roger heaved a shovel full of wet dirt out of his entrance.

"He can't be going to China, Wiggins; he's diggin' in the wrong direction. Looks like he's headin' for the East Coast to me," Case responded.

"You know that won't take a direct hit, don't ya?" Wiggins chided.

"Maybe not, lame brain," Roger replied, "but it will sure as hell take more than your little rat hole. It'll handle everything 'cept maybe a 120 with as many sandbags and beams as I've got on it."

"Say, Helle, can we move in with you? Looks like you got enough room." Case teased.

"Hey, you clowns ever hear the story of, 'The Three Little Pigs'?" Roger asked sarcastically. "Why don't you quit wastin' my time. This little piggy's got work to do, so you'll have to excuse me," Roger grunted as he threw out another shovel full of dirt.

"C'mon, I can tell when we're not welcome," Wiggins kidded.

When Roger finished his bunker, it was the talk of the firebase. The only problem with it was the fact that Roger could seldom squeeze into it. Whenever there was incoming, everyone else would beat him to it and crowd inside. About two weeks after its completion the familiar scream of "Incoming!" was sounded and men started piling into Roger's bunker.

"KawRunch...KawRunch!..KawRunch!" Rounds

exploded across the hill top.

"C'mon, you guys, I feel like I'm in a sardine can," Roger grumbled.

"Man, someone needs to clean their socks. This place stinks, Helle. Ain't you never heard of room freshener?" One of the men joked.

"KawRunch!" Another round hit nearby.

"How can you tell, Phelps?" Roger teased. "We're all startin' to smell pretty ripe if you ask me," he added.

"Wheeeeee!" The men flinched at the shrill wail of an incoming round.

"Whoomp!" The whole bunker shuddered from the impact.

"Run!" Someone yelled, as the Marines tore over each other to flee the bunker.

Only Roger remained. He emerged from the hole to check it out, only to find the tail fins of a huge 120 millimeter rocket sticking out of the top of the Bunker. It had buried itself several rows deep in the sandbags.

"Man, that thing could ruin your day, Helle," one of the Marines shouted at Roger.

"Whatdaya mean, your day? That thing could ruin your whole life," another Marine noted, as Roger walked towards the knot of men standing a safe distance away.

"You got a point there," Roger grinned and looked back.

A demolitions expert defused the dud and Roger moved back into his bomb shelter with his horde of unwelcome house guests never far away.

Chapter 14

After a week of incessant pounding, Roger felt like his brains were gradually turning to mush. He started volunteering for recon patrols to get away from the daily bashing. There really wasn't much for him to do as "Blackjack's" bodyguard anyway. In fact, the whole idea was a little absurd, when you considered the concept of protecting the Colonel from random mortar rounds and indiscriminate shrapnel.

The recon teams patrolled the mountainous jungles west of the Rockpile in the pocket bordering Laos and the DMZ. The Air Force had been dropping electronic sensing devices into the jungle to pick up seismic activity from trucks and men moving south. It was part of McNamara's high tech war, but it seldom worked. The real job was inevitably accomplished by Special Forces SOG teams, LRRP's and Marine recon squads. The small, five man teams were inserted along suspected NVA avenues of approach to track enemy troop movements snaking south through their network of jungle covered trails and concealed roads. They could call upon artillery from the Cam Lo artillery plateau, helicopter gunships, and Marine air support from Da Nang or Chu Lai.

Roger had pulled half a dozen of these specialized missions with a close knit team he had assembled. The five of them had mastered the unique rigors of recon, and had learned to function as a synchronized unit which excelled in stealth and mobility.

The five men in Roger's team finished painting their faces with the green and black grease sticks before heading over to the chopper pad for lift off. They were dressed in camouflaged utilities and wearing floppy bush hats. Roger had traded in his M-14 for one of the light weight M-16's which was better suited for close combat in the tight confines of the jungle terrain in which they were operating. Each of them was carrying a rucksack, three grenades plus a smoke canister, an extra sling of magazines and special dehydrated LRRP rations.

A barrel chested kid, called "Bear", was carrying the radio with an extra battery. He was short and stocky, but strong as an ox. A wiry little Puerto Rican from New York, named Caesar, was carrying the M-79 with an extra bandolier of high explosive and canister rounds. Roger, Red, and a muscular black marine from Georgia, whom they called "Spanky", were carrying M-16's and claymores.

They gave themselves a few finishing touches with the grease sticks and checked over their weapons.

"How do I look, Red?" Bear asked.

"You sure look pretty," the ruddy, red haired

adolescent teased his buddy.

"Oh..," Bear puckered his lips. " I'm sooo glad. I picked the color just for you, you brute."

"Knock it off, girls. We've got business to take care of. Everyone squared away?" Roger checked the faces of the men, who nodded their response. "Let's do it, then!" Roger ordered, as the men exited the bunker and headed over to the waiting chopper.

The team had been waiting two days for the fog and rain to lift, so they could get enough visibility to be inserted by chopper. It would be a seven day recon patrol. The men were tired of waiting and ready to go, as they reached the pad.

The pilot and co-pilot were sitting at their controls with their visors shielding their faces. Roger gave the pilot a thumbs up as the men crouched under the spinning blades and loaded into the waiting slick. The rotor screwed faster and faster, until the chopper lifted off a few feet, dipped its nose forward, and sailed over the scattered bunkers of the firebase. In seconds, they were skimming at ninety knots, above the rain forest at tree top level. Their Heuy rushed over undulating hills and valleys as they hurried northwest in the late afternoon. The valleys and draws were already pooling with greys, as the countryside darkened under the mantle of clouds.

The door-gunner pulled back the bolt on his M-60 and let it slide home, chambering a round as the chopper went into a tight bank and quickly hovered into a small clearing on a small mountain top about seven klicks from the Rockpile. The chopper was hovering a few feet off the ground when the signal to jump was given. The team stepped onto the skids, then jumped into the knee deep grass and quickly scurried off to the edge of the clearing. The pilot took the Heuy straight up and spun away to the east.

The whole insertion took less than a minute, then the silence returned. They huddled in the jungle fringe for a few minutes to see if everything was clear. Roger gestured with hand signals for the team to move out. They were somewhere west of the Nui Cay Tre ridgeline. He wanted to put distance between themselves and any NVA in the area who may have heard their chopper approaching.

They moved with a determined clip down the shadowy slope covered by double tier canopy. At the base of the hill they reached a narrow V shaped valley. At the bottom was a mountain stream flowing east. They quickly filled their canteens and splashed some of the cool water in their faces, then forded across and up another slope, where they set up a night defensive position. They had seen no signs of the enemy.

Early the next morning, they chowed down on some cold LRRP rations, buried their scraps, and started down the opposite side of the slope. Roger estimated they were about a klick from their insertion point. Everything was grey and dripping under the thick canopy. A light rain had returned in the predawn hours. It was leaking down through the foliage. They reached the bottom of the hill and skirted along the edge of long, horseshoe shaped valley covered by triple tier canopy. Roger was pulling point about twenty meters in front of the men. "Man, I don't know about you, Red," Caesar complained; "but these humps up and down these hills are killers."

"Hey, I hear ya," Red replied in hushed tones. "I feel like I have to keep making my body do things it don't wanna do," he added.

"I got the same problem. My ego just keeps writin' checks that my body refuses to pay," Bear grunted.

At the base of the hill, they entered the thickest jungle Roger had seen. The foliage was so densely packed, at first, it was almost claustrophobic. They penetrated the tangle only a few meters when they ran into a small trail which showed recent signs of use. He knelt to check out some prints on the trail. He wasn't an Indian scout, but he could tell they were from bata boots (tennis shoe like high-tops the NVA wore). The prints looked like they were at least a day old. The trail didn't appear to be a major one, so he decided to follow it instead of breaking brush to save time. Roger wanted to scout out the valley while they had daylight. The sides of the trail looked like walls of green as they made their way down the narrow corridor.

After a half an hour, they emerged from the clotted tangle into a semi-open area covered with thirty foot high bamboo. They quickly passed through it and were swallowed up by a towering forest of gigantic hardwoods. Everything was sweating from the humidity and rain filtering through the canopy. The ground was wet and spongy from the perpetual dripping, with shallow pools of brackish brown water standing in the lower depressions. Some of the enormous teak and ironwood trees were twelve feet in diameter. They stood solemn and majestic, overshadowing the Marines as they entered deeper into the prehistoric world. It looked like something out of an old King Kong movie to Roger. He almost expected some giant Brontosaurus to come crashing out of the jungle at any moment.

The fallen trunks of ancient trees littered the ground. They were covered with lime green moss and lichen. Gnarled vines and creepers twisted around the trunks of trees, like they were trying to strangle their competitors in a silent death grip. Others dangled like limp tentacles from limbs, or coursed off through the tangled trellises overhead. The jungle floor around them was covered with lush, broad leaves, the size of elephant ears, multi-fingered fronds, ferns of every size and description, and wild orchids.

It was dark and dense as they moved through the murky underworld of eternal shadows. What little light managed to penetrate the canopy diffused through the shaded greens, creating an eerie world of twilight greens. The fertile smell of rich humus and rotting vegetation permeated the moist underworld of living matter. The men moved silently through the towering rain forest, awed by the sheer grandeur of the scenery which enveloped them. It was like a picture out of a National Geographic magazine - majestic, almost enchanting. It didn't look inhospitable, but each of them knew that it was a place of deceptive beauty and unyielding danger.

They continued down the trail until the vigorous jungle growth began to thin. They had about thirty yards of visibility through the scattered shrubbery and trees. The team proceeded several hundred more yards before Roger moved the team off the trail. They took shelter in a cluster of huge moss encrusted boulders where they chowed down and took a short break. It was around noon. He conferred with his men. They decided to cut across the valley a little to their West, where the map gradients indicated the terrain started to narrow into a gorge then climb up a ridge south of them.   They planned to climb the ridge and check out a parallel valley on the other side. Roger had a hunch the NVA might be using it to funnel supplies West toward the Rockpile.

They headed west down the slender trail about a klick, until it started to climb up through clumps of brush and rocky outcroppings. They could hear the faint gurgling sound of water sluicing through the undergrowth as they followed the trail up. Roger figured they had climbed about forty yards above the valley floor when he detected the sounds of splashing waters. He signaled for the team to hold it up. He inched forward until he reached a rocky ledge overlooking a small waterfall. It was gurgling and bubbling from the water plunging into a deep green pool. The small grotto was dotted with delicate ferns and fairly-like plants clinging to the steep stone walls rising around the pool. It was a sheer drop of about fifty feet to the water without any way down. The opposite wall rose in a steep ascent through a snarl of tangled brush and sharp rocks. It looked impassible.

"We're gonna have to backtrack and try crossing the valley somewhere else instead of trying an end-run through this stuff. This will slow us down too much." Roger motioned toward the steep face on the other side of the stream. "We gotta keep alert. I don't know if any trackers have picked up our trail." Roger didn't like the idea of doubling back. He had already taken enough risk using the trail in the first place. He knew it was risky, but they were losing precious time and he needed to reach the top of the ridge on the south side of the valley before nightfall.

Roger led the team back along the trail. His movements were delicate, deliberate, as he carefully scanned every bend, every clump of foliage for warnings signs of the enemies presence. All the ambient skills of walking point were brought to bear. He didn't like covering the same ground twice. He felt exposed, as though invisible eyes were watching his every step. They made their way back until they reached the semi-open area they had passed through earlier. He pulled the team off the trail and checked out the map. He calculated the distance across the valley at about 2,000 meters until it started sloping up to a humpback ridge about two hundred meters high. He wanted to set up their night position on the summit where there would be less traffic if NVA were in the area - and he knew they were in the area.

Roger moved the team forward with the same catlike grace he had perfected on countless patrols as he glided past clumps of underbrush. He was several hundred meters into the valley when he pushed back some large leafy plants and noticed white lumps dropping onto his arms. He paused to check it out and winced at the sight of tiny white leeches in a caterpillar crawl up his sleeve. "Ugh!" he shook the little suckers off his arm and brushed off his shoulders like he was trying to pat off some dandruff. The ground was littered with thousands of inchworm like leeches. Their heads were raised in unison like they were homing in on the sound of an approaching meal. He shuddered at the thought of being fed on by the little vampires and hurriedly moved on.

About a thousand yards through the forest, Roger raised his arm to halt the team. He caught a whiff of something in the damp air. He sniffed the air like a wolf tracking his prey. He knew he had smelled something. He could just detect the faint smell of smoke coming from cooking fires somewhere in the valley. He couldn't tell for sure, but he guessed it was somewhere off to his left.

He moved more cautiously than ever. The enemy

was near. He could feel it. The jungle floor started to slope slightly downwards until it reached a clear stream flowing through the valley. It was probably coming from the waterfall, he concluded, though it didn't show on the map. It was crystal clear. The bottom was covered with sand and polished looking pebbles. It looked inviting to the men who hadn't bathed in centuries, but they couldn't afford the luxury of stopping.

They hurriedly crossed and continued south on a slight zigzag course, until Roger reached a wall of matted vegetation.   The first sounds were almost inaudible at first, then his ear pricked at the sound of Vietnamese. He motioned the men down and crouched under the overhang of some large broad leaves. He crawled a few feet into the wet wall of foliage and slowly parted the veil to see what was on the other side. There was a well used road only a few inches in front of his face. Three Vietnamese in dull green uniforms and canvas web-gear were walking casually down the trail with their AK-47's slung over their shoulders with the muzzles pointing down. They were chatting nonchalantly like they were taking a stroll. Roger watched them until they disappeared around a bend about a hundred feet down the road.

The muddy road was rutted by parallel tracks from vehicles and was covered by a natural trellis of vines and branches. The muddy ruts were filled with shallow pools of water. He inched his way back and signaled the rest of the team to link up. He whispered into each of their ears that they had found a "Red Ball Express" and indicated with hand language that they were going to cross. He knew they had stumbled onto something big.

Roger parted the curtain, looked both ways to see

if anyone was coming. One by one, they eased out of the wall of vegetation, darted across the road, and quickly submerged into the foliage on the other side. Roger huddled with his team about twenty feet into the vegetation with their backs against a huge log. He told them they were going to hole up a while and observe the road to see if they could get a better fix on things before calling in a sitrep.

He pulled out his terrain map and gave it a once over. It didn't appear that the road could have come through the rocky gorge they'd run into earlier. *"Man, this map's screwed up,"* he thought to himself. It wouldn't be the first time in 'Nam. It wasn't as if Rand McNally survey teams had been in those parts recently. He noticed a slight depression on the rounded ridge which dog-legged southeast from the gorge. *"The road probably passes over that depression heading west into Laos,"* he calculated.

The team hunkered down a few inches from the road, blending into the smothered vegetation with their camouflaged faces and cammies. About half an hour passed when Roger heard noises coming down the trail. *"Oh, great!"* He gritted his teeth at the sight of his team's muddy boot prints crossing the trail in front of their position. The sounds were getting closer. There wasn't anything he could do. *"I hope they don't see 'em,"* he thought. He looked down the trail and back at the tell-tale imprints of their jungle boots. Six Vietnamese were pushing bicycles along the edge of the trail. The bicycles were loaded with burlap sacks of rice. "Sssh." He cautioned the others. His heart was racing as they neared. *"God, don't let 'em see the prints,"* he tensed as they pushed the bicycles past and soon disappeared around the bend in the road. *"That was close,"* he sighed to himself.

A few minutes later, they heard the whine of a truck transmission as it negotiated the slippery ruts. An olive drab Soviet truck loaded with crates covered with camouflaged netting rumbled past, obliterating the prints in a splattering of mud.

"We've got something big here," Roger whispered. "Let's split. I'm gonna call in an air strike on the valley," he informed them. "We need to watch ourselves getting outta here. The place is crawlin' with bad guys," he cautioned.

He didn't know it then, but elements of the 324B Main Force NVA Division were grouping in the area. Senior General Vo Nguyen Giap, Commander in Chief of North Vietnamese forces and General Nguyen Chi Thanh, Field Commander of communist forces in South Vietnam had recently moved the 324B and 341st Main Force Divisions across the DMZ into Quang Tri province, in an effort to draw American units into uninhabitable jungle areas in an attempt to isolate and wipe them out. Roger knew that the valley had all the essential ingredients for a staging area - fresh water, a major trail, and excellent canopy cover.

The men backed away from the road and slipped through the jungle heading south. The scent of cooking fires still filled the air as they crossed the valley floor. Several times, Roger halted the team when he thought he heard something, but the jungle was still and dripping. They saw no more signs of the enemy. By 1700 hours, they had climbed up the hill and settled into a defensive position overlooking the valley.

Roger reached the crest of the hill and leaned his weary body up against a thick tree to relax the tension on his straps. They had been digging into his shoulders all day. He slid down the cool trunk with a sigh of relief. He and Bear called in a situation report and gave Battalion the coordinates of heavy enemy activity in the valley below.

From the concealment of the hilltop, they had a clear view of the crumpled mat of broccoli topped forest covering the valley. It stretched for two klicks northward before climbing up the ridge they'd come down earlier that morning. The skyscape was dark and threatening. It covered the valley like a slate grey blanket. A translucent shaft of light angled through the cloud cover several klicks away, highlighting a spot on the dark green matt with its flood light.

After scarfing down some cold chow, the men wrapped themselves in their ponchos for warmth and covered their faces with mosquito netting to protect themselves from the annoying swarms of insects which began to assemble. The darkness soon enveloped them, choking out the last vestiges of light. The five men took shifts with four dozing in a half-sleep and the fifth on watch. The night was quiet.

The following morning, they reconnoitered the next valley, but it showed no evidence of the enemy. That night, they pulled themselves up another ridge. It was a grassy, bald knoll ringed by trees. It would be suitable for an extraction if they needed one. It hadn't rained all day. They were into their third day of recon. They again divided up the watches and prepared to wait out the night.

"What was that?" Caesar whispered his alarm.

"Boom...Boom...Boom." The dull rumble of kettle-drums pounded in the distance. It was a rolling thunder moving through the blackness north of them.

"Sounds like an Arc Light," Roger noted. "I've

heard 'em before."

Thirty-two thousand feet up, three B-52's were releasing their payloads in a business like manner. The whole undertaking was mechanical, sterile, mathematic - done with radar and electronics. The crews never saw what they were killing. Their five hundred pound bombs carpeted the valley with mile long swaths of destruction, uprooting trees, gouging huge craters out of the jungle floor, and turning the prehistoric world into a pockmarked moonscape.

In the blackness, they could see the quivering orange glow from the impacts, four klicks north of them. Explosions were ripping through the unsuspecting ranks of NVA who had been peacefully sleeping in their hammocks moments before, or talking by their campfires, when a sudden rain of death fell from the sky without warning. The sledge-hammer blows drowned out the screams of terror. Men ran in a blind panic, trying to escape the drunken footsteps of an invisible monster staggering through the forest. Concussions were rupturing brains and shredding men as serrated shards of red hot steel sliced through trees and leaves and flesh.

The drum roll lasted a few moments, then the pounding abruptly stopped. The B-52's silently vectored North and headed back to Okinawa. The crews would be having steak and eggs before the dawn arrived.

"Looks like their gettin' their butts kicked!" Bear noted.

"Dong the Cong! That's what I always say," Red smiled a self-satisfied smirk.

"Get some," Caesar whispered.

Roger said nothing. He simply pulled his poncho tighter around him.

The men quieted down and drifted off to sleep.

The rumbling had long receded into the distance when Roger woke with a start. Little Caesar was taking the last watch just before dawn. Already, the expanse was beginning to lighten in the east.

"Aaayyh...Aayyh, help me! Get him off me!" The piercing screams of Caesar sent shock waves rippling through their systems. Roger instinctively rolled to his side and grabbed his M-16. Caesar was kicking and thrashing through the trampled grass. He was screaming bloody murder.

"Help me, you guys!" His panicked wail scared everyone.

Roger blinked his eyes in shock. He couldn't believe what he was seeing in the early morning light. At first, he thought he was having a nightmare, but it was really happening. He was temporarily stunned and unable to move - like he was riveted in place. *"What do I do?"* He thought. *"Gotta do something!"* He reasoned. It would have been almost comical, if it hadn't been so deadly. None of them had been trained for this.

"Help me!" Caesar face was a portrait of wide eyed terror. "He's gonna eat me!" He cried.

Caesar had been on the last watch with his back to Roger. He had only been about ten feet away when an enormous four hundred and fifty pound tiger had crept up and grabbed him. The tiger had been silently stalking through the grass with a subtlety and stealth none of the men knew anything about. Caesar hadn't even heard him, when it suddenly latched onto his left shoulder with his powerful jaws and clamped down. The only thing keeping the fangs from puncturing his shoulder was the protective plates in his flak jacket.

The tiger was about twenty feet away, shaking Caesar violently back and forth like he was trying to rip his arm off. Roger finally reacted. Roger and Red were on their feet, circling the tiger, not sure what they should do. The tiger was leering back at them with defiant green eyes.

"Get Outta here...Go!" Red shooed the animal with his rifle, trying to get him to release his grip.

"C'mon!" Caesar begged. "Get him off of me," he yelled. "Shoot him, shoot him!" Caesar howled.

Roger took careful aim and pumped five rounds into the side of the beast. The tiger let go and settled to his haunches, before rolling over onto the grass.

Caesar scrambled away on his hands and knees like a frightened crab.

"We've gotta move!" Roger warned. "Every gook in the area knows we're here now." The shrill screams and distinctive pops of the M-16's had alerted every NVA for miles around.

"Bear, gimme the radio!" Roger demanded.

Bear handed the handset to Roger and adjusted the squelch.

"Tiger Papa Six, this is Tiger Papa One, over." The usual rush of static filled the receiver. Roger considered how ironic their call signs were under the circumstances.

"Tiger Papa One, this is Tiger Papa Six...We read you, over."

"Tiger Papa Six, we need an immediate extraction, do you copy, Over?"

"We read you clear, Tiger Papa One. What's your situation, over?"

Roger paused a moment before responding. He figured the straight forward approach would be the best. "We shot a large tiger and woke up the whole countryside. This place will be crawlin' with bad guys."

"Say again, Papa One."   The radio operator wanted to make sure what he had just heard.

"We killed a tiger and need an extraction."

Back in the Battalion commo bunker, the early morning crew couldn't believe their ears.

"They gotta be stoned or juiced," a young lieutenant listening to the conversation injected.   "I better get the CO," he said as he left the bunker.

"What's your response, Tiger Papa Six?" Roger was starting to get irritated.   "We don't have all day, Tiger Papa Six... We're in some deep Sh--!"

"This better be damn good, Helle!"   Colonel Weston broke in.   "You tryin' to get off your patrol early, Corporal?"   Weston snapped.   "You been drinkin'?"   He didn't like having some shavetail wake him up that early or one of his patrols coming in before they were suppose to.

"No, Tiger Papa Six...Our position is compromised.   Imperative.   We need an immediate extraction, over."

"Corporal, you better have a tiger on board that chopper when you get back or I'll have your butt for breakfast!   Do we understand each other?"   Weston barked.

"That's an affirmative, Tiger Papa Six, out."
NVA were already coming up the slope a hundred meters below them when the Heuy angled in.   The door-gunner swiveled his 60 and nervously panned it along the crest of the hill.   "Let's get the hell outta here!"   He yelled under the clamor of the whacking blades.

Roger and the others dragged the limp carcass to the side of the waiting chopper and heaved it into the bay.   The unequivocal crack of AK's sounded from the slope as the pilot lifted off and skimmed over the tops of the trees on the opposite side of the knoll, whipping the branches back and forth in its down-draft. The door-gunner opened up and started chattering away at the hilltop just as a squad of NVA reached the summit and opened up on the departing chopper.

The men flinched at the sight of green fireballs floating past the chopper in slow-motion from tracer rounds. They pulled themselves in tighter as rounds pinged into the thin skinned hull. The pilot fought for altitude and slowly out-distanced the rifle shots as they climbed away to safety.

The men huddled in the open chopper with the huge tiger sprawled at their feet. They didn't say anything - just stared at each other with knowing looks and a glint of humor in their eyes.

"Well, he told us not to come back without one," Roger chuckled to himself.

Minutes later, they were down on the chopper pad, unloading their kill to the amazement of everyone assembled. News of the incoming chopper had raced through the firebase.

"Well, I'll be a Son of...." Weston stood with both hands on his hips shaking his head.

"Here's the tiger, like you ordered, Sir." Roger reported to the Colonel.

"Corporal, this takes the cake. First its apes, now a tiger. What's it gonna be next?" He threw back his head and roared with laughter.

"Semper Fi, Sir," Roger turned and winked at his men.

One of his aides was snapping Polaroids like a Japanese tourist - no doubt to send home with exaggerated war stories of how he killed the beast with his bare hands.

Roger escorted Caesar to the Battalion aid station at Dong Ha later that morning. He never did find out who confiscated, gutted, and skinned his prize trophy. The tiger hide probably ended up in some officer's quarters or den back in the States - the centerpiece of many antidotes and war stories for years to come.

Chapter 15

Roger continued to pull recon patrols in the mountainous jungles and secluded valleys northwest of the Rockpile, shadowing the enemy and calling in air strikes. For days, they slithered through tangled greens, laid buried in rotting humus or hidden in jungle-clogged ravines watching with unseen eyes as thousands of camouflaged NVA soldiers and porters snaked along trails.   He managed to make it back each time, swearing he would never go out on recon again. But after a few days on the Rock, he was craving a fresh fix of adrenalin.

Gradually, a battle scenario began to take shape. Observations from reconnaissance patrols indicated that the 324B and 341st Divisions were massing to encircle the Rockpile and wipe it out. The NVA had suffered steady losses over the weeks from the repeated artillery and air strikes, but the flood of men and material kept flowing south. The communists needed a major victory to boost sagging moral. The place they chose to do this was the Rockpile.

When Roger wasn't pulling recon patrols, his duty as Colonel Weston's body guard kept him around the command bunker a lot. During that time, he got to know a number of the field officers when they came in for their briefings. One of them was a Second Lieutenant he'd met in Phu Bai before the Battalion shipped north. Lieutenant Knox was the epitome of a Marine. He was the kind you would expect to see on a recruitment poster - handsome, sharp, standing ramrod straight in his dress blues and white gloves with his officer's sword smartly drawn at his side. Roger had seen a lot of young lieutenants come and go during his tour. Most of them were cocky, inflated with their own self-importance, and just a little too gung-ho for their own good. Some of them were more concerned with winning medals than caring for the welfare of their men. Knox was different. He was the kind of officer who didn't have to demand respect - Knox won it easily because he genuinely respected every man in his platoon. He had a quiet strength and an unassuming courage which made him a natural leader.

Knox was unlike any officer Roger had met. He was tough but never coarse, confident but never arrogant.   He was dedicated and fair. Roger would often find him in the solitude of his bunker quietly reading his Bible or praying. He had never met anyone in his life who was truly religious. He had seen a lot of guys carrying little Marine Corps New Testaments or wearing crosses and Saint Christopher medals, but these were viewed more as good luck symbols or talismans than anything else. Most of the Chaplains who would come out to the Rockpile to perform Mass or give short pep talks to the men didn't impress Roger much with their lofty sermons and tired moralizing.   But Lieutenant Knox was different. He was down to earth and relatable.   He wasn't a religious kook and he certainly wasn't a fanatic. He never tried pushing his religion down anyone's throat, or thumping on anybody about God, but he still affected his men with his resolve and strength of convictions.   To Roger, Knox's Bible reading and praying was not a token of weakness, but of some inner source of strength which seemed to sustain the man.   Roger knew that Knox had found "the faith", and he also knew that he was no wimp.

He really liked Knox, even if he couldn't quite figure him out. That bothered Roger in a curious sort of way. Knox had an understanding which seemed to transcend the complexities of 'Nam. He also had a curious sense of contentment even with the pressures leadership.   Roger admired him for that.   They gradually became close friends at the Rockpile and trusted confidants.

"How'ya doin', Sir? Gunny said you're lookin' for me." Roger leaned into the doorway of the half buried hootch and greeted the Lieutenant. The bunker smelled of mildew and rot.

Lieutenant Bob Knox was sitting on an empty ammo crate, reading a small, thumb-worn Bible. "Doin' great, Rog," Knox flashed his buddy a wide smile. "How's life treatin' you?"

"Life sucks, Sir, but I'm hangin' in there just the same," Roger replied. "You sure read that thing a lot. Must be somethin' interesting in it?" Roger half inquired.

"You oughta try it sometime. It won't kill you, ya know," Knox gave a knowing grin.

"You may have heard the scuttlebutt by now, Rog. The Battalion is sending a reinforced company on sweep to flush the enemy out of their hiding places. I'm short a squad leader and I wanted to know if you'd like to volunteer?"   Lieutenant Knox closed his Bible and looked up at Roger.   "I've already cleared it with Captain Damion and he's got the O.K. from the Colonel. It's up to you."

"Sure, Lieutenant. I've heard that the Corps is always lookin' for a few good men." Roger grinned. He was only too eager to jump at the chance to get off the hill.

"That's good. You'll be taking over 3rd Squad. Sergeant Reid is out with a bad case of malaria. The third herd are a great bunch of guys and Lewis is the best gunner in the company." Knox noted.

"Thank you, sir," Roger replied. "Say, Lieutenant, does that little book really help?" Roger asked as he started to leave.

"They don't call it 'The Good Book' for nothin', Corporal," Lieutenant Knox smiled.

"I'll keep that in mind, sir. I better shove off. The Colonel is probably wondering where I am." Roger ducked back out of the entrance and left.

The following morning, a column comprised of what was left of "D" and "B" companies left the battalion perimeter and advanced north across the *Cua Viet* River.

The following morning, they were deployed in a sweeping action through a bowl shaped valley ringed by hills. They were closing on the southern approach to the notorious Nui Cay Tre ridge. Roger was half way back in the column in 3rd platoon as it pushed across the valley floor. The forest floor was spotted with low vegetation. The extended branches of sayo and teak trees formed an interlocking series of umbrellas, partially shading the jungle floor. The rains had subsided for the first time in weeks, leaving a crystal blue sky poking through the openings in the trees. Glittering shafts of yellow sunlight beamed through numerous holes in the canopy. A delicate ground mist eddied around lush clumps of ferns and tropical plants, like a slow moving stream around rocks. The mist glowed a translucent white where the shafts of sunlight touched the floor. The morning warmth was almost refreshing after the dank chill of the monsoons.

The Marines were spread out with good visibility through the trees, but wary and watchful. They knew the enemy was close. Roger was on the left flank when word was passed back that First Platoon had stumbled onto a bundle of commo wire a hundred meters in front of them.

Captain Damion's radioman handed him the handmike as soon as the radio came to life. The Captain was tethered to his RTO by a coiled black cord attached to the transmitter strapped to the radioman's back. The two of them inseparable - like Siamese twins.

"Hold it up!" Captain Damion ordered as he held the handset to his ear. Lieutenant Morse relayed that they were following a multi-colored bundle of wire. After talking with Morse, Captain Damion radioed the other platoon leaders.

Roger could hear the distinctive rasp of Lieutenant Knox's radio a few feet away. Usually the jungle swallowed up the sounds, but the forest was open and still.

"I want your flank to slow it up a little, Lieutenant. Be on your toes. First Platoon found some commo wire." Captain Damion instructed.

Roger knew that there had to be a large force of NVA near, because only battalion size units or larger laid commo wire.

The column moved hesitantly through the forest. Occasionally, it lurched forward, compressing itself, and releasing itself again like a caterpillar. Roger could see the irregular line of advancing Marines scattered through the trees as they slowed their advance. The jungle was calm and expectant. The only sounds were the occasional screech of a parrot or curious monkeys scampering through the branches overhead.

Roger wiped some sweat off his forehead with his sleeve and quickly scanned the canopy. He didn't like the possibility of snipers hiding in the trees. Two hundred meters in front of him, the jungle floor began a gentle rise to a humpback Ridgeline north of them. Unknown to the Marines, a regiment of NVA was waiting behind its gun embrasures in reinforced log bunkers for the Marines coming their way.

Roger turned to his left to check out the lay of the forest when all hell broke lose. The distinctive crackling of AK's and 12.7 mm machine-guns opened up like a string of firecrackers. All around him, Marines were hitting the deck.

"We're under heavy attack, they're everywhere!" A frantic call came from the First Platoon leader. He was yelling in Captain Damion's receiver with a panicked strain in his voice. "We've got fire coming from everywhere!" Lieutenant Morse screamed.

"I want you to get a hold of yourself, Lieutenant! And do it now!"   Captain Damion snapped at the frightened Lieutenant.   "Pull your men back, Lieutenant, and redeploy.   Second and Third Platoon will link up and form a perimeter.   Do you understand? Over!"   Captain Damion asked the Lieutenant.

The NVA were firing a murderous volley from spider holes, bunkers and fighting trenches along their front. Captain Damion ordered the rest of the company forward and had them dig into a defensive perimeter. The fusillade to their front had reached such a voluminous pitch that Lieutenant Knox could barely hear Captain Damion's instructions.   It sounded like insane musicians were playing a discordant symphony of clashing cymbals and pounding drums. Damion reported to Weston, "We have 'em just where we want them, they're all the way around us!"

The mauled remnants of First Platoon were rushing back through the jungle carrying their dead and wounded.   The volume of return fire increased in intensity as the Marines answered back.   The deafening clap of AK's, M-14's, M-16's, frags, RPG's, M-60's and .51 caliber machine guns reached a sustained roar, which drowned out all but the loudest screams.   From the direction of the popping and cracking of small arms and the periodic "Krunch!" of grenades, Roger could tell that the enemy was gradually enveloping their flanks.   He also knew that they were outnumbered and in deep trouble.

Captain Damion ordered the company to consolidate their perimeter as he got on the radio and called for air support.   Marines hastily scooped out fighting holes with their entrenching tools and rifle butts.

"Falcon, this is Delta Six, do you read me, over?" Damion radioed the FAC pilot circling overhead.

"Delta Six, this is Falcon One, over." The FAC pilot radioed back.

"Falcon One, we've got a company pinned down with heavy fire coming from the hill north of us. We have NVA moving along our flanks, situation is serious, over!" Captain Damion kept his cool.

"Ah...Roger that, Delta Six. I've got fast-movers five minutes out, over."

Captain Damion was kneeling next to his radio man talking to the FAC pilot when a flurry of yells echoed along the front.

"Here they come!" The volley of fire reached an acoustical riot as a wave of NVA poured from their trenches into the front edge of the Marines.

"Falcon One, we need that ordinance now! They're coming at us hard!"

"Understood, Delta Six. Can you mark with smoke?"

"Negative, Falcon One. We're pinned down and the canopy is too thick." Damion was checking his position on the grid map laid out in front of him. "I'm going to mark my position with a flare, Falcon One." One of Captain Damion's men popped a hand flare and shot it through the canopy.

"I've got a visual on your flare, Delta Six. Where do you want the markers, over?"

Damion double checked his map and responded. "You can fire your marking rounds one hundred and fifty meters north of my flare, over." Damion could hear the little spotter plane thrumming overhead.

"Will do, Delta six." The FAC pilot brought his little spotter plane on course and fired two phosphorous marking rounds which impacted at the edge of the slope in a shower of white streamers.

"On the mark, Falcon One!" Captain Damion was in business now. "We need the first pass east to west. Do you copy?"

"Roger that, Delta Six...east to west. This is Gunslinger...Just sit back and enjoy the show," the flight leader broke in on their channel. "We're rollin' in hot. Keep your heads down!" The pilot instructed.

To the southeast, Roger could hear the banshee scream of Phantoms a couple seconds later as they knifed in low along the front edge of the slope and released four 500 pound bombs. Roger glanced to the front as the two jets roared past. The ground bucked and heaved from four enormous explosions which ripped through the jungle a hundred and fifty meters in front of them. The earth-rending concussions hurled fountains of dirt and jungle debris into the air, shaking leaves from the trees and sending shock waves rushing through their position.

"Lookin' good, Gunslinger," Captain Damion said.

"We aim to please, Delta Six. What's your pleasure?"

"Can you give us some cannon fire? They're still comin' at us. Same place, Gunslinger," Captain Damion requested.

"Read you five-by-five, Delta Six. Got C.B.U.'s and twenty mike-mikes. Where do ya want it?" The Phantom pilot relayed.

"As close as you can get it, Gunslinger....shove it down their throats!" Damion spoke into the hand mike.

"We got a special delivery for ya, Delta Six," the lead Phantom pilot replied.

The first few bombs had only temporarily

staggered the first wave of NVA. The frenzied automatic fire was still ripping along the front as Marines desperately fought to hold back the assault.

"They're comin' in again! GEEET DOOWN!" someone yelled as the men hunkered down and watched the front. The sound of the approaching jets increased in intensity. They came in hot. The chain-saw, rasping sound of the jet's twenty millimeter cannons could be heard as they came in low strafing the jungle. A second later, a daisy-chain of orange black explosions rippled through their front chewing up the ranks of NVA.

"Scratch some bad guys!" Captain Damion shouted into the mike. "What's your name?" Captain Damion asked the pilot.

"If you're ever in Da Nang, Just ask for Paladin...you know, have gun will travel," the Phantom pilot chuckled.

"Gotcha, Gunslinger...it kinda fits," Damion smiled at his radioman. "Jet-jockeys think their pretty hot," Damion winked at his radioman. "I owe ya a cool one, Gunslinger."

"The parties not over yet, Delta Six. Got hot stuff comin' in," Gunslinger radioed back.

The two jets roared off to the south and came screaming back for their final pass.

"We're takin' it a little further up the hill, Delta Six. Stay cool. It's gonna get hot."

"Napalm, comin' in!" the shouts echoed down the line.

The jets streaked in along the slope and released their pods of jellied gas which tumbled lazily end-over-end before splashing through the jungle with a wall of liquid hell.

"KawWhoooshh!" The molten balls rolled through

the greenery, consuming everything in their paths. It was acetylene hot. Men were incinerated where they stood. Others suffocated as the fireball sucked the air out of lungs and bunkers to feed its insatiable appetite. Through the scattered jungle growth, the Marines could see the boiling orange walls of flame churning and cresting with oily black clouds. In seconds, an invisible heat wave rushed over their position, slapping the men in their faces. It felt like someone had flung open the door of an enormous blast furnace. A hundred and fifty meters in front of them, a handful of NVA stumbled out of the inferno on fire and screaming. A couple staggered out of the pale of grey smoke looking like ghostly apparitions. Others lay half-cremated on the slope where they fell - their uniforms burned off and their skin charred a grotesque red-black. An oily black smoke rose from the blackened slope. Burnt foliage hung in tatters from charcoaled trunks. Small fires continued to burn. The acrid scent of burned flesh and petroleum floated through the forest in grim reminder of the fire storm. A mantle of oily smoke thickened and thinned as it floated through the jungle, gradually dissipating through the canopy.

"That's all we've got, Delta Six. I'll take ya up on your offer if you're ever in the neighborhood." The Phantom pilot radioed.

"You can take that to the bank, Gunslinger." Captain Damion responded. "Hey...and thanks!"

"D" Company tightened its perimeter and prepared for the next assault. Captain Damion knew that the air strike had only temporarily stopped the enemy.

"Falcon One, we're running low on ammo, need a resupply ASAP, over."

"Read you, Delta Six. What do ya need?" The FAC pilot responded.

"You can send us M-60 ammo, M-16, M-14, frags, claymores and batteries for the radio...Oh, and we could use some fresh barrels for our 60's and some water while your at it. We need dust off's for the wounded, over."

"Delta Six, I copy, but you can't get any choppers into your position...trees are too thick, over."

"We'll try blowin' an LZ, Falcon. We have serious wounded. They won't make it without a dust-off."

"We'll see what we can do, over."

"I'm runnin' low on fuel and daylight, Delta Six. I've got to return to base...I'll be back at first light, over." The late afternoon sun was dipping behind a cloud bank to the west, causing the valley to pool with grays.

"Roger, Falcon One," the FAC pilot banked his little prop and droned away to the south.

Damion handed the handset back to his radioman and checked his map, defining an area where they were dug in with a grease pencil. The company was spread out in an egg-shaped oval in the valley, hemmed in by high ground and a regiment of NVA.

The night was closing in fast. All along their front, sporadic rifle reports cracked. Litter bearers were picking up the wounded and carrying them to an improvised aid station the medics had set up in a shallow depression in the middle of their position.

About an hour after the air strike, the men on their southern perimeter could hear the reassuring sound of slicks slap-thumping towards them from the south.

"Delta Six, this is Maverick One, over." Captain Damion could here the "Dhup, dhup, dhup" of the chopper in the background as the pilot's voice crackled over the radio.

"Gimme the mike, " Damion instructed his RTO. "Maverick One, this is Delta Six, I read you loud and clear, over."

"We've got a resupply for ya, but we're gonna to have to drop it to you. Request that you mark with red flare, over," the chopper pilot responded.

"Aw...Roger that, Maverick One...shooting red, now," Captain Damion answered as one of his men ran in a low crouch about thirty meters south east of the aid station and popped a hand flare, sending a scarlet torch arching through the canopy.

"Got a visual, Delta Six. Keep your heads down, we're comin over," the chopper pilot warned.

"Heads Up!" Men nervously scanned the holes in the canopy for the shadow of the approaching Heuys.

The slapping grew louder as the choppers homed in on the spot where the flare had exited the branches. The two choppers beat in fast and thumped away to the east in seconds.

"Watch it!" Shouts echoed as boxes crashed through the trees and slammed into the jungle floor. One of them shattered on impact, scattering nylon bandoliers of .223 caliber rounds. Men rushed to break open the crates and load up on handfuls of M-16 rounds, grenades and linked belts of 7.62 ammo for the M-60's.

"Delta Six, we're comin' around again. We need another flare, over."

"Roger, Maverick One," Captain Damion acknowledged.

The lead chopper was two klicks out when a 23mm antiaircraft gun opened up with a necklace of green tracers. The tracers curved skyward toward the choppers, hitting the lead one in the engine compartment. "We're hit!" The chopper pilot shouted. The stricken Heuy was wobbling badly and trailing smoke as the pilot fought to stabilize the disabled slick. The tail chopper banked sharply to his right and swung away to the south.

"Delta Six, we're going down," The pilot shouted.

The Heuy was wobbling out of control in an erratic see-saw as it rotored down and crashed through the wooded canopy in a whirl of splintering blades and branches. The chopper landed on its side in a crumpled heap about fifty meters from Roger's flank. The gunner crawled from the wreckage. The crew chief and co-pilot scrambled out of the wreck, leaving the dead pilot tangled in the shattered plexiglass. A fireteam ran to retrieve the survivors. They were bruised and badly shaken, but alive.

Throughout the night, Captain Damion kept vigil by his radio calling in fire-missions around their position. Eight klicks east, 105 and 155 batteries at the Cam Lo artillery base responded. Gun crews feverishly loaded artillery shells into the breeches of their howitzers, re-checked trajectories and yanked their lanyards, sending high explosive rounds careening through the night.

All night long, the Marines listened to the guttural sound of shells freight-training overhead. They sweated and cringed in their shallow foxholes, shivering from fear and cold. Few slept that first night. Most spent the hours listening to the comforting concussions of shells impacting beyond their lines. They huddled in their holes with the forest floor bathed in a dull yellow light from parachute flares dropped from C-117 flareships circling overhead.

At dawn, the reassuring drone of the spotter

plane could be heard circling overhead. It was none to early.

On the morning of the second day, they started coming in human wave assaults, trying to overrun the Marines.

"Thoomp...Thoomp," the metallic sound of mortars leaving their tubes sounded through the perimeter.

"Incoming!" Shouts of Marines interrupted the morning stillness.

"Sssssssh...Crack, Crash!" Sixty-ones started air-bursting in the canopy, showering the Marines with red hot shrapnel. "Sssssssh...Karumph!" The sounds of explosions were followed by the fluted wail of shrapnel shooting through the air.

"Aaaywh! My leg!" A Marine screamed in agony.

"Sssssssh...Crack, Crash!"

"Corpsman!"

An M-60 opened up, followed by someone screaming, "Here they come!"

"Lewis!" Roger yelled.

"Yo!" the squad's M-60 gunner shouted back.

"Cover our left!" Roger ordered as he scanned the front.

"No sweat, Sarge," the gunner answered as he sighted down his barrel at the coming tide.

"TaTow..tatow, tatow,tat tat tatow!" Lewis' 60 opened up with measured bursts, followed by the scream, "This is it!"

"Here they come!" Others yelled as a platoon of NVA charged Roger's flank.

The shrill sound of whistles sounded. *"TIEN LEN!...TIEN LEN!"* (Charge!) Vietnamese screamed.

"Find your targets!" Roger shouted to his squad.

The rippling of automatic weapons picked up intensity.

Roger could see the shapes of NVA coming at them with their AK's blinking on and off. He flicked the selector switch on his M-16 to fully auto, placed one of the onrushing soldiers in his sights, and cut loose a burst which toppled the man backwards.

The human wave picked up momentum as more NVA poured from the hill. They were bent slightly forward like they were leaning into the wind. Bullets were lashing the air, as NVA and Marines screamed and fired.

"Tatow...Ta tow ta tow tattattatatatow," Lewis' M-60 raked the ranks of NVA. Soldiers stumbled and fell as the grazing fire found its mark and cut them down. Some pitched backwards. Others jerked and pirouetted in a spastic dance of death. More were coming. Roger aimed again and fired. Another soldier dropped. They were coming at a dead run. He flicked the selector to semi-automatic and fired again. Another soldier spun into a tree. He could see them clearly now in their dull green uniforms and pith helmets. He was picking his targets and dropping them at will. An NVA officer with his distinctive epaulets and brass buckle with raised red star was waving a pistol and motioning his men forward. Roger placed him in his sights and fired.

Marines were feverishly jamming magazines in their weapons and firing madly, but they just kept coming. It was a berserk riot - a pandemonium of bloodletting as the NVA collided with the Marines. It was a melee, a jungle brawl, a point blank shoot out. Roger fired at a soldier coming at him with his bayonet, blowing the mans chest open. Another was coming at him from his side. He swung and fired. A Marine beside him ran out of ammo and grabbed the hot barrel of his M-14, swinging it full force at one of the NVA soldiers. The wooden stock caught the man's head broadside, splattering it like a watermelon hit with a baseball bat.

The battle had deteriorated into a ferocious free-for-all. It was trench warfare at its worst - men screaming, kicking, gouging, swinging fists, cursing - men bent upon each other's destruction. They went at it like crazed animals. It didn't matter how they did it. Men shot each other at point blank range with pistols and rifles, bayonetted each other in the gut, caved in heads with rifle butts, slashed each other with knives, hacked each other with entrenching tools. It was gruesome hand-to-hand combat - up close, bestial, barbaric.

The onrushing tide had thinned, but they were still coming. Roger was on his knees trying to insert a fresh magazine into his M-16 when his bolt jammed. He was fighting his M-16 when he saw an NVA soldier coming at his side with a bayonet. He sprang to his feet and parried the blade with a vertical butt-stroke of his M-16, knocking the AK-47 out of the soldier's hand. The young soldier lunged at Roger, toppling them both to the ground. They rolled and thrashed at each other, tearing at arms and faces. The man was wiry and hard as ironwood, but Roger was bigger and stronger. They clawed at each other with clenched teeth, panting and spitting and grunting. They were locked in a death grip, each trying to out-strangle the other. Roger was on top with his hands around the man's throat. The NVA soldier was driving his knee into Roger's back, trying to knock him off. Roger squeezed the man's throat like a vice grip until the soldier's face turned red and his eyes bulged out. Roger was digging his thumbs into the man's windpipe with all of his strength. The NVA was straining to choke Roger back, but Roger's arms were longer. The man was weakening. Roger pulled back his right fist and drove it into the man's face, smashing his cheek bone. He swung again and again, pummeling the man's face until the soldier relaxed his grip and exhaled his last breath.

Roger hastily scanned the ground and found a discarded M-14, beside a dead Marine laying on top of an NVA soldier. He lined up the rear aperture sight with the front foresight, placed the blade on a soldier and fired, toppling him to the ground. He continued to fire at soldiers like he was an automaton, picking them out of the melee with mechanical precision, until there were no more left to shoot. It was over in minutes, leaving the surviving Marines exhausted and wrung out from the killing frenzy. Dead and wounded Marines and NVA were sprawled in a chiropractic nightmare around their position. A wispy, cotton-wool mist of gunsmoke floated in the air around them.

"Pop!....Pop!"   A Marine with a stone cold expression on his face was walking through the butcher shop, shooting NVA who were still breathing. Men coughed and swore. Some simply slumped in weak-kneed exhaustion to the forest floor. They were too tired to stand. Others stared in silence through blood-shot eyes.

Two M-60's stuttered in tandem along the perimeter.

The situation grew more desperate with each passing hour. They were surrounded and cut off. The Marines had repulsed repeated suicide assaults in fierce hand-to-hand combat, but the NVA just kept coming at them, gnawing on their flanks and steadily chewing them up. After one particularly brutal assault, Roger remembered an Old West painting he had seen hanging above a bar showing a panoramic scene of "Custer's Last Stand." He remembered the Calvary men slumped over dead horses, the swirling stampede of Indians on horseback, and the desperate looks of the last pocket of troopers firing through the drifting clouds of gunsmoke. He felt like he was there.

On the second day, Lieutenant Knox took a bullet in the stomach and was carried to the first aid station. The saucer-shaped depression was covered with wounded men unable to be medevaced. The shallow area was littered with the discards of exhausted corpsman who were running out of morphine and bandages. There was little with which to work and not much they could do for the wounded. Knox held on for a day, grimacing from the excruciating pain of a gut wound.

That night, one of the specially equipped C-47's the Marines affectionately called "Puff", from "Puff the Magic Dragon," showed up over head with its awesome compliment of electric gatling guns. Puff could spit out 4,000 rounds per minute which could hit every square inch of a football field with a controlled burst. The men watched with bated breath as the wavy crimson fingers of tracers probed the blackness. The pageantry of the aerial ballet was nearly hypnotic, as the men sat transfixed in their holes, watching the molten rivers of fire dance across the surrounding hills.

On the second day, B-52's started carpeting the terrain around them, walking their bomb loads within five hundred meters of their perimeter. The earth jarring concussions were so intense that the Marines literally bounced out of their holes. In typical Marine Corps humor, the men started joking about the B-52's turning them into pop-up targets for the NVA.

On the third day, Roger went to see how Knox was doing. He passed Captain Damion on the rim of the crater with the company command group. He was talking on the radio with his ever present radioman leashed to his side. Roger glanced at the Captain, but Damion didn't look up. He was too busy talking on the radio. Like the others, his face was gray with exhaustion, and smudged with dirty sweat and grime.

Roger found Lieutenant Knox laying on a poncho with a bloody compress tied around his stomach. Knox was pale and waxen looking. His eyes were tired and heavy lidded. His chest slowly rose and fell from short, labored breaths. Roger knelt beside him next to one of the corpsman.

"How's he doin'?" Roger quietly asked the corpsman.

"He's lost a lot of blood..if we could just get him out on a chopper," the corpsman pursed his lips.

Knox's eyes fluttered and struggled to focus on Roger. He attempted a feeble smile, dabbed his dry lips with his tongue and looked at Roger. "Does anyone have any fruit cocktail?" he asked.

Roger looked at the medic who looked back with sad, weary eyes.

"I'm sorry, sir. We're all out," the corpsman apologized.

"That's O.K." Knox exhaled softly, and died.

"Damn it!" Roger turned his head away and cursed. Even in death, Knox had died with a quiet dignity which touched Roger. But he couldn't understand why God would allow this to happen to one of His own. That troubled Roger more than anything.

For three days, they clung to their fragile position. The piles of dead and dying grew. Choppers kept braving the ground fire to resupply the Marines, but several of them were shot down in the process. Some of the supplies fell short. Others over-shot the target area and fell into enemy hands. Water bags burst. C-rations fell far too short. Out of sheer desperation, the Marines started stripping glutinous rice balls wrapped in banana leaves from dead NVA for something to eat.

By the third day, their situation had deteriorated to the critical point. They could barely keep from being overrun. Captain Damion was at the point where he was almost ready to call artillery in on top of his own position. Damion decided to order a do or die attempt to break out of their position. Under heavy covering fire from air strikes, the Marines, carrying dozens of dead and wounded, fought their way out of their pocket. They fought a running gun battle with the NVA until they reached a low bald knoll several hundred meters south.

The putrid, gaseous stench of decaying flesh and burnt cordite hung in the air from three days of fighting. The valley was littered with bodies and viscera which had begun to rot and bloat in the heat.

Towards the end of the third day, elements of the Second Battalion Seventh Marines, driving west from Cam Lo in a forced march, drove a spearhead through the NVA encirclement and rescued what was left of Roger's Company. The arrival of the reinforcements, coupled with old fashioned Marine Corps tenacity, forced the NVA to withdraw deeper into the mountains bordering Laos. Over half of the company was killed or wounded. Hundreds of NVA had died, their bodies dragged off by their comrades or blown to bits by high explosives.

When the relief column reached the beleaguered Marines, they found the survivors almost out of their minds from four days of carnage and hunger. They looked like walking dead. They were filthy, foul-smelling zombies - wasted and nearly disabled from exhaustion. Their eyes were dark and sunken, almost lifeless in their expression. Even the joy of being rescued could not erase the grim, almost catatonic looks on their faces.

Chapter 16

The battered survivors were still reeling from the after-effects of the battle, when the H-34's hovered in under sullen, grey clouds to take them back. Days drifted into months, doing hard time on the Rock.

A week after his return, Roger was carrying another Marine to a chopper when the NVA lobbed in several mortar rounds. The rounds bracketed the landing pad, sending splinters of shrapnel into Roger's legs and thigh. He was medevaced to Quang Tri, where his wounds were debrided and stitched. He was given a strong dose of antibiotics and sent back to the Rock with his second Purple Heart.

Roger continued to pull patrols and serve as part-time bodyguard for Colonel Weston. He also grew grizzled and hard from months of steeling himself against the loss and pain. By the end of 1966, he'd completed his thirteen months in 'Nam. He decided to extend for a second tour.

Half-way into his second tour, the First Battalion, Fourth Marines received orders to rotate to Okinawa to re-group.   The Battalion had sustained so many casualties that it had to be pulled off the line to be refitted.

A week before the Battalion was scheduled to leave the Rockpile, Roger volunteered to ride "shotgun" on a routine convoy transferring supplies over to Camp Carroll, about eight klicks southeast of their firebase. Camp Carroll was a strategic fire support base, off Route Nine and west of Dong Ha. It had previously been referred to as the Cam Lo artillery firebase, but it had been renamed "Camp Carroll" in posthumous tribute to a Marine Captain who had died in combat. It was a scarred plateau trashed with stacks of faded green sandbags, endless coils of concertina and artillery emplacements. The hill was pockmarked with 81 mm mortars, 105 and 155 mm howitzer pits. It provided fire support for operations in the DMZ. Camp Carroll was also a thorn in the side of the NVA.

Their resupply run was suppose to be a piece of cake - a "hop, skip and a throw" over to Camp Carroll and back. Three deuce-and-a-halves left the Rockpile in a cloud of ocher colored dust. They wove their way down the parched red rut the bulldozers had gouged out of the hilly terrain, linking the Rockpile to Route Nine.

It was another dusty, dry day - with memories of the monsoons long lost in the brain-baking amnesia of the hot season. The short trip was supposed to take a couple of hours. They would drop off the supplies, turn around, and be back on the Rock before dusk. But true to military form, two of the trucks broke down in the dust-choking heat. The Marines sweated and cursed for hours, trying to get the beasts running again.

The day had been calm, but Roger didn't like passing through Indian country with a small convoy of broken down deuce-and-a-halves. They were too vulnerable on their own, especially stalled out in the open. It was like a few defenseless wagons which had separated from the main wagon-train passing through Indian country under the watchful eyes of Comanche Scouts - easy pickins if the NVA wanted to massacre them. Late that afternoon, they pulled into Camp Carroll with their scalps intact, but soaked with sweat and dirty grime.

The sun was already sinking into a pastel haze by the time the trucks off-loaded. There was no way Roger was going to attempt a second run through enemy country at night. His small group of armed escorts and drivers were put up for the night in a half-buried hootch of plywood and canvas. They would head back in the morning.

"Zzzzzzsst whew.....Krunch!"
It was 2:00 A.M. Four hundred NVA sappers had launched a coordinated assault on the fire base. Roger rolled out of his cot and grabbed his M-16. "Incoming!" he yelled. "Move it! We're under attack!" Roger groped through the darkness, trying to get his bearings.
"Zzzzzzsst whew.....Krunch!"
"Oh crap!" someone cursed as he tripped on an overturned cot.
"Hurry, move it! Get your weapons!" Roger ordered. He could hear the rifle reports along the line. "They'll be coming through the wire soon," Roger warned from experience.
The NVA had taken out a couple of perimeter

bunkers and had started blowing corridors through the wire.

"KaRUNCH!" Slices of shrapnel ripped through the canvas, followed by the concussion slamming into the side of the tent.

"Out!" Roger shouted.

He emerged from the tent and scanned his sector of the hilltop. The velvet blackness was going on and off from sporadic explosions further down the hill. He made his way through the darkness with his M-16 at ready. He passed an 81 mm mortar pit. The crew was elevating the tube nearly straight up.

"THOOOMP!" One of the men dropped a round down the tube and quickly ducked back with his fingers in his ears. The mortar coughed out an illumination round which shot skyward. In seconds, it popped overhead, releasing a parachute flare which suddenly bathed the firebase in an incandescent green glow.

Roger scurried through the shadows until he reached a bunker along the perimeter which had been blown by a B-40 rocket. Charred sandbags were strewn around the smoking cavity where an M-60 gun team had been shredded by the rocket. Farther down the slope, a mob of NVA sappers was coming through the wire with blocks of explosives strapped to their bodies.

Roger dropped to one knee beside the ruins of the bunker and picked off one of the figures, dropping him into the twisted coils of razor wire.

"Ta tow tow tow tow tow," fluorescent streaks from M-60's slashed through the blackness in quick succession. The raking fire was dropping NVA right and left in the tangled wire.

The Marines had come alive along the perimeter and were firing away with small arms and hurling grenades down the slope. Roger took aim and fired at another sapper, spinning him off his feet like an erratic top.

"Pop   hisssss.." Another illumination round starburst overhead. Its garish green light cast distorted shadows across the perimeter, silhouetting the zigzagging figures which jerked and jitterbugged through the schizophrenic light show.

"KABOOM!" A bunker went up in a shower of sparks, sandbags, and flesh after a sapper dove through the entrance and detonated his bandolier of C-4.

Roger zeroed in on another NVA coming directly at him about forty meters away and fired. The round hit the sapper in the shoulder and staggered him slightly but he kept coming. The sapper was screaming at the top of his lungs with a fiendish grin on his face. Roger squeezed off another round which hit him in the chest, knocking him to one knee. But the sapper picked himself up and plunged forward. Roger couldn't believe his eyes. *"He must be doped up,"* he thought.

The sappers had shot themselves up with morphine and tied off their limbs with tourniquets so they could absorb more hits without going down immediately. Their objective was to breech the perimeter wire with wooden ladders and explosives to create corridors through the wire. Once through the wire, they would run through the firebase, throwing themselves into artillery pits, tents and bunkers to blow up anything of value.

Roger flipped his selector to fully automatic and fired into the onrushing sapper.

"WHAM!" A blinding flash erupted where the sapper had been. The burst had hit the sling of plastic explosives tied around his waist. The force of the blast blew Roger backwards, splattering him with a fine mist of blood and tissue. He was temporarily stunned by the concussion. His ears were ringing so loud he could barely hear the sounds of the battle raging around him.

He grabbed the side of the bunker. He was trying to pull himself up when an NVA sapper tackled him from behind, wrapping his arms around Rogers throat. They rolled into a pile of sandbags, thrashing and wrestling. Roger was dazed, but mad as hell. He tried to loosen the man's grip, but he couldn't break the choke hold. In sheer panic, he reached back, grabbed a thick clump of the man's hair, and pulled him over his head. Roger jumped on top of the sapper like an enraged animal and started beating the man's face with his fists - half out of fear, half out of hate. It was an adrenalin freakout. The sapper was tearing at Roger as he flayed away. Roger was cursing the man as his fist splattered the man's nose. The sapper's arms went limp. Roger glanced sideways and found an AK-47 lying beside another soldier in the dirt. He reached for it and slammed the butt into the sapper's face again and again until he caved in the front of his head.

The strident staccato of return fire was cracking around him. Scores of NVA had mobbed the perimeter. Dozens were already grotesquely snarled in the twisted strands of wire - some with undetonated satchel charges the size of backpacks still strapped to their bodies.

"BOOM! Wheeee!" a gunner in one of the 105 pits yanked the lanyard, sending a hailstorm of steel flechettes scything through the waves of NVA. The gun crews had lowered the barrels of their big guns and were firing beehive rounds point-blank into the assault. It was Missionary Ridge, the Somme, and Gallipoli as modern machine-guns and grapeshot literally mowed down dozens with the steel darts.

"**BOOM!**" another round cleared a swath through the perimeter.

Rifles crackled. Machine-guns chattered. Flares hissed overhead. The NVA threw more men into the wire. For two hours, the firebase fought for its life. By dawn, the Marines had broken the back of the suicide attack and driven the mauled sapper Battalion back into the jungle.

That morning, the battle-weary Marines, from cooks to gun crews, walked along the perimeter surveying the results. In places, the NVA were stacked like cord wood. Over a hundred and twenty lay sprawled where they had been cut down. The human time bomb Roger had detonated had been blown in half. Roger found his upper torso connected to his buttocks and legs by a thick spaghetti string of intestine thirty feet long.

The Marines found numerous blood trails leading down the slope where the NVA had dragged off their dead with meat hooks. Subsequent patrols found scores of shallow graves a klick outside the wire with a hidden cache of crude, wooden coffins the NVA had left behind. Colonel Weston choppered in that morning to get a first-hand look at the failed assault. In typical style, he could be seen walking around the perimeter wearing his pistol belt with his hands on his hips, taking in the scene. He bore an obvious look of approval on his face. His boys had done good. Marines were dragging the remains of dead NVA to a pit a bulldozer had scooped out of the dirt. Marines, their mouths covered with cloth, were throwing the limbs and bodies into the mass grave before the stink got unbearable.. In the late afternoon, Roger hitched a ride with Colonel Weston back to the

Rockpile.

A week later, the Battalion was transferred by truck convoy to Dong Ha and then to Da Nang by chopper. After a year and a half, he was going back to the world. After transitting through Okinawa, he got a thirty day leave and orders to report to the Marine Corps Recruit Depot at Parris Island, South Carolina. By coincidence, his brother, Ron, was going home at the same time for a thirty day leave, before reporting to Yuma, Arizona. After a thirty day marathon of knee-walking drunks, hell-raising, and chasing girls, Roger reported in.

He was assigned to the firing range as a Primary Marksman Instructor, teaching raw recruits the fine art of rifle firing. He had a lot of practical experience and sought to excel in his new responsibilities. In a few weeks, Roger's class of trainees had surpassed all the other training companies, with over a 90% qualification rate. As a result of his outstanding rifle range scores, Roger was summoned to appear before the Drill Instructor's Review Board.

"Sergeant, Helle, we've been reviewing your fitness reports as a rifle instructor," a Major sitting behind a desk with several other officers and NCO's looked at Roger with cold blue eyes. "We've requested your presence this morning to ask you if you would like to be a drill instructor?"

Standing ramrod straight at attention, Roger responded, "No, Sir, I'm sorry, Sir, I would not."

With a sarcastic challenge to his voice, the Major replied, "And why not, Sergeant?"

Roger didn't really know why; he just wasn't ready to baby-sit a bunch of pukes.

Before he could come up with an answer, the Major added, " Sergeant, did you earn those stripes, or were they given to you?"

Roger knew he was cornered. "I earned them, Sir!"

"Well, then," the Major smiled, "Now we're going to make you work for them."

Roger was "volunteered" for Drill Sergeant School against his will, but he made the adjustment and threw himself into his new responsibilities with a vengeance. Out of the 258 candidates entering the gruelling Drill Instructor's Training School at Parris Island, only 152 graduated.

A lot had changed since the free-wheeling days when the elite band of gnarled NCO's in Smokey-the-Bear hats ran roughshod over young recruits, dispensing their own brand of cruelty and intimidation.   No obscenity had been censored, no sarcasm spared in their efforts to break and re-mold the recruits. Marines were harassed and punched and sometimes beaten to toughen them up. The D.I.'s rationalized their harshness in the knowledge that nothing they dished out could surpass the demands of combat. Recruits were run ragged until they dropped from exhaustion, barfed their guts out, and sometimes even died. D.I.'s would scream in their faces, bite their noses, call them pukes, queers, maggots and every demeaning put-down conceivable during the recruits' torturous weeks at boot camp. For many of them, Parris Island would always be remembered as the Marine Corps equivalent of Devil's Island.

Roger's drill instructor days were more humane than when he had been a recruit. Much had changed in his absence, due to pressure from mothers and politicians who objected to the war and the military's handling of their sons. Even so, Roger joined the elite cadre of Marines which was given the task of molding flabby, gelatinous civilians into lean, trim fighting Marines.

Roger relished the role of taking Marines and putting them through their paces during the ten week purgatory of Parris Island with its sweltering summers, swamps, and sand fleas. At that point in his Marine Corps career, he had no illusions about the romance of war like he had when he stepped off the bus in his own pre-dawn arrival at boot-camp over two years before. Still, he was proud to be a Marine D.I. and he looked the part in his razor-creased trousers, with his Smokey-the-Bear hat cocked slightly forward in a rakish sort of look.

He was determined to instill that same esprit de corps in the hearts and minds of his charges. He was fair, but he worked his recruits on the "grinder" in endless hours of marching and close order drills. He was tough and uncompromising in his demands for perfection because he knew what many of them were going to experience in a few short weeks. Roger knew that the 'Nam would be even more uncompromising in its demands. He could curse with the best of them and stick his face in any recruit's to exact his demands, but, deep down inside, it wasn't blind dedication that drove him, it was the painful knowledge of what awaited those young men he was training.

Since his return, the 'Nam was never far from his thoughts even though it was half a world away. It tugged at his mind and replayed its images in the lonely hours of the night. It was as if it had followed him home.

America, too, was steeped in the reminders which

assaulted them every night on the six o'clock news. It wasn't something you could ignore. Since his return during the "summer of love", Vietnam had become a national nightmare. Political dissent, student riots, and peace marches combined with the turbulent forces of the late Sixties to foster a steady erosion of public support for a war perceived as immoral and unjust. Many back home had come to the conclusion that the only thing keeping the corrupt Vietnamese government afloat was the massive infusion of American dollars and adolescent blood.

America's commitment to the war was unraveling as she sank deeper into a quagmire of self-castigation. From college campuses to the corridors of Congress, from students to housewives, it became increasingly popular to distance yourself from Vietnam and those who were fighting in it. Men, who had been crossing fields of fire or humping through hostile jungle just forty-eight hours earlier, were sometimes greeted with taunts of "baby killer" and "murderer" when they stepped off their planes back home. For the first time, they encountered the full brunt of national contempt.

Few seemed to share the sense of patriotism Roger and his brother, Ron, had experienced when they signed their enlistment papers. They had both been eager to sign up, even dreading the possible disgrace of being disqualified as "4-F" during their physical. They feared that as much as they might have feared the loss of their budding manhood. When they joined the Marines, even the thought of resisting the draft was foreign to their way of thinking. That was something cowards would do, not patriotic Americans.

A growing chorus of Americans, including many from their peer group, began to think you were crazy if you even thought about joining, let alone, wanting to go to Vietnam. The former glory of serving in the armed forces had lost its luster. When their father's generation had gone off to war, soda jerks and bank presidents dropped everything to become citizen soldiers. They would stand in freezing lines around the block to volunteer to fight for their country. They would even lie and bend the rules to get in. Back then, a guy in uniform could always get a free cup of coffee or a ride anywhere. But, what had once been a symbol of honor had now become a mark of disgrace.

Roger began to feel increasingly alienated back home. It wasn't just the "spit and polish" harassment of stateside duty, it was the mood of the country. Men who had been to 'Nam like him were looked upon as social outcasts. Even when they put on their civvies and tried to fit in, they were often viewed as throwbacks to more barbaric times.

As soon as some guys reached the States, they tore their uniforms off like soiled graveclothes. Even so, Roger was not ashamed to wear his uniform and ribbons, even in public. He was still proud to be a Marine. What he'd done was right, as far as he was concerned, and he wasn't going to apologize to anyone.

He began to withdraw into the tight circle of his fellow drill instructors to recapture the camaraderie he'd known in 'Nam. Most of the D.I.'s had been there, too, and felt more comfortable with each other than by themselves outside the gate. The pressures in 'Nam had forged that kinship. They each secretly longed for the closeness they had left behind. These were honest relationships between men who really needed each other - who really cared for each other. They didn't talk about it, even in their most vulnerable sessions of bar talk, but each of them shared a sense of loss and guilt.

Roger started drinking heavily after "lights out", not so much to socialize or loosen up with his fellow D.I.'s, but to dull the painful memories. He had left the 'Nam, but the 'Nam hadn't left him. Hard as he tried, he couldn't escape the guilt of knowing that he had made it back and his friends hadn't. He just couldn't seem to put it behind him, or distance himself from their suffering.

A restlessness began to build within him, and, with it, a compelling need to go back to those he had left behind. He felt that he still owed that to Danny and Knox and the rest. He would turn on the T.V. set and see the black and white footage of guys dying, and he couldn't do anything about it. The weekly body counts grieved him. The images frustrated him. They tormented him with guilt for not being there. He couldn't stop recalling their faces, their names, and their deaths. He would see the mud-caked jungle boots of the dead protruding from under poncho liners and think of Danny, and the squad, and Knox asking for a can of fruit cocktail. He'd see the frenzied scenes of Marines shooting over a wall in Hue, or besieged at Khe Sanh and he could hear their voices calling for him. In some twisted way, he felt them pleading with him to come back and share in their sufferings - to atone somehow for his living when they had died.

The galling images of long-haired freaks, protesting by the thousands and burning their draft cards, angered him. A rage began to well within him at the sight of protestors spitting on the flag and waving the North Vietnamese flag in defiance. *"Is that what I was fighting for?"* he thought. *"Is that what my friends died for?"* America had turned her back on her young men who had gone to Vietnam in good faith, but Roger couldn't.   The sense of national rejection was galling enough, but the self-righteous criticism that his friends died in vain was a slap in the face he couldn't bear.

When the *My Lai* atrocities hit the front pages, the news media seemed to revel in its chastisement of Lieutenant Calley and, with him, every other Vietnam vet. It seemed like they were condemning them all. It didn't matter that Roger had seen both sides. He had seen the communist atrocities and the brutalizing of the innocents, but the news seemed conveniently to ignore that. It didn't seem to matter to the media that many men were serving out of the heartfelt conviction they were doing something honorable to help the Vietnamese. They seemed only to want to characterize those who served as a pack of sociopathic adolescents who got their kicks burning down innocent villages in "zippo raids", raping helpless virgins, and butchering babies.

It was one thing to come home to the loneliness of an empty terminal or bus station, with no welcome home banners or shouts of "we're proud of you!" So what if he didn't get any brass bands or ticker-taped parades, or yellow ribbons. Yeah, it hurt, but what hurt even more was the knowledge that good men were still dying in good conscience for what they believed was right. They were still giving themselves in service to their country. So what if a thankless nation called them on the one hand and held them in contempt with the other.   The nation might be able to ignore their sacrifices, but Roger couldn't.

His brothers-in-arms needed him. They could not come home, but he could go back to rejoin them. The Corps had ingrained that loyalty in him. "Semper Fi" was not just a motto, it was a sacred summons calling him back.

After a year and a half as a drill instructor, Roger served another year and a half as a criminal investigator for C.I.D (Criminal Investigation Department). It had been almost three years since he'd caught that near mythical "freedom bird" back to the world. He didn't like what he had found when he got back, and he didn't like himself much, either, for being there.

By January, 1970, the 'Nam had finally caught up with him. He had had enough and volunteered to return. He was sent to Camp Pendleton for several months of training, then shipped over for his third tour in Vietnam.

Chapter 17

Roger's chartered jet touched down on the runway at Da Nang in the spring of 1970. It was the year of the "Dog." He was assigned to the newly formed Second Combined Action Group, headquartered at Red Beach, where the Marines had first landed five years earlier. It was responsible for CAP units operating south of Da Nang.

Roger was given a short refresher course in Vietnamese, then assigned the responsibility of five villages near Hoi An, about twenty klicks south of Da Nang. His area of operation was a flat stretch of sandy red clay, pine scrub sand dunes, and paddy lands in Quang Nai Province, between Que Son and Hoi An. It was an area of coastal lands infested with Viet Cong sympathizers. The region was dotted with deserted villes and partially occupied villages drained of young men. The Marines sarcastically referred to the area as

"Pinkville." Roger was put in charge of three squads of Marines and a platoon of Vietnamese popular forces.

What he found when he arrived was very different from what he had encountered four years earlier. Roger gathered the squad leaders together to get a handle on the situation and quickly discovered that the unit's morale was shot. The squads had stopped going out on patrol and had basically relinquished control of the countryside back to the Cong. The Corporal in charge of the CAP platoon was a short-timer with little motivation to put his life on the line. The previous squad leader had gotten wounded and had been sent home. The whole ordeal had broken the spirit of the Corporal. Everyone had their breaking point and he had reached his. He just wanted to keep his head down, count off his days, and go home in one piece. Without aggressive leadership, the fighting spirit of the men had gone down the tubes. Roger had never encountered Marines so demoralized.

The loss of morale and motivation was not just the result of the wimped-out Corporal, but conditions back home as well. Not only had America lost her way, but the turbulent cross-currents of the late Sixties had taken their toll on the men still bogged down in 'Nam. Peace marches, Love-ins, psychedelics, "Flower Power", the "tune in, turn on, drop out" generation, race riots, assassinations and anti-war fervor had all combined to undermine the conditions in 'Nam. Though the brotherhood and camaraderie of the men in the field could still be as tight as ever, back in the rear areas drugs were rampant, racial tensions were at a flash point, and the troops were riddled with a prevailing sense of apathy. Men had lost the will to fight. Vietnam had no moral mission or meaning any longer to

most of them. No one wanted to go home in a box.
With the loss of popular support on the home front, no
one wanted to waste their lives in Vietnam. They just
wanted to stay alive.

After a couple of days of checking things out, he
relieved the Corporal of his command and sent him
packing to the rear where he belonged. Roger then got
to work on rebuilding the morale of his platoon and
instilling the fighting spirit they needed. America may
have lost her resolve, but Roger hadn't. He came back
to finish what he had started, and he needed his fellow
Marines to do it.

Roger knew he was putting his life on the line by
playing Sergeant Striker.   Fraggings had become
fashionable in some quarters. He half expected to
awake in the middle of the night to the sudden "thud" of
a grenade, anonymously tossed into his hootch. One of
his first missions was to lay it out to the men what he
would, and would not tolerate. Although the men's
morale was at a low ebb, he was pleased to find that
their discipline was still reasonably good. As he made
his rounds of the villages checking on the other squads,
some of the men began to come to him privately and
confide that they didn't like the way things had been.
They didn't like chickening out and giving ground to
Charlie. Since most of them were fairly new, they didn't
want to go over the Corporal's head, so they just backed
off and said nothing. Roger was sympathetic, but gave
each of them a firm warning that if he caught them
doing drugs or slackin' he would court marshal their
young butts just the same. He also gave them the
chance to transfer if they wanted without any questions.
Surprisingly, no one took him up on his offer.

A week after his arrival, word shot through the

CAP units that half a platoon of "dog faces" had been wiped out in a village in Que Son valley south of them. Because of Roger's previous experience with C.I.D., and the fact that the squad of soldiers was pulling similar CAP duty, the Battalion asked Roger to assist in the investigation. He was choppered to the village two days after the massacre had happened. His chopper landed in the small, dusty village where the soldiers had been butchered. The bodies had been dusted off the day before, but the village had been sealed off and Vietnamese military investigators were busy checking things out. Roger was led to a large bamboo hootch where the massacre had taken place. He entered the hootch and found the interior pierced by strands of sunlight filtering through cracks and bullet holes in the siding. The floor was scattered with woven mats and blood stains where the men had died.

The investigation was fairly simple. The investigators quickly pieced together a story from evidence gathered at the scene, evidence which included a pipe, a couple bags of grass and a box of Kool's containing several pre-rolled joints. Information gleaned from several of the men in the platoon who had stayed behind and through interrogation of the villagers helped confirm what had happened. For several weeks, members of the platoon had been making patrols at night outside of their base camp. Instead of following their patrol route, they had holed up in the hootch to get loaded on what the Vietnamese called "happy smoke." They had been calling in sitreps at the prearranged times to give the illusion that their patrol was progressing on schedule, but it was all staged hoax. They would spend several hours passing joints and getting stoned silly, then they would gather themselves together and head back to their perimeter.

The local V.C. had been watching them each night while the G.I.'s got loaded and laughed their heads off. About two weeks into their predictable ritual, the V.C. sneaked up to the hut and slit the throat of the guard who had dozed off. Three V.C., each armed with fully loaded AK-47's with thirty round banana clips, kicked open the door and sprayed the room with fully automatic fire, killing nineteen men. When they had stripped the bodies of weapons and valuables, they faded back into the night.

Roger spent a day assisting the investigation, then choppered back to his CAP unit. He was incensed at the sheer stupidity of these soldiers. If anyone had died senselessly in Vietnam, it was they, as far as Roger was concerned. Roger returned to his new unit more determined than ever to drive the object lesson home, so his men would not repeat the same fatal mistake. He also returned with a fresh vengeance to take the war to Charlie.

Roger decided that the best way to rekindle an aggressive spirit in the men was to build their confidence through results. He started taking the men out on night patrols around their cluster of villages. He was determined to reverse the "retreat" mentality by fighting back. Roger wasn't about to peacefully co-exist with the enemy. He knew you could only play that game for so long before Charlie broke the rules.

Over the ensuing weeks, the V.C. body count steadily mounted, and with it, the morale of his men. Roger's nighttime tactics had caught the enemy completely off-guard. The Marines were no longer sticking to their predictable rhythms, and the CAP unit's aggressive posture had thrown the enemy off balance.

Roger's night time forays were purposely irregular. Their cadence was uncertain, so Charlie couldn't second guess them. Roger was now playing Charlie's own game by his rules - the same deadly game of cunning and stealth. The Viet Cong had also grown comfortable with the lack of contact, and had been lulled into a false security. Through default, Charlie had been allowed to roam the countryside with impunity, but, suddenly that had all changed.

Roger's squads alternated their ambush patrols. When he wasn't walking point, he took out small "killer teams" of two or three men. Roger drew on his past experience from recon patrols in the dense jungles up north, and from instincts he'd refined on countless points, to kill his enemy. The killer teams would steal through the night and strike the enemy with hit-and-run tactics, then melt back into the countryside before Charlie could re-group. Night after night, Roger's "killer teams" slithered through the paddy fields and jungle fringes in their nocturnal hunt for the enemy. They would wait in silence for hours at the edge of a village for the V.C. to make their appearance, then they would spring their trap. They would watch for several V.C. to enter a hootch, then they would set a claymore to take them out when they emerged. They would lay half-buried in the weeds at the edge of a rice field and wait for several V.C. to make their way along an open dike. They would open up on them and then melt back into the safety of the jungle.

By the second month after he took control, Roger's CAP unit had run up the highest kill ratio in Second CAG. Their area of operation was quickly being sanitized of V.C. The combat proficiency and teamwork had wielded Roger's CAP squads into a small, but formidable fighting force. Their effectiveness had put a serious dent in Viet Cong activities in the area. As a result, the enemy had placed a price tag of a couple of hundred dollars on Roger's head. This was a substantial sum by Vietnamese standards. To a Vietnamese peasant, two hundred dollars was comparable to several years' worth of wages. An enterprising rice farmer could buy a new hootch and a sturdy team of buffalo with the bounty, and still have pocket money left over.

News that a V.C. contract had been put out on Roger's life gave him a greater aura of respect in the eyes of his men. It also gave him a sense of personal pride and satisfaction - not only because the reward money was a token of how devastating his presence had been to the enemy, it was also a lethal reminder of how many V.C. he had helped waste. Three years had separated him from the deaths of so many of his friends, but time had not diminished the hatred he felt for the enemy.

The team spirit was back and the small mobile CAP squads were functioning like a well oiled machine. Two of the squads were stationed in outlying villages a couple of klicks away. Roger took control of the third squad in a village south of Hoi An, along the Song Cai River. After the initial shake-down and attitude adjustments, each of the Marines soon found his combat equilibrium.

Like most of the small units he had worked with, his new CAP squad was an exotic blend of personalities and racial backgrounds:

Jesus Ortez was a Mexican-American from El Paso, Texas. He was medium in height, with a muscular build. He had reddish brown skin and jet black eyes. Ortez was a no nonsense kid who didn't take anything from anybody.   He had gotten drunk with several buddies after graduating from boot camp and had a large picture of an eagle with a snake in its mouth tattooed on his back.   He said he had gotten the inspiration from the Mexican flag.   Ortez was the squad's M-60 gunner, and could trim a killing zone with the best of them.

Gabriel Puentes, or "Gopher" as the rest of the squad called him, was a small, wiry Latino from Fresno, California.   Ortez and he had gone through Pendleton together and had become fast friends.   Gopher had the cunning and agility of a sewer rat.   At 5' 3", he was the smallest man in the squad, but he had the ferociousness of a pit bull.   Ortez had pulled him out of more than one fight because Puentes didn't like somebody making fun of his size.   When referring to Puentes, Ortez use to say, "Hey, man, it's not the size of the dog in the fight that counts, it's the size of the fight in the dog!"   Gopher had gotten his nickname because he was always eager to check out any tunnels they uncovered, armed only with a flashlight and a .45 automatic.   He had earned the reputation of being the squad's resident tunnel rat.   Just the thought of descending into one of those subterranean nightmares sent cold shivers through most Marines, so Puentes' fearlessness had won the respect of the others.

The squad's radioman was a blond haired kid from Kailua, Hawaii.   He had spent most of his teen years on a skateboard or surfboard cruising the sidewalks and beaches around Oahu.   Jack had done little more than surf for a year after graduation, picking up odd jobs for spending money until the Honolulu draft board caught up with him.   He had picked up the nickname "Wolfman Jack" after the popular, southern

California D.J. The name fit him like a glove, not only because he was the squad's radioman, but because he did a great impersonation with his, "It's the dog man. How's your boogalou hangin'?"

Francis "Monk" Carpulucci was a nineteen year old Italian from Chicago. Francis was soft spoken and as steady as a crowbar stuck in cement. He reminded Roger a lot of Danny. Francis never said much, but Roger knew that he was the kind of Marine who would always be there when you needed him. He was also deeply religious and took his Roman Catholicism seriously. It was rumored that he had almost gone into the priesthood. Francis wouldn't confirm it, but the rumor had earned him the nickname "Monk", just the same. Monk was the squad's "blooper" man.

Carl Jenkins was a pale looking kid with shiny black hair, from some podunk mining town in West Virginia. There wasn't much to look forward to in his Appalachian valley after high school except an uncertain future in one of the coal shafts, so Carl enlisted in the Marines. Carl was not particularly gifted in the I.Q. department. He was plodding in nature with a slow, sauntering gait. Jenkins also bore a remarkable facial resemblance to Goofy. His one outstanding quality as a Marine was the fact that he was an expert shot with a weapon. He had had plenty of shooting experience in the wooded hills where he grew up, fine-tuning his marksman skills shooting squirrels and varmints with an old single shot .22 his grandfather had given him on his thirteenth birthday. At fifteen, he'd graduated to a Thirty-ought-six and was regularly taking down deer during hunting season.

The squad's Corpsman was called, "Doc". They were all affectionately called, Doc. At twenty-three, Doc was the oldest man in Roger's CAP platoon. Doc had three years of college under his belt in Indiana when he decided to drop out and hitchhike to California to "find himself." That's also where his draft board found him. He didn't want to be a grunt, and he wasn't a strong enough conscientious objector to flee to Canada, so he joined the Navy thinking he would never set foot in 'Nam. After boot camp, he ended up at Great Lakes Naval Training Center, training to be a Corpsman. After graduation, he received his orders assigning him to the "Fleet Marine Force." That was the equivalent of saying he would be a Corpsman, tending Marine grunts in Vietnam. Doc didn't like it much, but stoically concluded it was fate and there was nothing he could do about it. He had served with a line company in Quang Tri and had been wounded twice, before volunteering to serve with a CAP unit. Doc was the squad's healer, confidant, counselor and father figure. His self-sacrificing character gave consolation and strength to the others. The Corpsmen were often the fine line between life and death and gave the others a unique sense of security. Doc was their lifeline to the world and they always knew that he'd be there if they needed him.

"Spider" was a lanky black rifleman from Oakland, California. He had long muscular arms and legs and looked like he could have been a pro basketball player. It was his long limbs that won him the handle, "Spider." His Dad had migrated to the Pacific Northwest from Mississippi during the late thirties to work in the shipyards at Bremerton Seattle. When the war broke out, he joined the Navy and ended up loading ammunition ships at Port Chicago. The only action he saw was in the aftermath of the big explosion that devastated the Port in 1944. After the war, he settled in

Oakland and got married.

Ronald Brown, alias "Spider", was born in 1951. Growing up as a black kid in the East Bay during the turbulent Sixties wasn't easy. The racial tensions and peer pressure of the times were pretty tough on a black kid's attitude.   Oakland was the birth place of the militant "Black Panther Party" and the soapbox for Huey Newton and Eldridge Clever. He went through puberty under the shadow of their defiance against white racism and support of black pride. Martin Luther King, Jr.'s assassination and the race riots in Watts, Newark, Detroit and Hunter's Point had helped fuel the backlash of blacks. The constant political agitation in People's Park and along Telegraph Avenue, a few blocks away in Berkeley didn't help matters.

Ronald had been especially bitter about the inevitability of the draft. It seemed like blacks were getting sucked up in disproportionate numbers by the "green-machine" to feed its insatiable appetite. Whole blocks were being emptied of draft age adolescents. When he hit eighteen, Ron decided to join the Marines instead, just to throw the first punch.

He had excelled in boot camp - more out of black pride than red-blooded patriotism. He wanted to be better than any white boys. What he encountered in the Corps started to smooth the rough edges off his defiance. The Corps didn't seem to care he was black. For the first time in his life, he excelled at something that won the respect of others, even whites. By the time he had reached Roger's CAP squad, his defiance was subdued. The kinship and closeness forged in combat was a great leveler of racism. Blacks, whites, Hispanics, orientals and red-necks shared a unique bond in the field that transcended racial barriers and cultural differences.   Spider was one of the more dependable members of the squad.

The Viet Cong had tightened their tactics as a result of the CAP squad's effectiveness. Roger's small killer teams were still wreaking havoc on the V.C. in lightning "hit and run" ambushes at night. The Marines had moved from the safe predictability of their villes to aggressive predators who stalked the night. Spider and Monk became Roger's main men on his night killer teams. Each of them had honed their killing instincts under the watchful tutelage of Roger. Working together, they were racking up more confirmed kills than many line companies saw in weeks.

Chapter 18

"Any suggestions?" Roger asked Spider and Monk. The three of them had gathered to finalize plans for their night killer team. They were dressed in camouflaged fatigues, and floppy bush hats. Their faces and hands were smeared with camouflaged grease sticks. Monk was carrying an M-79 with flechette rounds and an extra bandolier of high explosives for back-up. Roger had a Savage 12-gauge shotgun. The barrel had been sawed off for better mobility and spread of the .00 riot shot in his shells. The shotgun was modified so he could carry the maximum number of shells. Spider was carrying one of the light weight AR-15's with the shorter barrel and magazines taped back-to-back for faster reinsertion. Each was carrying two frags and a claymore. They were going light for agility and speed.

"It's been a week since we scouted out the river along this stretch," Spider suggested as he pointed to an area on the map. "Maybe we can catch some dinks crossing at night or trying to move contraband up the river by sampans," he added.

"Whaddaya think, Monk?" Roger asked.

"Sounds good to me. Its kinda marshy closer to the coast and the way Highway One dog-legs here," he traced a curve in the road with his forefinger, it forms a good spot for them to be operating in. We always seem to get our limit when we snoop around in this pocket between the highway and the river. We've got excellent cover along the bank. If there are any V.C. coming across, they won't know what hit 'em," he concluded.

"Tag 'em and bag 'em," Spider smiled. "That's what we're here for," he commented.

"Yeah," Monk nodded in agreement.

It was 2200 hours when the three men slipped out of their compound and moved through the shadows of their village, before striking out across a series of fields. The point on the river they had selected was three clicks away.

It was a muggy, moonlit night with puffy, cumulus clouds drifting beneath a luminous orb. The three men moved quickly through the night, pausing every so often to look and listen - sometimes waiting in the shadows for the moonlight to disappear behind the clouds. They had traversed this area many times and almost could do it in their sleep. They knew every trail, hideout, and alternative route in case something went wrong. Once they had committed themselves to the mission, they assumed a vow of silence. Movements were orchestrated with familiar hand signals and fluid body language, which each understood.

The night air was choked with humidity, making breathing difficult. Even nearing midnight, they felt like they were sucking air through mud. The air was so saturated with moisture, it seemed to muffle sounds, like they were being swallowed up in a vacuum.

They moved at a brisk pace for over an hour, before they reached a thick wall of leafy brush and coconut palms along the river.

Roger settled onto his haunches just inside the wall of vegetation above the river bank. He motioned to his men that they would move through the foliage and set up an ambush site covering the river. The spot he had selected was a couple of hundred meters down stream from a small fishing village.

The three men quietly pushed through the leafy tangle for about thirty meters until they reached the opposite edge. The air hung in hot layers like a heavy blanket over the river. The rich smell of river bottom choked the air. The grassy bank was about twenty feet above the water's surface. The bank sloped down to the water's edge in a gradual descent.

Roger scanned the river in both directions, but nothing was moving. A familiar abandoned hut was sitting about fifty meters upstream. A crude, wooden foot bridge, perched on short stilts, ran from the back of the bamboo hut about twenty feet out in the river. What caught Roger's attention was a flicker of yellow light glowing through a woven matt hanging over one of the windows.

"Might be V.C.," Roger whispered, "let's check it out." He gestured toward the hut. They moved cautiously along the fringe of vegetation until they reached the hut. Monk hung back to keep them covered. Roger and Spider inched closer to get a "look-see." They reached the side of the hootch and stopped to listen. Roger could just make out some low muffled sounds coming from the inside. He gestured with his hand that he was going to get a better look. As delicately as possible, he pushed aside the woven mat covering the window with the tip of his shotgun and peeked through the crack. He was shocked by what he saw. In the warm yellow glow of a kerosene lantern, he could see a nude Vietnamese woman lying on her back on a wooden bed staring at the ceiling. The woman had her right arm cocked with the back side of her hand resting on her forehead. She was wearing a black shirt which was open, exposing her breasts. A North Vietnamese soldier was sitting on the end of the bed pulling up his dull green trousers. Another soldier was leaning up against the wall next to the bed fully dressed and smoking a cigarette. He was looking at the woman with a blank expression on his face. His AK-47 was slung over his shoulder. He was wearing his web gear. Roger looked back at the other soldier who was buttoning his fatigue shirt. His pith helmet, assault rifle and web-gear were propped at the end of the wooden bed.

"Bastards," Roger thought. *"They just raped some innocent village girl,"* he concluded. Roger stepped back into the shadows along side of the hootch and indicated to Spider that he was going in through the front door. He instructed Spider to cover him. Roger rounded the corner and positioned himself firmly on the dirt foot path leading up to the rickety, wooden door. He took a deep breath and gripped the slide action of his pump shotgun. He glanced back at Spider who had his M-16 in firing position right behind him, then kicked the door in. *"DUNG LAI! DUNG LAI!"* (Don't move!), Roger shouted. The sudden break-in momentarily paralyzed the soldiers with fright. A split second elapsed, then the

soldier leaning against the wall jerked upright and tried to unsling his weapon. Roger's eyes darted between the soldiers. Events were racing out of control, again. Roger pivoted with his shotgun and fired. **"BOOM!"** the blast slammed the man against the bamboo siding, blowing a hole through his chest. He let out a gasp and slid down the wall leaving a bright red smear. "Click, click," Roger worked the slide action, quickly chambering a fresh shell. He turned to the man beside the bed just as he reached his AK-47 and started to bring it up. **"BOOM!"** The .00 shot shredded the man's face and chest and somersaulted him off the end of the bed. Roger's ears were ringing from the confined noise of the blasts. "Click, click," he mechanically chambered another round. The room was filled with gun smoke.

He turned to look at the young women who had brought her right arm over her breasts in shock. For a split second, Roger felt good that he had rescued someone innocent like Mai. He felt sorry for the young woman. But the glare on the woman's face didn't add up. Roger started to lower his shotgun when the women reached under the straw mat she was laying on and started to pull out a pistol. Everything had slowed to slow motion. *"You rotten bitch!"* Roger swore to himself as he squeezed the trigger, hitting her in the chest. The impact of the blast on her small frame shoved her off the bed and left her crumpled in the corner.

All of a sudden, rifles crackled across the river. Spider was screaming. The enemy had opened up on the hut. Roger threw himself to the dirt floor as bullets splintered through the brittle siding. Spider opened up on fully auto until he spent a magazine, then inverted it and emptied the twin into the treeline across the river. Monk had responded with the blooper and lobbed several rounds into the miniature blinking strobes.

When Roger hit the dirt floor, he fell across the hind end of a mangy looking dog. The dog let out a whelp, bit the back of Roger's hand, then backed under the wooden pallets of the bed. Roger turned to his side to see the dog snarling at him with a rabid look on his face. His lips were curled in a vicious snarl, exposing yellowed fangs covered with foam and dripping saliva. The dog was staring at Roger and quivering as he defecated in place.

Roger unholstered his .45, cocked the hammer and blew the dog back under the bed. Roger reached under and grabbed one of the dog's legs. He pulled the remains out, hoping that there was enough left to do an autopsy on it, to see if it had rabies.

Less than a minute had passed, when the firing stopped and the enemy force across the river broke contact. Spider crawled into the hootch and found Roger holding what was left of the dog. "You O.K.?" Spider asked. "What happened?"

"Damn dog bit me," Roger held up his hand to show the small puncture wounds.

"What the....," Spider swore as his eyes locked on the body of the woman. "Did the gook chick get in the way, Sergeant?" Spider questioned.

"Can ya believe, she tried to shoot me with a pistol," Roger pointed to a Chinese K-54 pistol laying beside the wooden bed. "She wasn't being raped, Spider. She was gettin' it on with the two soldiers. She was doing her patriotic part to build the morale of the heroic freedom fighters," Roger added sarcastically. "We'd better search the bodies most ricky-ticky and get outta here before the bad guys decide to come back." They rummaged through the clothing of the two soldiers and checked the clothing of the woman which was neatly piled in the corner. They found a picture of her in an officer's uniform and a document showing that she was a nurse. Their unauthorized R & R had cost them dearly. After gathering the weapons, they slipped into the darkness and headed back through the night.

They later determined that an NVA unit had been brought into their area of operation as a back-up for the local Viet Cong. They were in the process of crossing the river when Roger's killer team found the threesome in the hut. The woman was a North Vietnamese nurse who would have killed Roger quicker than a blink if she had had half the chance.

The following morning at their CAP compound, Sergeant Tre, Roger's Popular Forces counterpart, informed him that the price on Roger's head had been raised to five hundred U.S. dollars. Sergeant Tre also informed Roger that his men had pieced together a number of rumors and bits of information from relatives in the surrounding villages that a large force of Viet Cong had set up a base camp just outside of their area of operation. Word was, the Viet Cong were planning an operation to isolate and destroy Roger's three CAP squads.

Roger knew that he would have to act first, before Charlie had time to launch their ambush. He contacted Second CAG Headquarters and informed them of the situation. Because of ongoing operations, the Battalion was short of reserves. His Company commander told Roger to hang tight and pull back his patrols. He said that CAG headquarters would mount an operation when they could get ARVN and South Korean Marines to back them up. Roger knew that his men could do the job themselves, if they had the element of surprise on their side.

He was so insistent, that his company commander finally relented. His words to Roger were, "If everything goes all right, we can all take some of the credit. If you screw up, I don't know anything about it. Do I make myself clear, Sergeant?"

Roger immediately began preparations to hit the base camp. But the following morning, he got word from Da Nang that the tests on the dog carcass had come back positive. The dog was rabid. He would have to undergo the painful series of rabies injections to protect him from the disease. Without the excruciating series of shots, he would die of hydrophobia in a couple of weeks. This turn of events put a serious crimp in his plans to attack the Viet Cong base camp.

For the first six days, Doc administered the shots in the field. But the injections in the stomach were excruciatingly painful. The large gauge needle left huge black and blue welts. The medicine made Roger sicker than a dog. After six injections, Doc sent Roger to the aid station in Hoi An to finish the series. Before he left, he instructed his men and Sergeant Tre to continue their preparations to take out the V.C. base camp.

When Roger reached the aid station, his CAG company commander was there waiting for him. He took one look at Roger and said, "Helle, every gook in the area has been tryin' ta kill ya and they've had about as much luck as a blind man crossing a freeway at rush hour. But, some runny nose mutt gets ya with one bite!" His company commander busted up at the absurdity of the situation.

"Hey, Doc," Roger asked, "If I bite someone, they'd have to get rabies shots, wouldn't they?" Roger was determined to get his CO back.

"Well, yeah, that's right, Sergeant, " the Corpsman responded.

Roger looked at the Captain with a mischievous grin on his face.

His C.O. didn't say another word. He never teased him again about the dog.

After eight more days of injections, Roger's stomach felt like he had been laying under a pile-driver. "Hey, Doc, those horse needles are killing me. How would you like me stickin' those suckers in your stomach?"

"Sorry, Sergeant. I'm not the one who got bit by the dog, remember?" The Corpsman said as he gave him a sadistic grin.

"Well, at least this is the last one," Roger noted.

"Not quite," the Corpsman responded. "You've got another seven to go."

"You're just jokin', right?" Roger had a worried look on his face. "I thought you only had to get fourteen of those things," Roger whined.

"No, I'm serious. Back in the States, they only give fourteen shots in the series, but here we had two Marines die of rabies afterwards. I guess gook rabies is pretty heavy-duty stuff, so we've been giving twenty-one, just to make sure."

On the twenty-first day, the Corpsman came in with his stainless steel tray holding the injection paraphernalia. "One more, Sergeant, and you're outta here."

"Wait a minute," Roger protested, "I've already had twenty-one. Check out the knots on my stomach!"

"We only count twenty, Sergeant Helle," the corpsman was enjoying this. "Better safe than sorry," he smiled as he swabbed Roger's stomach with an alcohol prep.

"That's easy for you to say," Roger grimaced as the Corpsman injected the needle into his stomach one last time.

After his twenty-two shots, Roger returned to his CAP compound feeling like someone had beaten his stomach with a baseball bat. He immediately resumed his plans to attack the V.C. base camp. It had been quiet during his absence, but Roger knew that it was only the calm before the storm. Precious time was running out.

Roger and Sergeant Tre took a walk down the main street of their village. It was a sizzling hot day. The air smelled of baked dirt. They went from door to door, chatting with familiar faces and stopping in some of the stalls to talk to the villagers. They were trying to gather any loose talk or bits of information about what the V.C. were up to.

Roger and Tre started across the street followed by a gaggle of chortling children who wanted Trung Si Helle to give them candy or cigarettes. Roger was smiling and talking to Sergeant Tre, as he reached into his shirt pocket to pull out some chewing gum to give to the kids. Several mothers in black pajamas and conical hats were standing in the doorway of a nearby hootch, smiling and talking.

He bent over to push a stick of gum into one of the kids mouths when he caught something out of the corner of his eye that seemed out of place. A Vietnamese man was leaning casually against the side of a thatched hootch, staring at him. He was wearing an olive drab poncho liner which hung down below his knees. Roger straightened slightly, but tried to act like everything was normal.

The man was staring intently at Roger.   The intensity of the look triggered Roger's instincts.   The man didn't fit the normal rhythms of the village.   His symmetry was off.   Roger's reflexes poised to respond. Out of the corner of his eye, he detected the man shift his body weight and gently push himself away from the wall.   There was a movement almost imperceptible under the man's plastic poncho.   Roger looked up.   The normal movement of the village continued around him. The kids were still laughing and grabbing.   The women were still smiling and talking.

"The children," Roger thought.   That's when he saw the tip of the flash suppressor protruding from beneath the hem of the man's poncho.   Roger glanced at the children and shoved them aside with his arm. Sergeant Tre flinched with alarm.   Roger's eyes shot back, locking onto those of the V.C.   The barrel of the AK-47 was coming up when Roger reached for his .45 automatic.   He pulled his pistol out in a smooth draw. He cocked his knees, holding the pistol with both hands, and fired.

"BAM!" The slug hit the man in the center of his forehead, blowing off the top of his skull in an explosion of brain and bone.   The man flew back, dropping the assault rifle.   The kids screamed and ran for cover. Sergeant Tre blew a whistle to summon help.   Roger walked toward the body.   It was laying in a shallow trench between the hootches.   The dead V.C. was staring at the dirt with a surprised look on his face.

"V.C. try to collect money on your head, Trung Si Helle," Sergeant Tre said as he pointed to his head for effect.

"Not this time, Sergeant Tre," Roger added as he

holstered his pistol.   "We're going to have to move quick.   If the V.C. are this desperate, to try a hit in broad daylight, it means that they're getting ready to make their move," Roger noted.   "We're going to have to hit them before they hit us, Sergeant Tre."

"Yes, Sergeant, I think you are right," Tre responded.

"Are your men ready, Tre?"   Roger looked the Sergeant in the face.   They had grown close over the few weeks Roger had known him.   Tre was one of the most dedicated Vietnamese soldiers he had met.   His brother had died in the South Vietnamese army, fighting in Pleiku during the '68 Tet offensive.   Tre hated the Viet Cong with a passion.

"My men are ready and eager, Trung Si Helle." Tre gave Roger a proud, determined look.

"O.K. then, we go in the day after tomorrow."

Chapter 19

The evening of the village shoot-out, Roger gathered Sergeant Tre, his PF squad leaders, and the squad leaders from the other two Cap squads under his command. They spent several hours fine-tuning their plans for the attack on the V.C. base camp. They would combine the thirty-five men from the PF platoon and the forty-five men from Roger's three squads of Marines. They planned to sweep west in two columns, to a remote pocket tucked into the hilly terrain six klicks from their CAP compound. They would move out in the evening of the following day in a two pronged assault which would surround the suspected base camp in a double envelopment.

The following afternoon, the men readied their gear, cleaned weapons and rehearsed the plan of attack. Then the Marines had assembled in the main CAP compound in Roger's village.

"...Somethin's happening here...what it is ain't exactly clear...There's a man with a gun over there, tellin' me I got to beware.....We better stop! Children, what's that sound?   Everybody look what's goin' down......Paranoia strikes deep, into your life it will creep..."

Wolfman was listening to a Panasonic tape recorder while the squad inventoried their gear.

"Man, I used to listen to that song back in the world, and it sounded a whole lot different back there," Doc noted absently.

"Know what ya mean," Spider responded, as he pushed .223 rounds into one of his magazines. "The pigs was the man with the guns. They was always hasslin' the brothers," he paused. "Not so sure who the man is any longer."

"Things are a lot different in the 'Nam," Ortez added.

"You, got that right, my man," Gopher said. "After what happened in the village yesterday, you gotta wonder who the man is."

"I hear ya, Gopher," Spider agreed.

At 0800 hours, the two platoons assembled. They were pumped up and ready for action. The squad leaders gave the men a final once over, then the two columns moved out. The PF platoon took the northerly route while Roger's Marines headed south.

The weather was at the muggy transition time between the end of the dry season and the advent of the rainy. Although the rains had not yet started, the sky was threatening and overcast with dirty grey clouds. The night was hot and sultry. The smell of rain was in the air.

The columns moved with precision and stealth

through the darkness, keeping in contact by radio. By 0330 hours, they had moved into position. They fanned out in a broad horseshoe ambush, just inside a treeline surrounding an open field about a hundred meters in diameter. The pungent smell of wood smoke and fish sauce floated from the clearing. There were no sounds coming from the camp, but they could tell that the V.C. were there. They could smell them.

Roger and Sergeant Tre had positioned their M-60's and fire teams in an L-shaped ambush with the open end butting up to a steep hill. They were concealed in double tier canopy with an open killing field in front of them. The jungle was dripping with moisture which had condensed on the leaves in the early morning air. Crickets, mosquitos, and flying insects whined and buzzed around them.

The field was covered with shoulder high stands of elephant grass, stubby trees and trampled down areas. Camouflaged netting and brush was set up to conceal the base camp from spotter planes.

The men waited and listened. They would strike at first light, when they could see what they were shooting at.

Between 0400 and 0430 hours, several V.C. squads came back from patrols. At one point, the rustling of brush sounded, as a squad of eight V.C. approached down an animal track. They passed within inches of Roger's men who were lurking in the foliage. Much to their relief, the V.C. passed by. The V.C. were probably too worn-out from the patrol to notice the Marines. All they wanted was some hot rice and tea.

The camp was a staging area for a platoon of main force Viet Cong and a bivouac site for other V.C. and NVA units passing through the area. The local V.C.

would serve as escorts to guide other units through the area as they filtered south. That morning, there were about sixty V.C. in the camp. Most were asleep in hammocks strung between spindly trees.

By 0450, the clearing began to lighten with the violet half lights of predawn. The camp began to stir to life. The ambushers could hear a few Vietnamese talking in a low pitch in the still morning air. It was 0455. Word was passed long the line with hand signals. They would open fire in five minutes. The Marines and PF's tensed in anticipation. Men flipped their selectors to fully automatic, machine-gunners chambered rounds and checked their belts. Men glanced at their watches, wiped sweat from their brows, took deep breaths and tightened their grips on their weapons.

"Tatow tatow tatatatat..!" At 0500, the first 60 opened up, followed immediately by an eruption of automatic fire which cut across the field at waist level. The startled V.C. bolted from their sleep and ran in a frantic free-for-all, as the machine guns and M-16's mowed them down. The withering fusillade of automatic fire chopped through the shoots of elephant grass like a weed-eater, neatly trimming the grass with a deadly manicure. "Bloop...**CRUNCH!** Bloop...**CRUNCH!** Bloop...**CRUNCH!**" the M-79 grenade launchers were lobbing rounds into the frenzy of running V.C.

"FOORWAAARD!" Roger screamed, followed by the shouts from the other squad leaders. "Yeaaah!" The Marines and PF's rushed through the grass, firing as they went. V.C. swiveled, pitched, and toppled around them. The onrushing tide of Marines stormed across the clearing, overrunning the startled V.C. in the lightning assault.

"Chieu Hoi! Chieu Hoi!" Frightened V.C. threw

down their weapons and surrendered, begging the Marines not to shoot them.

The ambush was over in a couple of minutes. The predawn attack had completely taken the enemy by surprise.   The CAP unit accounted for twenty-six confirmed V.C. kills, fifteen wounded, and ten P.O.W.'s. Only a half dozen V.C. had escaped. A quick search of the area found two blood trails leading off through the brush.

The attack was a complete success. The Cap unit had only three wounded.   Only one PF was seriously wounded. They captured numerous AK-47's, carbines, satchel charges, Chinese grenades, a 12.7 mm machine-gun and several light machine guns.   Besides the weapons, they confiscated a ton of rice in burlap bags, medical supplies, maps, important documents, and field radios.   They had effectively eliminated an entire reinforced platoon.   They had captured so many weapons and stocks of ammo, they couldn't carry it all. Some of it was blown up in place.   The rest was concealed until they could return to search the area more thoroughly in a couple of days. They loaded up what they could and started back an hour after the attack had begun.

Roger was basking in the euphoria of his unit's victory. He had worked hard to be the best Marine he could be, and he was savoring his hard earned success. It was his finest moment - his moment of triumph. He had put it to Charles the way Charles had put it to Danny and his squad - point blank, cold blooded, blunt. He felt no remorse, only stone cold satisfaction. It was payback time and he had collected, big time.

CAG   headquarters   was   stunned   by   the

overwhelming success of the CAP raid. Roger's unit had done what many larger units never did in a year. Rumors quickly trickled down through the grapevine that the Second Combined Action Group was seriously considering Roger for a battlefield commission for his leadership skills. Roger couldn't be happier.

Three days after the raid, Roger mustered his men to mount a follow-up attack on the V.C. base camp, to destroy the cache of weapons and ammunition they had left behind. Roger wanted to obliterate the base camp. They had left a number of tunnels he wanted to blow, to prevent Charlie from using the area again.

On the night before the mission, CAG headquarters radioed Roger that he was to report the following day to the Battalion CO. Roger suspected that the summons to Da Nang was to announce his commission. He was looking forward to a little time in the rear to get snockered and celebrate his anticipated appointment. Even though the mission back to the base camp was already in motion, he felt confident that he could be back in time to catch a late afternoon jeep to Da Nang.

Around 0400 hours, Roger's platoon of Marines and PF's began to assemble in the CAP compound. He had ordered each of the men to carry either a block of C-4 or at least two incendiary or white phosphorus grenades. Since he was pulling point on this mission to blow up the camp, he felt that he should set the example by carrying the most explosives. He had carefully stocked his demolition bags with four five-pound blocks of plastic explosives, six incendiary grenades, six willie-peters, a box of blasting caps, and half a dozen spare magazines. His two "demo" bags were bulging with explosives. He was obsessed with the need to finish the job this time. The raid had seemed so perfect in its execution and results. This morning's mission would be the final exclamation mark.

The men were smokin' and jokin' and fooling around with each other in the pre-dawn darkness. Their spirit's were buoyant with the thrill of victory. They were preening and strutting like prized fighting cocks, ready to get back in the ring. They were bad, and they knew it. They'd socked it to the Cong and hurt them bad. Roger's men were also savoring the fortunes of war, which had shifted so decisively in their favor.

Roger strapped down the ties on his demo-bag, made some final adjustments, then hefted one on each side, crisscrossed around his neck and shoulders. His bags looked pregnant, but he was dressing light. He was wearing camouflaged pants, a Marine utility hat, a flakjacket, and his jungle boots.

He found his men assembled in the compound, waiting for his order to move out. It was early, but the air was already humid. Only a few puffy clouds floated overhead. It promised to be another oven-broiler day, before the rains returned.

"You pullin' point with all that stuff?" Monk asked, slurping down the last of some pear juice out of a C-rat can he'd just opened with his P-38.

"Is the Pope Catholic?" Roger responded.

"Whaddaya got in that thing, a tank?" Gopher joked.

"Let's just say there's enough bang in here to finish what we started," Roger answered.

"Hey, Sarge, just make sure you're far enough away when that thing goes off, so we don't get it too," Spider teased.

"No sweatty-da, Spider. You're so damn skinny, all you have to do is turn sideways and the shrapnel won't have anything to hit!" Roger grinned. "O.K., saddle up!" he hollered.

The men quickly shifted their weight to position their rucks, then filed off with Roger in the lead. They pushed across familiar terrain, over a green tapestry of rice paddies and untilled fields. By 0730 hours, they had left the last farmable land and started into the jungle area where they had found the base camp.

The morning sun was blistering in its intensity. The sun's heat supercharged the humid air, creating a hot sticky sauna, which caused men's clothing to cling to their skin like hot fly-paper. The men were covered with sweat and brine, which burned their eyes and blurred their vision.

By 0800 hours, Roger reached the edge of a field about a hundred and fifty meters across and fifty meters wide. It funneled up to a stand of trees on the far side, and was surrounded by a thick wall of tangled brush. They were almost there. All they had to do was cross the field, break through a few yards of treeline and the clearing was on the other side.

Roger paused at the edge of the field. He carefully scanned the area before resuming point. The field was covered with knee-high grass, thickets of stubby brush, and small scrub trees. He inched forward a few meters down a trail that cut across the field, when he suddenly froze. It was barely noticeable, but his trained eye detected it. Three leaves were impaled on a short stick forming a three pointed star at ground level. Roger knew that it was a V.C. warning that a booby trap was near. He slowly crouched and ran his eyes along the ground, scrutinizing every blade of grass until he saw what he was looking for.   A taut nylon fishing line crossed the trail about twelve inches off the ground. He carefully followed the line with his finger tips.   He pushed back some blades of grass and found the booby-trap in a nearby bush. The line led to an old pineapple grenade, tucked into a bamboo cylinder, tied to a bush. The pin had been pulled. It was waiting for some unsuspecting G.I. to trip the line and snag it out of the cylinder. Once out, the spoon would fly free and the grenade would go off.

Roger stood and motioned to Monk with his hand to watch out for the booby trap. About twenty meters more, he nearly fainted from a sudden jolt of adrenalin. He had just missed stepping on a Bouncing Betty. His footfall was coming down when he noticed a bent branch just off the trail. The trip-wire was concealed in the grass. *"That was close,"* he sighed. The Bouncing Betty was designed to maim more than kill.   Once the detonator was triggered, a small, explosive charge popped the mine up to groin level where it exploded, blowing off legs and testicles. Roger marked the mine with a stick and motioned again to Monk to watch out.

His pace had slowed considerably. The morning's euphoria had evaporated as the bush reality settled in. Point was not the place to get cocky, no matter how good you were. Charlie was close and he could feel it.

It was 0815 hours. He was fifty meters from the treeline. Roger had reached a dry stream bed, about six feet across, when he paused to wipe some beads of sweat from his forehead.

"Thunk!....Thud." An object flew out of nowhere and hit him on the thigh. It bounced off of his leg and thudded into the dirt at his feet. He looked down and saw an M-26 fragmentation grenade laying on its side.

"It must have fallen off of my flakjacket," he thought. *"NO! That can't be right......It hit me....IT DOESN'T HAVE A SPOON! OOOH..."*

"BLAAM!" The orange-grey explosion kicked up a cloud of dirt and dead grass, blowing Roger backwards and riddling his body with shrapnel. He felt like he had been hit by a logging truck. He struggled to his feet in a daze.

Forty meters in front of him, an enemy soldier had stepped from the treeline with his rifle raised. It was aimed directly at him. He saw the AK-47 blink twice, just a milli-second before the rounds tore into his right elbow and stomach. He toppled backwards, landing on his demo-bags.

"Oh, God!" he panicked. His entire life flashed before him. He was seized in a swirling whirlpool which was sucking him into a vortex. He was blinking from the blood and the sun's glare. He couldn't move. The shadow of an enemy soldier towered over him. He couldn't talk. His face was hamburger. His lips were bleeding profusely. He was gulping and spitting blood. *"NOOOO!"* he cried out in silence as the soldier drove the bayonet into his stomach. It felt like he was being run through with a red hot poker.

Chapter 20

How much time had passed was unclear, but he knew one thing beyond a doubt; his entire body was convulsing with waves of pain. He was laying on his side, doubled up in a fetal position - his legs drawn up because of the intense cramping in his stomach from the AK round lodged in his upper groin and the bayonet puncture just below his navel. His blood-smeared hand could feel a moist, rubbery knot of intestine protruding from the gaping hole. In his mind, it seemed like time had ground to a slow agonizing crawl, but only a couple of minutes had passed since the shocking realization that the spoonless M-26 grenade lying in front of him had not accidently fallen from his flakjacket.

With all the determination he could muster, he struggled to one knee, then stood, reeling on unsteady legs, like the battered stance of a heavyweight just risen from the count. His was not an act of bravery, but the sheer adrenalin-induced will to survive.

Blood seeped from dozens of shrapnel wounds peppering his body. The entire front of his body was covered with blood, some areas already caked and coagulating in the intense heat. His right arm dangled limply at his side, his elbow shattered by the impact of the first round. The skin on his left inner arm, shoulder, and neck were still burning from the molten phosphorous which had leaked when a shard of shrapnel ruptured one of the Willie-Peter canisters in his demo pack. The remains of his fatigue pants were drenched nearly black from blood. They hung in tattered shreds from legs which had taken the full force of the grenade blast. He didn't know it then, but both legs were fractured in several places. Bloody pockmarks and jagged lacerations covered the length of his legs where chunks of flesh had been gouged out by the blast.

Half-coherently, Roger began the longest trek of his life. Still clutching the sticky knot of intestine trying to balloon from his belly, he half-limped, half-stumbled back to his men, back to safety. The pain was excruciating. Every nerve in his body screamed in agony, but he kept going. One desperate, all-consuming thought drove him on; *"If I can just reach my men, I might make it."* But, he also knew, too, that his life force was draining from him faster than his effort to reach his perimeter. He covered only a few yards when he started to drift. He stumbled and fell, sending sharp jolts of pain through his body.

Again, he somehow struggled to his feet, tightly gripping his stomach, as warm blood oozed between his fingers. He pushed himself forward across the no-man's-land, only vaguely aware of the random rifle reports around him. He was exhausted and reaching the limits of his endurance. Again he fell, and again he rose to his feet and propelled himself forward for one final attempt - just a few feet more, but he could go no further. He started to pass out, then collapsed in a state of semi-shock from the loss of blood and traumatic wounds covering his body.

He was sprawled on his back, in stunned silence, for what seemed an eternity. He lay there staring skyward through tear filled eyes, seeing only those same graceful clouds drifting high overhead. He closed his eyes and wondered, *"Why now? This is it,"* he concluded, half-afraid to let go, half-relieved that the torment was coming to an end. A tumble of tortured thoughts cascaded through his mind - sorrowful memories of another place half a world away, painful thoughts of fractured dreams and youthful innocence, lost before its time...

The sound of the grenade's concussion caused Roger's squad to hit the deck. Only Monk had seen the blast and Roger's being blown backwards. He had watched with relief as Roger rose to his feet. He wiped his brow and whispered incredulously, "Man, I just don't believe this. That is one lucky sucker!" But his relief was short lived. Roger had no sooner gained his footing when Monk saw him jerked backwards, followed by the distinctive report of AK rounds. "Damn!" he swore in frustration, feeling helpless and unable to respond for fear of tripping a full scale ambush.

He stared to his front, transfixed in horror, at the sight of an NVA soldier, standing over the spot where Roger had gone down. The scene was almost hypnotic, as he watched the figure raise his bayonetted assault rifle skyward. "Jesus," he muttered. "He's going to kill him." The sight of the plunging bayonet was too much for the Corporal to stand by and do nothing. Ambush or not, he wasn't going to let that gook get away with it. Monk took aim with his M-16 and squeezed off a burst which tore into the khaki clad soldier, lifting him off his feet and hurling him backwards.

"C'mon, Doc, lets get him." Without questioning, the two Marines bolted from their position, under the covering fire of the other men and darted for their fallen Sergeant, in a low crouch. They were nearly out of breath when they reached Roger's body. Doc clutched Roger's flakjacket while Monk grabbed Roger's left wrist.

"Careful...easy does it!" Doc instructed as they secured Roger's body.

They dragged his mangled body back across the field to the safety of their lines. Roger's team and the PF's had deployed in a tight protective perimeter, concealed by scrub and secondary growth. The enemy had chosen not to pursue the matter, and had melted back into the densely packed jungle on the opposite side of the field.

No sooner had they reached their men, when the desperate fight to save Roger began. Doc tore into his medical kit and extracted a shot of morphine which he promptly injected into Roger's thigh, then attached the empty syrette to Roger's fatigues. He then tied off the steady stream of arterial bleeding from his right elbow with a green tourniquet. The wound looked like raw hamburger embedded with fragments of splintered bone and exposed tendons. There was no way he could clean and debride the shattered arm properly in the field. All he could do was wrap it with compresses. Roger was covered with so many wounds, it was impossible to bandage them all. Only the major bleeders got immediate attention. Everyone was contributing their field dressings to help stop the bleeding.

"Is he gonna make it?" Jenkins questioned.

"Shut up!" Doc snapped, as he tied off another compress.

"He doesn't look good," Jenkins shook his head.

"You heard me," Doc warned.

"Yea, why don't you quit beatin' your gums, JERKins, and press on this compress!" Carpulucci ordered.

"My name's not Jerkins", Jenkins protested.

"Then stop actin' like one," Monk snorted.

"I'm sorry, Doc. I didn't mean nothin'," Jenkins apologized.

Roger was only semi-conscious of the motions and sounds around him. Everything seemed to be swirling in a weird trance-like ballet. "Gotta get a chopper," Roger groaned.

"Keep quiet!" the normally passive Corpsman ordered.

Roger could hear the static rasp of the radio as it crackled to life. Wolfman pressed the side bar of the handset and spoke, "Gringo One, this is Gringo Two. Gringo One this is Gringo Two. Do you read, over?"

"Roger, Gringo Two. What's your status?"

"We need an immediate dust off. Do you copy, over?" The radio gave an uncooperative hiss as the incoming voice broke off. D.J. adjusted the squelch knob as he coaxed the PRC-25, "C'mon baby, don't quit on me now," he muttered to himself.

"Say again, Gringo Two," the voice came through clear.

"We need a dust-off, Gringo One! Our sergeant

is hit bad!" Wolfman shouted into the mike.

"Can't do. All available choppers are committed. Have one outbound in about 45 minutes, over."

"Damm it, we need a dust-off now, you mother, or our sergeant isn't going to make it! Do you read me?"

An agonizing delay followed before the radioman came back. "Read you five by five, Gringo Two. Gotta hold of a supply chopper enroute to Da Nang. He's diverting to your position. About ten klicks out. ETA in five minutes. Wants you to mark with yellow smoke. Best we can do Gringo Two, over."

"Roger that Gringo One, and thanks man - I owe ya."

"Good luck with your sarge, Gringo Two. Gringo One out."

The young radioman lowered the handmike and sighed a measured air of relief. "Well, that's a start," Ortez commented.

"Most definitely," Wolfman agreed, as he thought to himself, "I've had enough of this crap. If I ever get outta this stinkin' armpit, the closest this boy is ever goin to be to the action is havin' a board between his legs waitin' for a long smooth wave that ain't never goin' to quit."

While Roger's radioman was calling for a dust-off, Doc fought the clock to stabilize Roger. After securing the compresses to his arm, abdomen, and the major leg wounds, he administered a blood expander by inserting a needle into a vein on the back of his left hand and taping it down.

"His lips are turning blue, Doc," one Marine noted. His systolic pressure was dropping fast. Many of his veins had already collapsed from the loss of blood.

He had already lost well over a quart. Though still conscious, his eyes were dilated and glazing over with that glassy-eyed look of oncoming shock. Doc had to move fast. Unless he could get his falling blood pressure under control, he would slip into irreversible shock and die of kidney or liver failure in a matter of minutes.

Doc probed his arm for a good vein. "Do something useful and hold this!" he barked, as he handed Jenkins a bottle of .02 milligrams of epinephrine and saline solution and inserted the needle into his left wrist.

The enormous loss of blood had caused the vessels to automatically constrict in order to compensate for the loss. Doc injected the saline and epinephrine in the hopes of constricting his vessels again, but this time, to increase his blood pressure. "Hold it up!" Doc snapped, opening the regulator all the way as the clear fluid flowed through the plastic tubing into Roger's vein.

While an anxious squad waited for the medevac chopper, Doc took out his bayonet and a pair of tweezers and started scraping away the remaining bits of phosphorous, which were still eating into Roger's arm. Exposed to air, phosphorous burns with an insatiable heat which burns through everything, even under water. When it touches your skin, it sticks like glue and literally eats its way through your flesh, until it either burns itself out, or the oxygen is cut off. It had been known to burn itself so deeply into the skin that it smothered itself, only to re-ignite in the operating room when the surgeons opened up the wound.

"How bad is it, Doc?" Roger slurred, "am I goin to make it?" The numbing effect of the morphine had only taken the edge off the pain.

"Lay still and don't talk. You'll be O.K." Doc

tried to reassure him. But, Roger couldn't ignore the concerned look on Doc's face.

"I can hear the chopper now!" Ortez shouted. The men huddled around Roger could just make out the resonant "dhup-dhup-dhup" of the approaching Chinook in the distance, thumping through the moisture laden air.

"Trung si, Helle, Trung si, Helle," Sergeant Tre stood nearby, with tears streaming down his face.

"Spider, toss me a smoke grenade," Ortez said. A couple of seconds later there was a muffled "pop" from a smoke canister. It released thick coils of bright yellow smoke in a low stream across the ground before billowing sluggishly upwards. The din of the chopper's twin rotors grew louder as it lowered into the waiting Marines, churning up a cloud of dust and loose brush. No sooner had the landing gear of the chinook touched down, than the tail ramp lowered and the Crew Chief rushed out with a stretcher. Watch it!...easy now," Doc cautioned, as Roger's men lifted him onto the canvas stretcher, carefully maneuvering the I.V. bottles. Under the buffeting downdraft of the chopper blades, the stretcher bearers carried him up the tail-ramp and laid him on the floor of the chopper, next to one of the walls.

Still awake, but drifting in a morphine induced haze, Roger felt like he was floating in a liquid pool of his own blood. The Door-gunner glanced down at Roger with a stone cold expression, then looked away - his dispassionate face hardened against the hopeless sight of another butchered Marine, littering the floor of the chopper bay.

Against the acoustic backdrop of the slapping rotors, he could hear the hydraulic whine of the rear-ramp retracting. The fuselage began to vibrate as the pilot throttled down and increased the engine torque on the aging chinook. The twin rotors screwed faster and faster until the chopper lifted off and slowly gained altitude, as it lumbered off across the field and veered north over the treeline.

Roger had never felt so alone and lost in all his life, as he lay on the floor of the chopper bay enroute to the 95th Evac Hospital at Da Nang. Everything was a confused collage of impressions: the steady hammering of the chopper blades, the wet clinging sensation of his soaked fatigues, the freezing cold feeling from the rush of wind blowing through the open bay, the tight tearing sensation of the tourniquet, the sickening metallic taste of blood, the dull ache in his gut.

He was physically spent. His system was pleading to shut down and end the ordeal. He was so weakened from the loss of blood and the trauma of his wounds, he just wanted to close his eyes and go to sleep. Instinctively, he knew that if he shut his eyes he would never open them again. He endured the torment and fought back the tide of blackness which threatened to engulf him, as the chopper beat its way North over the pine scrub dunes and coastal paddy lands South of Da Nang.

A change in the pitch of the rotor blades caused the large chinook to gain altitude as it floated over the distinctive escarpments of Marble Mountain. Several hundred feet below, office pogues and suntanned REMFs frolicked in the incoming surf caressing the sands of China beach. To the few who even noticed, the sound of Roger's chopper beating its way overhead was just a momentary distraction from their fun in the sun. To Roger, his reality of Vietnam was as foreign to the beach bathers below as surfboards were to water buffalo.

The pilot descended towards the huge red cross painted on the helipad at the 95th Evac, and eased the chopper down before a waiting covey of medical personnel. As soon as the ramp lowered, a team of orderlies rushed into the cargo bay to retrieve Roger's stretcher. An Army nurse rushed through a series of rapid examinations with clockwork proficiency, checking his vitals with agile fingers as they carried him to a waiting gurney.

Even though he was drifting close to death, the impressions of those next few moments are indelibly etched in Roger's memory: The sweet smell of kerosene from the engine exhaust, the warm prop blast from the slow, whacking blades, the frantic flurry of orders, someone calling out his blood type, another shouting, "What's his tag read?", a female voice asking if he needed a cut down, the pulling sensation as an orderly cut away his jungle boots with surgical scissors, and the determined look of the gurney team as they pushed him across the landing pad.

Strangely, the sensation of the gurney bursting through the double doors of the E.R. caused Roger's mind to flash back for an instant to a more innocent time as a kid. Ron and he had cashed in enough coke bottles to pay for a ticket on the "Chamber of Horrors" ride at a traveling carnival. They had laughed their heads off at the garish props and loud sound effects. This time, the ride was not a laugh-filled trip through a raucous carnival ride, but a hellish descent into a charnel house.

Though gravely wounded, Roger was just another casualty among many. The receiving room was filling with casualties from fire-fights, as dust-offs steadily arrived to deposit their human cargos. The receiving room was rapidly transforming itself into a churning mass of pandemonium. Orderlies scurried to patients with bags of whole blood while nurses feverishly hooked up I.V.'s, adjusted tourniquets or sucked out trach tubes. Here and there, orderlies were cutting away mud-caked jungle boots and blood soaked fatigues, while doctors in splattered green smocks tried to stop someone's bleeding or desperately pounded on the bare chest of a young soldier whose heart had arrested.

Partly naked Marines were sprawled across wooden receiving tables, amidst an assortment of stainless steel trays, sterile utensils, and rubber tubing, while a collection of plasma bags and saline bottles dangled from overhead hooks. Some of the wounded were writhing in agony, others were screaming out for more morphine, while others were simply crying.

The interior of the ward was a grisly portfolio of snapshots. Teenage soldiers had been carried in with the shredded stumps of traumatic amputations, sucking chest wounds, and cavernous holes from gun shot and shrapnel wounds. Along one of the walls, a mound of body parts was piled on an abandoned stretcher. Soiled field dressings and discarded bandages littered the blood smeared floor. Besides the visual and audible horrors, he would never forget the nauseating smell of body fluids, paddy funk, and sour sweat which filled the room.

In one isolated corner, lay several zippered shut body bags. They were tagged and waiting for transfer to the morgue unit in Da Nang and eventual transit home. They would join the steady stream of reusable aluminum caskets flowing home to military funerals in thousands of grieving crossroads scattered across America.

The emergency room exam and X-Rays revealed a body riddled by seventy-two major shrapnel wounds, massive internal hemorrhaging from the bullet wound to his upper groin and bayonet puncture through his small intestine, a devastated right elbow in probable need of amputation, three fractures to each leg from the concussion of the grenade, and 3rd degree burns covering his upper left arm, shoulder and neck.

After having the extent of his injuries determined, Roger was wheeled into the operating room where his wounds were scrubbed and debrided, the larger pieces of shrapnel and the bullet in his stomach removed, the intestinal damage sutured, and his facial lacerations sewed up.

As the nurses arranged the trays of surgical instruments and prepared his body with antiseptic solutions and sterilized drapes, Roger felt he had lost all control of his fate. The image of the surgeon overhead, outlined against the backdrop of the bright operating lights, reminded him of the menacing shadow which had hovered over him little more than an hour before, intensifying the feeling of utter helplessness which now overwhelmed him.

The last words he would remember, as the black rubber mask covered his mouth and nose, were those of the surgeon;

"We're going to have to put you under now, son....."

Chapter 21

Roger's body was left on a gurney in the hallway outside the operating room, where they had deposited him after surgery. The team of surgeons had done everything they could to save him, but his prognosis was grave. There was little hope that the severely wounded Marine had enough strength left to make it. He had been wheeled to an isolated end of the hallway to die in peace, like a broken-down boxcar, shunted off to rust on some abandoned siding.

Years later, he learned from Gunnery Sergeant Purcell, an instructor he had befriended at C.I.D., what had happened. When Purcell had come to check on Roger's condition, he had found him in the hallway with a tagged body bag neatly draped over the foot of his gurney - grim testimony to the doctor's certainty that he wouldn't make it. He told Roger that he was so overwhelmed with shock at the sight of Roger, all he could do was stand there, crying at the foot of his gurney, saying over and over, "It's going to be all right, it's going to be all right."

In spite of the doctor's resignation, something deep inside of Roger refused to let go. His will to live was stronger than his desire to die. To the amazement of one of the orderlies, Roger was still showing vital signs when he checked to see if he had quietly passed away in his anesthetic coma.

He was transferred to an adjoining Intensive Care Unit for observation.   As far as the doctors were concerned, only time would tell whether he would make it or not.   One thing was sure - countless others, less seriously wounded than he, hadn't made it this far.

Over the next six days, Roger lingered at the point of death, slipping into, and out of, an incoherent dreamscape. His mind was a kaleidoscope of bizarre hallucinations,   ghostly   phantoms   and   tortured impressions. At times, he was falling backwards down a dark shaft.   At other times, he was standing in suspended animation, with that grenade laying at his feet, unable to move. He was screaming in his mind, straining to escape, flailing and kicking to break free, but it was like he was trying to swim through some thick fluid. No one was there to hear or help.

He spent six days of passage through this incoherent nether world, only vaguely aware of his surroundings. At one point, he remembered seeing a nurse in her starched white uniform looking down at his bed like a marble statue. He could vaguely remember pleading with her to tell him why the room was filled with a cloudy mist? - like it was some overwhelming mystery that had to be explained. He kept asking her why everything was so cloudy. It sounded to him like his voice was far away, like he was talking underwater or down a long pipe. She just stood there, deaf and dumb, staring at him. Then, he realized he was floating above her, looking down at his own body lying on the bed, and the nurse couldn't hear him because he was too weak even to speak. Once again, he lost consciousness.

It took five days for word of Roger's situation to reach his twin brother, out in the field. Ron was a forward observer with Mike Battery, 4th Battalion, 11th Marines. His battery was dug in along Highway One, outside Hoi An, about fifteen klicks south of Da Nang. Word was slow in reaching him through the Battalion Chaplain because of the usual bureaucratic ineptness of paper pushers who couldn't find their rear ends with both hands. The fact that Ron was out on an operation in the emerald paddy lands west of Hoi An slowed things, also. When word finally reached him, he caught the first available supply chopper to the 95th Evac, where he began the frantic search for his wounded brother.

It didn't take long for Ron to track down his brother. All of the nurses were more than willing to cooperate with the 6'4" Marine, fresh from the bush, standing before them still clad in his salt encrusted, sun bleached fatigues. The fierce intensity in his eyes gave sufficient warning he was not to be messed with or given the run around.

Ron soon located the Intensive Care Unit where they had placed his brother. Like most Evac-wards in 'Nam, it was the usual Quonset hut surrounded by sandbags and fifty-five gallon drums filled with dirt. It was attached in a cross formation to a central nurses' station, along with two other huts containing only the most critically wounded. Their conditions either stabilized enough on these wards to medevac them eventually to Japan, or it was the end of the line.

"Can I help you, Sergeant?" the nurse asked.

"Yes, Ma'am," Ron responded. "I'm here to see my brother, Sergeant Helle." She hesitated for a brief moment before replying. Normally, a blonde haired, round-eyed woman would have been an instant distraction to a red-blooded grunt with healthy glands like Ron, but none of those impulses mattered at the moment. "Is my brother here, Ma'am?" Ron pleaded impatiently.

She looked at him with compassion in her eyes, and with a soft voice replied, "Yes, Sergeant, he's on ward B. If you'll wait just a moment, I'll take you to him."

Before she could rise, Ron strode from the nurse's station. In an instant, he had surveyed the lay of the units with practiced eyes, and promptly headed toward the appropriate ward with the nurse at his heels.

Ron removed his utility cap as he opened the door and entered. The antiseptic smells of the ward were an ominous token of things to come. The ward was lined on both sides with ten beds covered with crisp white sheets. Each bed was filled with a gravely wounded Marine. In the center of the ward was another nurses' station. What confronted the battle hardened grunt was the most disconcerting scene he had ever witnessed.

Young men, whose limbs and faces and manhood had been blown away in a milli-second by the searing blast of shrapnel or a high velocity round, lay in quiet repose. They just lay there with catheters and trach tubes running in and out of their bodies, tethered to life support systems and I.V.'s, or suspended by trapeze cables and pulleys to stainless steel scaffolding and Stryker frames. Some had thick, mummified stumps while others lay under sheets with the bedding awkwardly depressed where limbs once had been. Others were horribly burned from ruptured gas tanks, napalm or phosphorus.

A troubled torrent of thoughts coursed through Ron's mind as he scanned each bed. *"They are just kids like me - young men a fraction of their former self. Just teenagers barely out of puberty who are never going to walk again or know a woman or hold their child or even be let out in public....God,"* he groaned, *"What kind of life do they have to look forward to? - Years of painful therapy, prosthetics, monthly disability checks, and the dismal seclusion of some lonely bedroom or forsaken V.A. ward for crippled vets? And what about my brother?"*

Unlike some of the wards with their jocular patients and lighthearted antics, this ward was tomb quiet - a reflective silence prevailed. It was almost as if a solemn refrain or mournful commentary to lost innocence hung in the air, as Ron passed each bed, unable to recognize his brother.

A doctor and nurse were standing at the far end of the ward with their backs to him. They were both looking down at a clip board. They hadn't noticed his entering the room. Ron had nearly reached them when the doctor turned. "Can I help you?" he asked in a hushed voice, as he glanced over Ron's shoulder at the first nurse entering the ward.

"I'm Sergeant Helle's brother. I want to know where he is....Now!" he demanded.

At that moment, Roger was laying a couple beds down. He had drifted in and out of his coma for days, but was conscious when his brother entered the ward.

Roger's body looked like he had been pulled from a head-on collision with a cement truck. His face was badly lacerated. It was so engorged with contusions that his eyes were swollen nearly shut. Through tiny slits, he could barely make out the image of his brother's passing by his bed. He wanted to say something, but nothing would come out.

He couldn't move or talk. He could only hear. He couldn't see what was happening, but what he overheard was like the sound of dirt falling on his own coffin.

The doctor placed his hand on Ron's shoulder and broke it to him as gently as he could, "Sergeant, I'm afraid your brother isn't going to make it. We've done all that we could. There is nothing more we can do." The nurse standing by the doctor's side placed her hand on his elbow to steady him, as she and the doctor guided him to Roger's bed.

Ron was stunned at the sight of his brother. He didn't even recognize him. His brother looked more like a butchered piece of meat than the robust Roger he had known. He was lying on the bed with his wounds exposed to the air, like a freshly autopsied cadaver in a morgue. He moved alongside of Roger's bed, unaware that Roger could see him through the tiny slits.

When the comprehension finally hit home that it was indeed his brother, hot tears began to flow down his face. The overwhelming flood of emotions was too much for him to bear. His knees buckled and he fell to the floor, burying his face in the sheets, sobbing with a gut-wrenching pathos which welled up from deep within his soul. "Oh, God, please, please save my brother," his heart pleaded.

Roger could see and hear, but he could do

nothing.   Scalding tears seeped from the slits of his eyelids.

The last thing he remembered before he blacked out was the desperate promise he made to God; "Oh, God, if there is a God...**PLEASE**...if you'll just let me live, I'll do anything you ask".....

Chapter 22

Twelve thousand miles away, a Western Union telegram arrived, notifying Roger's parents that he had been wounded in action:

MR.& MRS. HERBEN HELLE, A REPORT RECEIVED THIS HEADQUARTERS REVEALS THAT YOUR SON, SGT. ROGER LEIGH HELLE USMC, SUSTAINED INJURIES ON 13 JULY, 1970, IN THE VICINITY OF QUANG NAM PROVINCE, REPUBLIC OF VIETNAM, FROM HOSTILE FIRE WHILE ON PATROL. HE SUFFERED MULTIPLE TRAUMATIC WOUNDS FROM SHRAPNEL AND BULLETS TO ALL EXTREMITIES. IN THE JUDGEMENT OF THE ATTENDING PHYSICIAN, HIS CONDITION IS OF SUCH SEVERITY THAT HIS PROGNOSIS IS POOR. YOUR GREAT ANXIETY IS UNDERSTOOD. PLEASE BE ASSURED THAT THE BEST MEDICAL FACILITIES AND DOCTORS ARE BEING PROVIDED AND EVERY STEP IS BEING TAKEN TO AID HIM. YOU ARE ASSURED THAT HE WILL RECEIVE THE BEST OF

CARE. YOU SHALL BE KEPT INFORMED OF ALL SIGNIFICANT CHANGES IN HIS CONDITION. LEONARD F. CHAPMAN, JR. COMMANDANT OF THE MARINE CORPS.

Two days after he was placed on the I.C.U. ward, the Commandant and Sergeant Major of the Marine Corps passed through the 95th Evac, decorating wounded Marines. They could have been passing through Mongolia, as far as Roger was concerned. He was hopelessly lost in a no-man's-land of pain and drugs. He couldn't talk or move or even acknowledge their presence. Everything was blurred, like a picture out of focus. He could barely comprehend the Commandant pinning a Purple Heart on his pillow. The Sergeant Major laid a little souvenir knife and nailfile, with his name engraved on it, on his bed stand. There was something pathetic about the guys on the ward, with no hands or arms receiving one.

Wounded soldiers and Marines lingered at the point of death in the beds around him. Roger's bed was next to the nurse's station. The closer the bed was to the nurse's station, the more serious their condition. The ward was filled with others who had been delivered with horrendous burns, amputations, and traumatic disfigurements. Some were blind, others limbless, still others faceless. When the drugs wore off, men moaned and screamed from the unrelenting pain which racked their bodies. Some were barely kept alive by life support systems which drained and sucked from every orifice - sucking and pumping up and down, in and out.

Roger's battered body lay on the hospital bed with plastic tubes dangling from I.V. bottles of saline, antibiotics, Demerol and morphine. Roger was sustained by intravenous feedings through plastic tubes which injected needed nutrients into his body. Other tubes removed unwanted wastes from his bladder and bowels. Some of his wounds were covered with gauze and surgical tape, but most had been left open and raw. The doctors were reluctant to wire them shut for fear they wound turn gangrenous, if sutured shut too early. The litany of his wounds was overwhelming; seventy-two major shrapnel wounds to his legs, arms and groin; both legs and both arms were fractured in three places; a bullet shattered right elbow; perforated and torn intestines from shrapnel; a traumatic bullet entry; and a bayonet puncture. He had sustained third degree burns on his left arm and shoulder and second degree burns on his upper arm and neck from white phosphorus. Besides the initial wounds, he was suffering complications from internal bleeding, hemorrhaging from the rectum and penis, and multiple infections. The physicians would later inform him that the multiple shrapnel slivers in his testicles would make it impossible for him to father children. The multiple fragment wounds, traumatic tissue damage, intestinal rupture, third degree burns, fractured bones, not to mention a critically weakened body, provided the perfect breeding grounds for infection.

Day after day, Roger drifted through a purgatorial half-state, lapsing into and out of, a fitful consciousness. It was a surreal world of distorted nightmares and incoherent dreams. At times, he felt like a drowning man trying to reach the surface after going down for the third time. At other times, he would break the surface for a fleeting moment of reality and stare through lizard slits for a few moments. Then he would black out again and be assaulted by ghoulish images of men screaming, crying, and dying around him. He would see the death masks of his departed friends and the dismembered heads of the enemy he had killed, swirling around inside his mind in a macabre death dance. Sometimes he would suddenly bolt awake from the sheer terror of his nightmares or the electrifying pain stabbing his body, only to lapse back into unconsciousness and be assaulted again by images of the grenade laying at his feet, or the soldier standing over him with the bayonet. His was a psychological and physical hell.

For a week, Ron maintained his vigil beside Roger's bed - praying to a God whom he didn't know, but instinctively knew, was the only one left who could save his brother's life. For a week he watched for any sign of life, encouraging him when he came to, and when he passed out, urging him to hang in there, telling him that he could make it.

After two weeks of I.C.U., the doctors told Ron that his brother was going to make it. Roger's condition had stabilized enough for his doctors to risk the medevac flight to a better equipped hospital in Japan.

Ron returned to his artillery unit. Three weeks later, his firebase was hit by a sapper attack. Ron had just emerged from a sand-bagged bunker with his M-16 when a sapper ran by and hurled a Chicom grenade at him. The potato masher hit Ron in the back and bounced back into the bunker where eight Marines were huddled. Without hesitating, Ron dropped his rifle, dived through the entrance, and landed on top of the grenade, trying to smother the explosion with his body. "GRENADE!" Marines shouted in panic as they ran out of the bunker, stepping on top of Ron who was lying in the dirt, waiting for the grenade to go off. Agonizing seconds passed, but the grenade didn't explode. The

E.O.D. men later disarmed the grenade. They found that its fuse had burned down to the powder, but for some inexplicable reason, it had not gone off. Diving on a grenade to save others was grounds for an automatic Medal-of-Honor, but since the grenade hadn't gone off, Ron was awarded the Navy Cross and a battlefield commission for his heroism. The grenade may not have gone off in the eyes of the review board, but it had as far as Ron was concerned.

The day after Ron returned to his unit, Roger's stretcher was placed on a medical bus and taken to the airfield, where he was loaded onto a C-141 "starlifter" medevac jet. His condition was still listed as "critical", but the medical policy in Vietnam was to evacuate the wounded as soon as possible to a transit hospital out of the war-zone and back to the States, for prolonged care and therapy. Roger was given strong doses of pain killers to numb the agony of the flight. Stretcher after stretcher was carried into the bowels of the waiting jet with men secured to I.V.'s of saline, antibiotics and pain-killers. The fuselage walls were lined with tiers of stainless steel bunks to help immobilize the wounded during their transit to Japan. Most of the men were amputees, or burn patients, facing months of multiple operations and physical therapy, and a lifetime of adjustment to their disfigurements and trauma.

The medevac flight to Japan was the first leg of Roger's painful pilgrimage home. Six hours after taking off from Da Nang, the huge jet touched down at an air base outside of Tokyo.

On their arrival, the wounded Marines and soldiers were sent to several military hospitals clustered around Tokyo. Roger was sent to the U.S. Army's 249th

General Hospital at Camp Zama. His strength slowly began to come back, and with it, an acute sensitivity to the constant pain assaulting him. The pain had reached such overwhelming proportions that he wondered if it would ever stop. Even the strongest would clinch their teeth in agony and cry, and sometimes scream. The severity of his wounds introduced him to the widest range of physical torment - sharp, piercing, stabbing, pinching, gnawing, burning, throbbing, tearing, remorseless, unforgiving, mind-numbing pain - pain which showed no mercy, respected no person, mocked the administration of narcotics. Roger had degenerated to the point where his all-consuming desire was for the next shot of morphine or Demoral to ease the torment.

He spent a month enduring the daily ordeal of having the blood caked dressings peeled away from seeping sores, and having raw wounds scrubbed and debrided of dead tissue, scabs and pus. He underwent several surgeries to mend his perforated intestines, repair some of the damage done to his shattered elbow, and remove shrapnel still left in his body.

The hospital was modern and well-equipped, with the latest, state-of-the-art diagnostic equipment and procedures. The staff was friendly, professional, and trained to prepare the men for their first steps back to the world. They provided the best of care, but there was only so much medical science could do to prepare the wounded and maimed for their eventual journey back to a world fraught with new insecurities and fears. Between them and home stretched an invisible void filled with terrifying unknowns and unanswered questions.

None of them was as young and confident as they

may have been when they were first heading for Vietnam. The brutal realities of combat had shattered their myths of invincibility and brought them an emotional vulnerability none of them had known before. Though the spirits of most of the men were high, in spite of the severity of their condition, they all shared a nagging uneasiness of what the future held for them. The prospects of rejection, disability, and a lifetime of limitations privately tormented each of them.

He spent a month in Japan, oblivious to his surroundings - lost in a delirious twilight-zone of pain and pain-killers. His face was swollen and lacerated from the grenade blast. His lips, cheeks, and eyes were engorged with blood, inflamed and swollen a purplish black and blue. The force of the blast had ripped his lips and cheeks open and knocked out two of his teeth. His face constantly felt like it was on fire. The nurses would fill surgical gloves with crushed ice and lay them on his face to take down the swelling, but it still looked like a water-balloon about to explode.

Roger had maintained a constant, low-grade fever from staph infections since his arrival. Besides the seventy-two major shrapnel wounds, his body was covered with hundreds of small punctures from slivers of shrapnel which had imbedded themselves in his flesh. The blast had also peppered his body with jungle bacteria and dirt. The ruptured intestines from the bayonet and bullet had riddled his stomach cavity with excrement from his bowels. In spite of the daily scrubbings, debridings, and antibiotics, the doctors couldn't get his temperature below the 100 mark. They wouldn't release him for a medevac flight home until it was under 100 degrees.

Besides the unrelenting pain, Roger felt like he

was dying of thirst. The massive intestinal injuries made it impossible for him to drink fluids or eat solids. The nurses would dab his swollen, cracked lips, but they would not let him have any water. His every waking moment was consumed with a desire to drink water. Even when he slept, his thirst haunted him. Between his nightmares of the grenade going off at his feet, he experienced a recurring dream about his being back in 'Nam. In the dream, it was raining so hard he could only hear the sound of water pelting his body. He was running around with a bucket in a monsoon downpour, trying to fill it up with water before the rain stopped. Over and over in the dream, the rain would suddenly stop and he would lift the bucket to his lips, only to find that it had holes in it and all the water had drained out.

At one point, he was laying in his bed when the ward nurse laid an ice-filled surgical glove on his face. She then started down the opposite aisle, checking the temperature of each of the patients. With slight, painful movements of his facial muscles and head, he gradually maneuvered the little finger of the glove within biting range. He worked it over to his mouth and began sucking and pulling at the latex with his teeth until he was able to grab enough to bite a tiny hole in the glove. The cold sensation of the tiny drops of water trickling into his mouth was almost sensual, it felt so good. The pain on his lips was excruciating, but it was worth it - even if he was risking his life doing it.

Fortunately, the nurse came to take his temperature before he drank too much water, or it would have killed him.

"How are we feeling today, Sergeant?" she asked as she removed the bag of ice and inserted the thermometer between his lips.

"O.K.," Roger mumbled the words, upset that he couldn't continue drinking the precious drops of water.

"Let's see now," she said as she pulled out the thermometer and checked the reading, unaware that he had been sucking on the glove. The ice water had cooled his mouth and helped keep the temperature reading down. "Well, it looks like your temperature is down this morning, Sergeant. You might be going home sooner than you think." The Captain smiled and headed for the next bed.

Later that day, Roger was taken to an Air Force base on the outskirts of Tokyo and loaded onto another C-141 for his evac flight back to the States. He was strapped to a stretcher along one of the fuselage walls. Because the physicians had left many of his wounds open and unsutured, he was laid on the stretcher without any hospital pajamas. He had only a sheet to cover him.

When the jet landed in Anchorage for refueling, the flight crew retracted the rear ramp to off-load several patients. Roger thought he was going to freeze to death when the frigid night air flowed into the fuselage and chilled his naked body. He was flushed and burning up with fever. Beads of sweat had broken out on his forehead and his sheet was soaked in cold sweat. A flight nurse was checking the patients when she noticed that Roger's lips were turning blue and he was shivering. She immediately pulled off the wet sheet and got some blankets to cover him up. After tucking the blankets around his shoulders to ward of the chill, she wiped his brow with a towel. They monitored him closely for the rest of the flight.

Roger looked at the young nurse and grimaced in pain, "Thank you." He was still barely able to talk.

During the flight, his temperature flared to nearly 103 degrees. His condition had deteriorated since Japan. His body was losing the battle against the virulent infection spreading through it.

Roger's medevac flight landed at Glenn View Naval Air Station north of Chicago and braked to a stop, after an exhausting twenty-two hour flight. Those who were lucid enough to comprehend what was happening were excited at the prospects of finally being home and having survived - even Roger. When the Loadmaster retracted the rear ramp of the huge jet, the dim cavern was suddenly bathed in the promising light of the afternoon sun. Roger half expected a brass band to strike up a rousing rendition of the Marine Corps anthem to welcome the wounded back. However, the homecoming was uneventful and routine.

Except for several Air Force and naval officers who boarded the jet to check over the paperwork and supervise the unloading of the wounded, there was no one waiting for them. Each of the stretchers was unstrapped and carried off the plane by Corpsmen. The stretchers were laid in a neat row next to each other on the hot tarmac until the buses could arrive to carry them to the hospital. Even though he was in a drug-dazed stupor, he can still remember how lonely and forsaken he felt, lying on the concrete runway with no one there to say, "Welcome home, you did a good job!" All the wounded had on that hot, homecoming afternoon was each other. In some ironic way, it was fitting, in light of what they had shared together. They would always have each other.

Chapter 23

By the time Roger arrived at Great Lakes Naval Hospital, he had been in his stretcher for almost twenty-four hours. He was running a high fever and was absolutely drained from exhaustion, fever, and pain. He was only half coherent as they wheeled him through the hospital to one of the massive wards. *"If I can only get some sleep, I'll be better,"* he thought as he gazed at the green tinted walls through bloodshot eyes.

No sooner had he arrived at admitting, when one of the physicians began to examine him to determine the severity of his wounds. His high temperature was a dangerous indication that something was serious. "Sergeant, I'm afraid we are going to have to remove your bandages and casts. This is going to be painful but we can't help it. You're running a high fever and we have to check your wounds for infection," the young navy doctor warned Roger.

Roger was immediately wheeled into a surgical room where a doctor and a couple of nurses began to cut away the caked dressings covering portions of his body. Slowly at first, they methodically peeled away the soiled gauze and cloth netting which was caked with dried blood, sticky scabs, and dead skin.   Roger grimaced in agony as each bandage was literally torn away from the tissue to which it had bonded. When the doctor removed some soiled gauze dressings on Roger's left leg, he recoiled from the putrid smell of infected flesh. Gangrene infection had already begun to spread its insidious rot through Roger's leg.

"I'm very sorry, Sergeant, but it looks like you're going to lose this leg. Gangrene has already set in. Why they didn't detect this in Japan is beyond me," he said as he shook his head.

Roger was stunned by the doctor's diagnosis. "Please, Sir, you can't take off my leg!" he pleaded. "I've come too far. You've got to try to save it. Please, don't cut it off!"

The young doctor looked at Roger with pity and said, "Sergeant, we'll try, but I want you to know that your leg is already badly infected. We can only wait so long. Unless we can stop the infection, it will spread through the rest of your body and kill you. If you don't respond to treatment soon, I will have no choice but to amputate your leg. Do you understand?"

"Yes, sir. Just try."

After the first of many more scrubbings, Roger was taken to Ward 3 South - the dirty orthopedics ward where patients with severe staph infections were deposited.   His first impression of the ward was unsettling. It was larger than any ward he had been on during his transit home. It had eighty beds - forty along each side of the ward. Each had a little American flag draped at its foot. It would be the home for Roger for the next six months of reconstructive surgery and physical therapy.

Over the next few days, Roger's dressings were peeled away from the raw, oozing wounds and scrubbed with surgical brushes to remove the pus, dead nerve endings, and infected tissue. The procedure was unbearable in its intensity. Scrubbing the raw wounds and burn patches was like taking a wire brush to exposed nerve endings. The scrubbings caused the open wounds to bleed from ruptured capillaries. Several orderlies had to hold Roger's bucking body down on the table while his wounds were being cleaned and rewrapped with fresh dressings. By the time the daily torture sessions were over, Roger was dripping with sweat and completely wrung out.

After the first day's scrubbing, a lady volunteer from the American Red Cross helped Roger make a free phone call to his next of kin. She dialed the number in Toledo that Roger gave her and gently held the receiver to his ear. The phone rang three times before a voice answered.

"Hello!" the voice sounded annoyed on the other end.

"Mom?...Mom, it's me, Roger," he groaned out the words. "Mom...I'm home, " Roger's voice cracked as he broke into tears, "Mom, I'm home!"

"We're glad, son, we've been worried sick," his mother responded.

They talked for a long time.

Roger was introduced to one of his first pleasurable experiences during his painful trek through the hospital. It was part of his treatment to counter the infection eating away at his legs. One morning, a nurse showed up beside his bed with a wheelchair and pushed him down to a room equipped with a special whirlpool bath. The whirlpool was used to gently remove unwanted tissue and infection from open wounds. The gentle, swirling action of the jacuzzi jets soothed and softened his tender sores, as it slowly stripped away dead tissue, scabs, and bacteria. After being manually scrubbed and scraped hamburger raw, the whirlpool was actually enjoyable.

After two weeks of intensive treatment, his doctor checked the gangrene and informed Roger that he would keep his leg.

"Thanks, Doc," Roger told the doctor when he announced the good news.

"Hey, don't thank me, " the doctor had told him, "Thank God. I just did my job. He did the healing."

"Yeah," Roger muttered absently, suddenly flashing on the promise he had made back in 'Nam.

Two and a half months after being wounded, the doctors wheeled him into surgery to close the wounds which pockmarked his body. Two-hundred ninety-six stainless steel sutures later, he was wheeled back to his ward. Months of cleansings, skin grafts, plastic surgery, and physical therapy followed.

One morning, while he was being taken to P.T. to work on his arms and legs, a young doctor passed him in the corridor and noticed the ugly, ropey looking scars covering his upper lip and face. The severe lacerations from the grenade shrapnel had disfigured his upper lip into a curled snarl. Most of the guys on Ward 3 South joked about their disabilities and wounds, no matter how grotesque they appeared or how debilitating they were.

It was their way of lightening the atmosphere on the ward and coping with their fate. One of the guys started kidding Roger about the curl of his lip, telling him that he looked like Elvis Presley. Roger took it as a perverted compliment and picked up on the humor by doing an imitation of Elvis every time the guy made a wise-crack.

"Nurse, wait just a minute, please. I want to take a look at your patient here," the doctor said, as he bent over and carefully examined Roger's facial scars. "Umm huh," he pondered. "I think we can fix these. What's your name?" he asked before continuing his impromptu exam.

"Ah, Helle...Sergeant, Helle, Sir." Roger responded sheepishly.

"Well, Sergeant Helle. This is your lucky day. Your lip looks a little worse for wear, but I'm going to give you back a new face."

"I don't know, Sir," Roger replied. "I think the old one is kinda sexy. You know the guys back on the ward say I look a lot like Elvis now," Roger gave the doctor a sly grin.

"Well Elvis, how about comin' up and seeing me later this afternoon, so I can take a better look at that face of yours," the doctor instructed before he turned and strode down the hall.

After visiting the surgeon later that day, Roger was moved to Ward 9 South, to begin a series of plastic surgeries to remove the knotty scar tissue and reconstruct his face. Four operations later, his face was greatly improved and any resemblance to Elvis was gone.

Between the agonizing moments of surgeries, debridings, and skin grafts, were long interludes of dull pain and duller monotony. Apart from the constant companionship of the fellow patients who shared a common kinship of suffering, the only diversions were from radios and T.V.'s scattered through the ward. Relatives and friends would occasionally visit, but the visits were usually brief and the conversations stilted and strained. The visitors tried to act composed, but the discomfort in their eyes was evident. They could not hide the shock and revulsion they felt.

The sight of maimed and disfigured young men, stumps, draining wounds, and the smells of antiseptics and sour body fluids were unnerving even to those with the strongest constitutions. The ward was a sobering experience for mothers and fathers, sisters and brothers, wives and sweethearts. Suddenly to come face to face with the fragility of human life and be inches away from bodies which had been so ruthlessly violated, was too much for some. Each visit was an emotional ordeal for everyone involved.

There were always a few "whiners" on the ward who were drowning in their own self-pity, depression, and loneliness, but most endured their private ordeals with a quiet dignity which moved Roger deeply. They never complained nor felt sorry for themselves, even though they had so much which they could feel sorry about. Even with so little left to bolster their egos or reaffirm their manhood, they hung in there and toughed it out together. They were the bravest men Roger had ever known.

Even in spite of their courage and nobility of spirit, the wards could be some of the loneliest places on earth. Time crawled by in agonizing increments. Watching the ward clock doing slow laps was like watching paint dry. Endless days of boredom and T.V. monotony blended into each other.

Sometimes, the distraction of the radios and T.V.'s would drown out the private reflections of men who contemplated their futures outside the ward. At other times, the silence on the wards was oppressive-especially at night when Roger would lay awake for hours staring at the ceiling or at the dim yellow glow from the nurses' station.

Roger tried to keep his spirits up, but even he couldn't fight back the occasional tides of loneliness and melancholia which engulfed him. His heart was filled with mixed emotions about what life would be like when he left the hospital. He would turn on the T.V. and see the news coverage of tens of thousands of protestors marching on Washington and students waving the Viet Cong flag and shouting, "Hell no, we won't go! Ho, Ho, Ho Chi Minh, the NLF is going to win!" These actions tore at his emotions.

Though the hospital was a refuge from the political strife raging outside the gates, it was hard to forget the war with so many gruesome reminders surrounding him. The perpetual suffering evoked painful memories and summoned thoughts back to the rice paddies and jungles.

Even in the sterile sanctuary of the ward, they could not completely insulate themselves from the alienation and loneliness they felt as they watched the evening news. Roger would listen to the television interviews of people criticizing those who had fought in 'Nam, calling them murderers, and he wanted to rip the T.V. set off the wall. The news media only seemed to talk about what the men in Vietnam were doing wrong. "What about what we did right?" he fumed. All they cared about was the atrocities. *"What about the innocents the V.C. slaughtered? Why doesn't someone care about them? Why?"* he thought, as he looked around the ward at the mutilated young men and wondered what war the media were talking about. The men laying beside him were quiet heroes who didn't deserve such contempt. *"Why doesn't someone care about us?"* he steamed.

One particularly lonely day around Halloween, Roger was sitting in a wheel chair in the corridor outside of Physical Therapy, when a Navy Chaplain walked down the hall. Roger looked up and caught his eye. The balding Captain, with a middle-aged spread, looked at Roger and said, "You don't want to talk to a Chaplin, do you?" shaking his head like he was trying to say, "No, of course not, you don't need one." The Chaplain obviously had better things to do than talk to a wounded Marine.

Roger didn't know if he needed to talk or not, but he answered, "Yeah, you're right. I guess I don't need one."

"Well, you take care of yourself and have a good day, son," the Captain turned and continued down the hall.

The brief encounter troubled him. He knew deep down inside that he needed something, but he just couldn't put his finger on it. He really didn't know much about God. He had gone to a Lutheran church when he was a kid. He had even been baptized, but it all seemed so boring and mysterious. He had never felt the need to talk to a Chaplain, especially after he got the impression that the fat one going down the hall didn't want to get involved. Maybe God was like that, too, he thought to himself. He always seemed so distant in 'Nam. Maybe that's the way He was. The only Christian he had ever met was in 'Nam. He had always wanted to talk to Knox, but Knox was dead. Still, Roger sensed he needed someone who cared enough to understand.

The fellow patients supported each other because they shared an empathy birthed in the womb of mutually shared suffering and hardship. Even with their support, it was impossible for them to absorb all the hurt he felt knotted in his gut. He had come back whole and he had come back wounded, and his second homecoming was even more empty than the first. The rejection was still there, and the unanswered questions about the war and why young men were still killing and being killed.

One morning, the guy next to him was listening to WLS out of Chicago when he tuned into the words, "C'mon all of you big strong men, Uncle Sam needs your help again...He's got himself in a terrible jam, way down yonder in V-i-e-TNAM....So put down your books and pick up your guns...Whoopie, we're gonna have a whole lot of fun.....And it's one, two, three, what are we fightin' for?....."

Roger slapped the bed with his palm and snapped, "Turn that crap off! I'm sick and tired of hearing about the war!"

"...*Be the first one on your block to have your kid come home in a box...*"

The startled Marine next to him shut off the radio. Roger's outburst had galvanized the attention of the ward. A few traded glances. No one said anything. They all understood. Roger had spoken for each of them.

From the moment he regained consciousness, he had feared the prospects of being sent back to 'Nam after he was patched up. The foreboding was eating him up, and with it, the guilt of not wanting to go back. The nightmares of the grenade poised at his feet tortured him in the lonely hours of the night. The flashbacks of his squad sprawled along the dike haunted him. Others were still over there, while he was safely sheltered in the hospital. It wasn't rational, but it didn't matter. He had barely made it back, but he knew that some of those he had left behind wouldn't, and there was nothing he could do to help.

In Late Fall, the paperwork finally caught up with him at Great Lakes. He was awarded his fifth Vietnamese Cross of Gallantry and a Bronze Star for the actions involving the destruction of the Viet Cong base camp.

A couple of weeks before Christmas, Roger's mother placed a notice in her church bulletin about his receiving the Bronze Star and his convalescing at Great Lakes. When Roger heard about it, he thought he would take his first weekend leave outside the hospital. He was progressing well through physical therapy, but he was still wearing a cast on his right arm and braces on his legs.

The church was an old stone edifice to which his parents had dragged him as a kid. He hadn't been to a service in years. The excursion outside the hospital was an adventure, as far as Roger was concerned. His showing up at church was not an act of consecration, merely a chance to parade in his Winter-greens and make a statement of his manhood and pride as a Marine. He caught a bus downtown and walked a couple blocks to the church. He hobbled down the sidewalk with his cane, proudly wearing his rows of ribbons.

As he approach the steps leading up to the cathedral, two older ladies brushed past him and pulled to an abrupt stop in front of him, blocking his path.

One with a puckered face looked at him with absolute disgust. "You got what you deserved, you baby killer!" Her voiced cracked with contempt. Her companion spat at his feet, then they strode down the sidewalk.

"Actually," the other turned, "They should have killed you!"

Roger was nearly paralyzed with shock. He felt like he had been ambushed all over again. He was dumbfounded - burning with anger and hurt at the injustice of it all.

Chapter 24

After six months at Great Lakes Naval Hospital, Roger was medically retired from the Marine Corps and discharged with a hundred percent disability rating. The hospital had issued him a set of crutches, but he refused to use them. His right arm was still partially paralyzed and he was limping, but he was determined to walk out on his own. He left the safe familiarity of the hospital and went home to his parents in Toledo. The visit was awkward and short-lived.

He soon found that returning to the world wasn't easy. Coming back to the world was the easy part, acclimating to normalcy was not. He may have returned, but his mind was trapped in a time warp called "Vietnam." Vietnam had left its indelible imprint upon his senses and reflexes. He had lived too long in the pressure cooker suspense of Vietnam just to step back into the world like nothing had ever happened. For two years, his life had been wound tighter than a steel spring. Unwinding would not be easy. His instincts and physical senses had become so acute that he couldn't adjust overnight to the normal sights and sounds around him. The backfire of a passing car, a stroll through a crowded shopping mall, walking across a lawn, the sound of a helicopter overhead, being suddenly awakened at night - all triggered lightning responses which had been conditioned by the sustained intensity of Vietnam. He had lived on the lethal edge for too long. Stepping back on the well-worn treadmill of predictability, without missing a step, was a psychological absurdity. He had been an adrenalin junkie for too long to come suddenly off the run cold-turkey. The high-speed momentum of 'Nam had been too much just to slam on the brakes.

Roger applied for a job at the Pinkerton Detective agency. He figured that his experience in criminal investigation would look good on his application forms. He was right. He was promptly hired. Roger found the hazards of the job exhilarating in a perverse sort of way. He had been hooked on the lethal rush of combat. His role as a detective helped him play out the obscene obsession he had for danger and excitement - anything to get the juices flowing. He was carrying a gun again and putting his life on the line and he thrived on it. Several of his fellow detectives were 'Nam vets and they seemed to fill the vacuum left by those he had left behind. He found himself living on the edge once again.

He threw himself into his work. After hours, he would hang out late, drinking and partying and picking up women for one night stands, anything to forget the past and bury the memories of 'Nam. No one seemed to care about Vietnam. No one wanted to talk about

Vietnam, like it was a curse or something, so he dug a grave and buried it. Even so, the thoughts and flashbacks kept resurrecting themselves in the quiet hours of the night. As hard as he tried to escape his past, the more it seemed to gain on him. It pursued his every move, like a malevolent presence, and dogged him with the relentlessness of bloodhounds.

Roger's dedication to his job began to produce impressive results. He was solving cases, making arrests, and quickly accelerating up the career ladder. He was rapidly becoming a workaholic. In June 1971, he was asked to open a Pinkerton office in Fort Wayne, Indiana.

With all the success, he still felt empty and unsettled. He had changed the window dressing of his life, but his heart was still filled with anger and hurt which nothing seemed to cure. It looked like his life was going somewhere after all, but the changes were only cosmetic. On the inside was a festering abscess of emotional pus, poisoning his life.

In October of that year, he walked into a bank in Fort Wayne for a business appointment and noticed a pretty, young secretary who caught his eye. Roger tried to put the make on her before he left, but didn't seem to get anywhere. She wasn't like the "easy scores" he was picking up in the bars after work. She showed just enough interest to bait the hook. She was confident and hard to get and that intrigued Roger. Shirley was a new and exciting challenge. After a month of asking her for a date, his persistence finally won out.

Eleven months later, they were married on September 9, 1972. The marital bliss and euphoria quickly wore off. Roger had assumed that the hurt would evaporate in the warmth of Shirley's love, but it didn't happen. It wasn't her fault. No human could heal that kind of hurt. The plastic surgeons back at Great Lakes had done wonders reconstructing his lacerated face, but no earthly surgeon could remove the scars in his heart. All his working and drinking and love for Shirley could not heal a wounded heart which was hemorrhaging with hate and bitterness and guilt - especially guilt. It was like trying to put a band-aid on a bullet wound. He tried to act cool and Marine macho, but inside his soul, he was an emotional war-zone.

Roger proceeded to turn Shirley's life into a living hell. He floored the career accelerator even more, and poured himself into his work to ignore the turbulent emotions eroding the underpinnings of his life. He was trying to compensate for the failure and guilt he felt by paying penance through his work. When he wasn't working, he was hanging out late at night at the bars, getting drunk and trying to forget. Shirley did everything she knew to be a loving wife, but Roger's neglect and indifference was killing her. The tenderness of her love was being ground beneath the crush of Roger's work, neglect, and pent-up anger. He was not only running from 'Nam but from the pressures of his marriage. He knew he was failing as a husband and he just couldn't face that fact.

To those whom he worked with, he seemed so together, but Shirley knew how miserable and tormented he was inside. He was consumed with a cancer of bitterness and raw hate which was eating away at his system. Shirley knew it, and Roger knew it. He'd look in the bathroom mirror in the morning after shaving, see the man staring back at him, and know that he was a hypocrite. He was hiding behind a shallow veneer of pride and success, but behind that mask of "togetherness" was an emotional cripple.   A lifetime of hurt and frustration was bottled up inside, just waiting to explode. He hated what he saw in himself, but he was too proud to admit it, or talk about it, even though he longed for the abscess to be lanced and drained and somehow healed.

Shortly after their marriage, Roger was transferred to Omaha, Nebraska to take over the investigation department at the Pinkerton office. Roger's obsession with work began to make ripples through the upper echelons of management. He was advancing quickly through the organization because of his devotion to work and his success rate at cracking cases.

While his career was flourishing, his marriage was withering. Shirley's life had deteriorated to a barren round of duties and nights of loneliness and neglect. She begged Roger to spend more time with her, but he let her know that his job came first. Roger told her the marriage would have to wait, but Shirley had reached a point of quiet desperation she could bear no longer. The fighting, neglect and tension took its toll. Roger's anger was slowly destroying everything around him.

Shirley endured two years of his emotional and mental abuse, hoping he would change. He had vented his pent-up frustration on the one he loved the most. He was unconsciously punishing himself by driving away the one person closest to him. Somewhere along the line, they had become strangers and drifted apart, neither knowing what to say or what to do. Roger pursued his work while Shirley's love wilted, shriveled, and slowly died.

He had tried to run from his painful memories of 'Nam, but it was always gaining on him. Had tried to bury it under an avalanche of paperwork and busyness, but the phantoms would always emerge to remind him, and haunt him. Nearly two years had passed since his wounding. The war in Southeast Asia was still grinding on, and he was still paying interest on his guilt.

In desperation, Shirley finally confronted him, one morning before he left for work. "Roger, I can't go on like this. We've got to do something. You know it, and I know it. We don't seem to be able to talk. Maybe we could see a marriage counselor or go talk to a pastor together. I'm willing if you are." She was pleading with all her heart.

Roger gave her a cold look and said, "Hey, go ahead, if you need to....It's your problem anyway," and left for work. The chasm in their marriage grew wider as they drifted even further apart. His work became his companion by day, the bars his surrogate wife by night.

Shirley packed her bags and left for her mother's to think things over.

Roger had been working a major investigation linked to organized crime. The case had brought him dangerously close to nailing key figures in a major crime ring. A week after Shirley left, he got a phone call at his office; "Helle, this is the only warning you get. Back off the case or you're a dead man!...Click!" the anonymous caller slammed the receiver down. Roger's heart was pounding in his chest from the threat. But, it was more than fear which he felt - it was that familiar rush from pushing it to the edge.

That afternoon, Shirley called and said she was coming home. She wanted Roger to pick her up at the airport. On his way there later that evening, a big Buick pulled up along side of him on the freeway and ran him off the road into the median. At first, he thought the guy was a drunk driver. Roger floored the accelerator, shooting rocks and dirt in a rooster-tail as he fish-tailed out of the grassy ditch in pursuit of the other car. He caught up with the Buick a couple miles down the Interstate. He was madder than hell and ready to flip the guy off or force him over and make a citizen's arrest.

He pulled up alongside and rolled down his window to yell at the guy to pull over. Just then, someone in the passenger seat rolled down his window and stuck out a revolver. Roger saw the barrel and stomped on his brake just as the gun popped with a bright flash. Roger's front window exploded in a shower of glass as he screeched to a stop.

When Shirley got off the plane, she found Roger talking to two Omaha police detectives. Neither said anything as they drove back to their trailer. There wasn't much left to say. Shirley laid awake most of the night, sick with loneliness and fear, loneliness from the knowledge of a failed marriage, fear from the death threat stalking them both.

On Thanksgiving Day, 1974, Shirley had hoped against hope too long. She didn't have anything left to give. Roger's neglect and coldness was more than she could bear. She had found out through the grapevine about an affair Roger had had while on a business trip to Sioux Falls. That was the final straw. She had put up with more than most women would take. She had born his neglect, but she wasn't going to bear the bitter insult of his unfaithfulness, too.

Shirley knew something was tearing Roger up inside, and their marriage with it, but she didn't know what to do or what to say. She also knew she deserved better than he was willing to give her. She just couldn't live with it any longer. She had loved Roger with all of her heart - that was why she had stayed with him as long as she had. The passion and feelings that had once been there were now buried under untold layers of hurt.

On a grey, Thanksgiving morning in the living room of their small trailer home, she confronted him with his adultery. Her final words to him were; "I love you, but I can't live with you any longer. I'm leaving for good this time." She picked up her handbag and suitcase and left, leaving Roger standing in that empty trailer, finally defeated.

Shirley's departure was like getting run through with a bayonet all over again. His life had reached rock bottom. The crush of his career and tortured emotions finally caved in around him, burying him in despair and hopelessness. The failure he had feared all of his life had finally come home to stay. He had lost his friends in 'Nam, and now he had lost his wife. He had always felt he had somehow failed his friends, but he knew that he had failed his wife. He had loved them both, but his remorse was too little, too late. Roger was no longer the tough, proud Marine. He was broken and devastated by a loss he could not bear.

A couple of days later, he bought a puppy for Shirley as a present and had it delivered to where she was staying with a little card which said, "I love you, Honey." Shirley didn't respond. Night after night, Roger tossed and turned in the cramped loneliness of his empty trailer, thinking about Shirley and wondering what he could do to get her back. He couldn't eat. Nothing seemed to matter any longer - not even his job. It seemed like all the color had faded from his life, leaving only dismal greys and winter bleakness.

A couple of weeks after Shirley left, Roger went

to a party at the Omaha Ski Club. No sooner had he walked into the cocktail lounge, when he saw Shirley sitting across the room at a table, having a drink with another man. Roger just stood there in the middle of the lounge like a marble statue, staring at Shirley in disbelief. He was boiling with rage and ready to walk over and kill the guy she was with. One of Roger's partners at work saw what was happening, came up to him, and put his hand on Roger's arm, "C'mon, Roger, take it easy, man! Its not worth it." Shirley looked up and saw Roger staring at her with jealousy and hurt in his eyes. Roger just turned away, walked over to the bar, and started knocking down doubles.

A few minutes later, Shirley came up to him as he stood hunched over the bar, looking glumly into his drink. "I wanted to thank you for the little poodle you gave me, Roger. He's really cute."

Roger didn't say anything, trying to ignore her. Shirley got the hint and walked away. She came back later that evening and tried to talk to him, but each time he gave her the cold shoulder. The third time she touched his arm and said, "Don't you think we better talk, Roger?"

Roger choked back the emotion and finally broke, "Yeah, Shirley....I do."

"Let's go home, then," she said as she took his hand.

They drove to her new apartment. He ended up staying the night. The next morning, they went to a shopping mall together to window shop. Both of them felt awkward and nervous, not knowing what to say or where to start. The whole morning was strained as they walked the mall in silence, pausing to look at the displays and seeing the reflections of strangers in the glass panes staring back at them. Finally, after a couple of hours of strained silence, Shirley turned to Roger and said, "Rog, I've been giving our marriage a lot of thought, lately...."

"Yeah, I know what you mean, " Roger cut her off in mid-sentence.

"I'm not finished. I just want you to listen to what I have to say," she said firmly.

"O.K. Honey, I'm sorry," Roger apologized.

"Roger, I know that unless we put God first in our lives, we don't have any hope left that our marriage will work," Shirley spoke, with a conviction Roger couldn't ignore.

"I know, Shirley, but I don't know what to do," Roger said. He was like a little boy who had lost his way home and didn't know where to go. However, he knew in his heart that she was right.

"Roger, I think we should go to church or talk to a pastor."

"I don't know, Shirley. The last time I wanted to talk to a chaplain, he acted like I was a leper or something. The last time I went to church, two old ladies spat on me and called me a baby killer."

Shirley paused a moment and said, "Isn't that what they did to Jesus, Honey...spat on Him and rejected Him, too? I know God cares, Roger. If anyone can understand, I think he can," Shirley looked at him with tears welling in her eyes. "I know He's the answer. I think He's what has been missing all these years."

At that moment, looking into the depths of Shirley's eyes, Roger thought of that hospital room back in Da Nang, with his brother kneeling beside his bed sobbing and the words of desperation he had uttered on that deathbed; "Please, God, If you'll let me live, I'll do anything you ask, Please, God..." He realized, too, that God had kept his promise and he hadn't.

That night in the bedroom of her apartment, they both knelt beside her bed, broken and spent. They were holding each other's hands. Roger was not a religious person, he didn't know how to pray like they did in those boring services he had gone to as a kid, but he opened his mouth and uttered the humblest of prayers, " God, I've tried to do it my way....I've really messed things up. I can't do it anymore, Jesus. Please help me and my wife....I love her so much." Warm tears were flowing down both of their checks. "Please, God, forgive me for all the hurt I've caused....I need your mercy. I need you, Jesus."

At that moment of brokenness, it felt like an enormous weight had lifted from his shoulders. It was like he had been humping back in 'Nam through the muck and jungles, with a thousand pound pack on his back for a hundred years, when it suddenly slipped from his shoulders. He had come home with a garbage load of hate, bitterness, and guilt, and now it was gone. He didn't have to carry it any longer. Something decisive and powerful had happened in a heart bruised with hurt. There were no flashes of lightning or claps of thunder. There were no tingling sensations or rapturous visions of the heavens rolling back and a host of angels singing a celestial chorus, but something real and life-changing had taken place in that humble apartment. That night, for the first time in four and a half years, the nightmares stopped. They never returned.

That prayer brought momentous changes to Roger and Shirley's lives - some subtle and almost imperceptible, others swift and dramatic. Their marriage turned around and began to heal. In 1976, he came back to his office from a meeting with a client and found a plant with a card in it from Shirley which simply read, "The rabbit died!" He sat there like a dunce for a couple minutes trying to figure out whose rabbit had died, when it suddenly dawned on him. He was going to be a father! Months later, the first time he held little Josh in his arms, he remembered what the doctors had said when they had told him he would never be able to have children from the shrapnel he had taken in the groin.

Chapter 25

"Are they Russian?" the gnarled old mama sanh asked the driver. The old woman's mouth was set with toothy snags. They were stained pomegranate black from years of chewing betelnut. Her face was leathery from years of sun - her features etched with fear.

"Khong phai dau. Ho la nhung nguoi linh hoa ky." (No, they are Marines...) The young driver answered the old woman. They were generations apart. She still remembered the war. He was too young to know.

Our group of veterans had spent most of the afternoon in the steamy paddy lands south of Da Nang looking for Hill 55 - a former Marine outpost during the war. Twenty years had refoliated most of the former scars and eroded the positions manned by Marines years before. Our group had pulled to a stop outside a little village somewhere in Que Sanh Valley. It had been in the middle of the fighting years before. We had climbed a nearby knoll to check out the surrounding country-side. Several old women from the village had approached the bus to ask about our group. It had been many years since they had seen any foreigners in that remote area. But the years had not dulled the painful memories of more brutal times when soldiers and Marines, NVA and Viet Cong had clashed in the fields and hills around them. Our arrival had conjured up ghosts from the past.

"Troi oi ho se tro lai sao?" (Oh, God, are they coming back?) one of the old women asked, fearing a resumption of hostilities.

"Khong dau, Ma sanh a. Ho khong phai tro lai de danh nhau dau." (No, no, Mama Sanh, they have not come back to fight) the driver tried to calm their fears. *"Ho dang tham vieng nhung hoi ho da tung di qua trong thoi gian chien tranh."* (They are visiting the places where they fought during the war).

The driver's assurances brought relief to the old women, who greeted our return to the bus with reserved smiles.

Each of the men on our *"Vets With A Mission"* team had come back to see the places which had played such a pivotal role in their lives. The smoke had long cleared from the battlefields, the refuse of war collected and sold as scrap to the Japanese, the dead buried on both sides, but the memories were still alive. They had faded some over the years, like old snapshots tucked away in a shoe box in some bottom dresser drawer, but time had not erased their intensity.

Each man had a personal reason for coming back. Our group had returned for some basic reasons, nostalgia, curiosity, and a need to put our past in perspective. But, it was more than just sentiment which drew us back. We had not come as tourists or sightseers, but men on a pilgrimage of healing. We had each weathered the turbulent years of aftermath. Each of us had faced the demons from our past. Each had come to terms with the lingering wounds we had carried home. But, now, each of us felt the need to bring that healing full-circle to former friends and foes, who also shared in the suffering we all endured.

It had been a momentous journey which had taken us on an emotional roller-coaster. Our *"Vets With A Mission"* team had come without a lot of fanfare, but media attention had been attracted to us like iron filings on a magnet. *Sixty-minutes* had already interviewed each of the men in Da Nang, and planned to film a reconciliation dinner in Saigon at the end of the trip. We had visited many places with names familiar to many Americans - Khe Sanh, Camp Carroll, Dong Ha, Quang Tri, Phu Bai, Hue, Da Nang, Marble Mountain, China Beach, Que Sanh, Tam Ky, Saigon, Cu Chi, Tay Ninh. They were places filled with memories too deep to express, and each of the men had a story to tell.

Bill Baldwin had served two tours as a grunt, fighting in the mountainous jungles of Quang Tri Province bordering Laos. He'd come back in the hopes of remembering the name of his best friend who had been killed by a sniper's bullet near Khe Sanh. The trauma of that loss had wiped the name from his memory and he wanted it back.

Big Mal had spent only six weeks in country as an M-60 gunner when his company was overrun by a regiment of NVA one night west of Tam Ky. The Marines had fought a vicious night battle in fierce hand-to-hand combat before beating back the hordes of NVA. Mal had spent a terrifying night hunkered down behind his M-60, chewing up the ranks of NVA storming their position. He had taken two rounds in his right leg and had nearly lost it. He still walked with a noticeable limp.

Mike had come back to see the tunnels of Cu Chi where he had fought as a tank driver. He had met a middle-aged Vietnamese man at a bridge where he had been wounded who had served with the Viet Cong in the same area when Mike was there. They had talked for awhile, then the man had asked Mike to please wait a moment. He ran back to his hut and returned with a medal he had been awarded during the war. He pinned it on Mike's shirt, stepped back and saluted him in a humble gesture of respect between brothers-in-arms - former enemies who could now shake hands and reconcile.

David Knight was the senior statesman of our team. He had served as an infantry officer in Korea. At the age of thirty-seven, he volunteered from the Army Reserve to serve the men in Vietnam as a Chaplain. He had never felt comfortable during his tour in the Mekong Delta in the safe confines of a rear area chapel, and chose instead to walk beside the men when they went to battle. David won the Silver Star for heroism, for leading a number of wounded soldiers back to their lines during a fierce fight.

One was a landscaper from Tulsa, another a cement contractor from Boston, another a heavy equipment operator from Fontana, another a pastor from Spokane. Each had come to terms with their past and "gotten on" with their lives. But each wanted to do something more to heal the wounds left behind.

All were proud to be Vietnam vets. None had returned as an act of political penance. None had a need to atone for the sins of the past, though each shared the same heartfelt desire to heal the wounds of war. It was only because of the healing they had found in Jesus's love that they could meet, face-to-face, with their former enemies, and show them that same love.

Roger had also come back with a compelling sense of unfinished business. He had come back with Shirley, Josh, and Jamie. He had brought his family back with him, to pay a final tribute to those who had died by his side.

They had sweated their way over the heights of Hai Van pass in the old dilapidated Russian bus. The day was brutally hot. One of our group had already collapsed the day before from heat stroke. Roger was looking for familiar landmarks alongside the road as they headed north. He was going back to the village where his squad had been wiped out twenty-three years before.

"This is it...right here, right here!" Roger told the guide when he saw the old French fort alongside Highway One. A few words were exchanged and the driver pulled the bus over to the side of the road, by a nearby village north of Phu Bai.

Roger was determined to walk out to the village, but he was concerned about his nine year old daughter, Jamie. The sun was blazing in a sapphire sky overhead. Little Jamie was just as determined as her dad to visit the village. As the rest of the group wandered around the village with their interpreter, Roger, Shirley, Josh and Jamie walked along its edge, looking for the large dike leading out to the village fishing. They came to a shallow canal about twenty feet across. Roger was looking for a place shallow enough to cross.

"Eeeeck!   What is that?" Shirley shuddered, pointing to four inch slugs slithering across the slimy shallows.

"They're leeches, Honey," Roger noted.

"Cool," Josh exclaimed.

"Can they jump, Dad?" little Jamie asked innocently.

"No, don't worry, the water's not deep enough for them to get you," Roger consoled them, as he found a narrow path through the mud with fresh sandal prints.

Roger chuckled to himself at the sight of little Jamie wearing a conical hat to protect her from the sun's intensity. Shirley and Jamie took off their sandals and held them as they slopped through the mud to the other side, praying none of the leeches would get them.

They crossed the canal and headed down the large dike until they came to a small Buddhist pagoda beside the trail. Half a dozen Vietnamese peasants were resting in its shade. No one smiled as they passed. They offered only curious stares and guarded nods. They continued down the dike through the open rice paddies, toward the fishing village two miles off the highway.   They passed several Vietnamese farmers squatting in the shade of some trees along the dike, smoking hand-rolled cigarettes and trying to stay out of the afternoon sun. They gave Roger a wary look, but said nothing. They continued on through the merciless heat and humidity. They passed a young boy swatting the hind-quarters of a mud-caked water buffalo pulling a wooden cart.

Roger kept pouring water on Jamie's head to protect her from heatstroke. He couldn't believe what troopers both of his kids were. He only let them have little sips of water to save enough for the return trip. He was getting worried that they might get faint and dehydrated from the heat.

The trek brought back poignant memories - the fertile stink of the paddies, the sun's intensity, the look of the people, the smell of Vietnam, the old feelings of pulling point. With the memories, were the old fears that came with walking point down that same dike, which his men had patrolled countless times in the past. Each time his squad had approached the fishing village, they had drawn rifle shots from local V.C. Every time the shots would crack, they would dive in the shallow paddy water next to the dike. The reflexes were so ingrained and so deeply imprinted in Roger's memory, the familiar surroundings triggered them once again. He led his family forward, half-expecting shots to ring out from the village, half-prepared to leap into the muddy water. All the feelings of walking point were there again. The closer he came, the tighter the knot in his stomach got.

As he walked along that sun-baked dike, thoughts of his comrades flooded his mind. Memories of Pope, Danny, Knox, and his squad filled his emotions.

Jamie and Shirley were flushed from heat and soaking wet. They were sweating profusely. Roger and Josh were drenched, too. The sun kept beating down. He kept stopping to pour water on Jamie's head to cool her off. He was concerned about his family, but none of them wanted to turn back. They had come too far. Josh and Jamie knew how important it was to their dad.

After about a mile, they passed a Vietnamese fisherman casting a nylon net into a canal beside the section of dike. A little further on, they came upon a couple of boys with woven baskets, wading through the muddy shallows, scooping up small fish with their hands. After an hour of slow moving through the heat, they drew near to the village. It was a couple of hundred yards away, but in the distance, they could already see villagers beginning to gather. The closer they came, the larger the crowd of curious villagers grew. Emotions began to swirl around them as they neared the village.

The villagers gathered around Roger's family. They seemed awe-struck by the sight of the fair-skinned foreigners. They were especially taken with Jamie's sandy-hair and freckled face. They, too, seemed caught up in the drama which was unfolding before them. Roger was older now, but they could clearly see the marbled, white scars, covering his legs and arms, and they knew he had been there before.

The covey of villagers followed Roger and his family along the dike until they came to the spot where twelve of his men had died. The brush and bamboo along the trail had grown over the years. But, he could still make out the spot along the paddy dike where he had desperately clung to the muddy bank and helplessly watched as his men died in a sudden spasm of violence. With what little Vietnamese he remembered, he tried to explain to the villagers that he had been a Marine many years ago, and his squad had been wiped out on the very spot they were standing. He finished explaining and looked into the paddy water where God had spared his life and was choked with emotion. Roger withdrew a small American flag from his pocket and knelt with his family on the trail to thank God for saving his life that day. The villagers stood reverently around him, not understanding the words he spoke, but honoring the solemnness of the moment.

"God, I want to thank you, again, for sparing my life. If you spared my life for such a time as this, then help me to have the courage to be faithful to whatever you have called me to do." Roger stuck the little flag into the dirt and stood. He scanned the faces of the villagers and felt something he had never before felt for them. He could see the oppression and pain of lifetimes etched in their sad weary faces. They, too, had lingered in the shadows of 'Nam. They, too, had endured the nightmares. The blood of their sons had mingled in the same paddies and jungles. Their simple lives had been torn by war.

An old villager was standing in the crowd staring at Roger with sad eyes. Roger went up to him and bowed with his hands folded in a greeting of respect for an elderly person. *"Chau Ong,"* Roger said. He gave him another flag he had in his pocket. An old Vietnamese woman was standing nearby holding a little girl. She began to sob. She stepped forward and gently took Roger's hand in hers. She stood there holding his hand and weeping quietly, while she looked at her granddaughter. Roger could not tell if she could feel his loss, or if she knew about the events twenty-three years before, but he could sense her empathy and concern. He could feel the warmth of the villagers and their compassion for him.

At that moment of overwhelming emotion, he looked into their tear-filled eyes, and felt compassion for them, too. They, too, were survivors. They also had suffered the pain and grief of loss. The aftermath had taken its toll. The years which separated them had done little to relieve the harshness of their lives. The South had lost the war, but the North had lost the peace.

Roger had come to terms with his past. He come

to terms with his guilt and hate, because he had come to terms with God. In that little fishing village, he had done something more. He had come to terms with his enemies. Roger had forgiven them with the same love with which he had been forgiven. He had made his peace where it started.

Roger had returned with those who understood the most - his wife and children, his fellow vets. They were a small piece of America come to honor her fallen sons. It was a fitting memorial - not of death, but of life. Standing there on the spot where his men had fallen, with his wife and the two children the doctors said he would never have, it did seem that life had risen from the dead. They had come back with him as a gesture of love - a requiem understood by each of us.

We had laid to rest the painful memories, but we would never forget. We would always carry them in our hearts. The guilt of a nation was gone. We had learned to live and love again. Our lives had taken their course. The cadence had resumed, but we would never leave them behind. We would be the custodians of their sacred honor - a witness to their memories - their brothers. Their sacrifices would not be forgotten. We would always be one in spirit, brothers-in-arms. The covenant was still unbroken.

We would never forget.

Glossary

AK-47 - A Soviet assault rifle

APC - Abbreviation for "Armored Personnel Carrier"

ARC-Light - A B-52 Bomb strike

Artie - Slang for artillery support

ARVN - Abbreviation for "Army Republic of Vietnam"

B-52 - A long-range heavy bomber

"Beaucoup" - French for "Many"

Beta Boots - High-top tennis shoes worn by North Vietnamese soldiers

Betelnut - An opiate chewed by some Vietnamese. It stains the user's lips red and teeth black

B-40 - An antitank rocket used by the enemy

Blooper - Slang for an M-79 grenade launcher. Derived from the sound it makes.

Body Bag - A plastic zipper bag for corpses

Bouncing-Betty - A mine designed to pop about three feet into the air and explode at waist-level

Bronze Star - Our nation's fourth highest medal

Bush - The outer field areas where soldiers operated

CAC - Abbreviation for "Combined Action Companies"

CAG - Combined Action Group

CAP - Combined Action Platoon

C.O. - Commanding officer

C-rats, C's, - C-rations or prepackaged military meals eatin in the field

C-4 - High explosive putty-like material

C-130 - A cargo plane used to transport men and supplies

C.B.U.'s - Abbreviation for antipersonnel cluster bombs

Charles, Charlie, Mr. Charles, Victor Charlie - Slang expression for the Viet Cong

Chicom - Of Chinese communist manufacture

"Chieu Hoi" - "Open Arms" or expression of surrender

Claymore -   Mines rigged to spray hundreds of steel pellets

Concertina Wire - Barbed wire that is rolled out along the ground to hinder the progress of troops

Commo Check -   Radio communications check

C.P. - Abbreviation for "Command Post"

Cycalos - Pedicabs

Dapsone - Malaria tablets

Demo-bag - Small packs used to carry explosives

Deuce-and-a-half - Two and a half ton trucks

"Dung Lai" - Vietnamese for "Don't Move!"

Dust-off -   A medical evacuation flight

E.O.D. -   Abbreviation for "Explosive Ordinance Disposal"

FAC - Abbreviation for "Forward Air Controller". Used to spot the enemy and direct fire support

Fast-movers - Slang for jets

Five-by-five - Term used to indicate you were receiving loud and clear

Firebase - Bases established to provide artillery support for ground units operating in the bush

Fire-mission -   Artillery support which has been requested

Flakjacket - A protective vest worn to protect the chest area from shrapnel and bullets

Flechette Rounds -   Canister rounds containing small steel darts

F.O. - Abbreviation for "Forward Observer"

Frags - Slang for fragmentation grenades

Freedom Bird - Slang for the flight that took you home after your tour was up

Friendlies - Friendly Vietnamese

Gooks, Gooners, Dinks, Slopes, Zipper-heads - Derogatory slang for Vietnamese

Greased - Slang expression for "killed"

Grunt - Slang for any combat soldier

Gunship - A Huey helicopter armed with machine-guns and rockets

Halazone Tablets - Water purification tablets

H.E. - Abbreviation for "High Explosives"

Huey - UH-1 helicopter. Used extensively in Vietnam to transport men and supplies

H & I - Abbreviation for "Harassment and Interdiction"

Ho Chi Minh Sandals - Crude sandals made from rubber tires

Ho Chi Minh Trail - The main North Vietnamese supply route running from the north to the south through Laos and Cambodia

Hootch - Slang for any form of dwelling place

Humping - Slang for marching with a heavy load through the bush

H-34 - An older helicopter used by the Marines

Indian Country - Slang for "enemy territory"

I.V. - Intravenous Injection

Kalashnikov - An AK-47 rifle

K-Bar - Marine Corps knife

K.I.A. - An abbreviation for "Killed In Action"

Klick - Short for kilometer (1 kilometer = 1,000 meters)

LRRP - Abbreviated form of "Long Range Reconnaissance Patrol"

LURP Rations - Special dehydrated rations

L.Z. - Abbreviation for "Landing Zone"

Mama Sanh - Term for elderly Vietnamese woman

Medevac - A helicopter extraction of sick, wounded, or dead from the battlefield

M-14 - A automatic rifle used early in the war

M-16 - A standard automatic weapon used by American and allied ground forces

M-60 - A machine-gun

M-79 - A portable grenade launcher

Napalm - Jellied-gas bombs dropped by airplanes

Navy Cross - Our nation's second highest medal for valor

NLF - Abbreviation for "National Liberation Front" - The political designation for the Viet Cong

Nouc-mam - A strong smelling, fermented Vietnamese fish sauce

Number One - "Very good"

Number Ten - "Very Bad"

NVA - Abbreviation for "North Vietnamese Army"

O-1E - A small, single engine propeller driven plane used by Forward Air Controllers

P-38 - Slang for a G.I. can opener

Pedicab - Three-wheeled bicycle used as a taxi

Papa Sanh - A term for an elderly Vietnamese man

Pogue - A Marine assigned to a rear area

Pith Helmet - Helmet worn by some NVA and V.C.units

Point, Pointman - The lead man in a column or patrol

Policed - Term for "cleaning up"

PRC-25 - A radio used by American ground units

Punji Stakes - Sharpened bamboo stakes usually dipped

in excrement and usually placed in pits

Purple Heart - A medal awarded to those wounded from hostile fire

Recon - Reconnaissance

Red Ball Express - A major enemy road used to funnel supplies

REMFs, REMPs - Abbreviation for "Rear Echelon Mother F------"

Rock-and-roll - Slang for "Fully Automatic"

R.P.G. - Abbreviation for "Rocket Propelled Grenade"

R & R - Abbreviation for "Rest and Relaxation"

Ruck, Rucksack - Back pack carried by American infantry units

Saddle Up - An order for soldiers to put on their packs and move out

Sappers - Enemy infiltrators whose job was to detonate explosive charges within our positions

Satchel Charges - Explosive packs carried by sappers

Scuttlebutt - Marine Corps or Navy term for "Rumors"

Silver Star - Our nation's third highest medal

Sitrep - Situation report

Short-timer - Someone whose tour in Vietnam is almost completed

S.K. - A Soviet carbine

Slick - Slang for a Huey

S.O.G. - Abbreviation for "Special Operations Group" - an elite Special Forces unit

Sortie - A bombing mission

Spider Hole - A camouflaged, one man foxhole or firing pit

Stand Down - A period of rest and reorganization after an infantry unit is pulled in from battle

Tail-end-Charlie - The last man who covers the rear of a column

T.A.O.R. - Abbreviation for "Tactical Area of Responsibility

Tracer - A bullet with a phosphorous coating designed to burn and give a visual indication of its' trajectory

Tracks - Any vehicle with treads

Triage - The process of sorting out patients according to the seriousness of their wounds

V.C., Viet Cong - South Vietnamese Communists

Web-gear - Canvas suspenders and belt used to carry an infantryman's gear

Willie-Peter, W.P. - White Phosphorus

X.O. - Executive officer

Roger L. Helle

Roger Helle was retired from the U.S. Marine Corps, in 1970. He worked for Pinkerton Detective Agency for eight years. He left Pinkertons to found **Teen Challenge of The Midlands**, a Christian program dedicated to helping young men and women, families and Vietnam vets find escape from the tangled web of drugs, alcohol abuse and emotional pain. Since 1978, literally thousands of young men, women and families have found hope in the midst of their despair.

Roger also counsels Vietnam veterans and their families, and works with several Christian veterans groups to help others find peace from their Vietnam experience.

In early 1989, Roger teamed up with William Kimball and his ministry, *"Vets With A Mission"*, to take a message of healing and reconciliation to the nation of Vietnam. After numerous trips, with many more planned in the future, the healing continues among people on both sides of the world. *"Vets With A Mission"* humanitarian projects help meet the needs of orphans, the poor and the struggling Christian church in Vietnam.

William R. Kimball

William Kimball has written numerous books and articles. His sensitivity to the subject of Vietnam is a result of his own firsthand experiences as a motorman with the 1st Air Calvary Division and his own personal ordeal when he was medically evacuated from Vietnam in 1968. William is extensively involved with the healing of the Vietnam experience, both on the home-front and in Vietnam.

"To everything there is a season, and a time for every purpose under heaven... a time to kill, and a **TIME TO HEAL**...a time to love, and a time to hate; A time of war, and a time of peace."

(Ecclesiastes 3)

"Moi bien chuyen deu duoc chi phoi Theo mua, ya thoi gian cho moi du dinh duoi vom troi....Luc de chem giet, va **LUC DE HAN GAN DAU THUONG**....Khi de yeu, va khi de ghet; mot thoi gian cho chien tranh, va mot thoi gian cua su thanh binh."

(Truyen-Dao 3)